ECO-PERFORMANCE, ART, AND SPATIAL JUSTICE IN THE US

In *Eco-Performance, Art, and Spatial Justice in the US*, Courtney B. Ryan traces how urban artists in the US from the 1970s until today contend with environmental domestication and spatial injustice through performance.

In theater, art, film, and digital media, the artists featured in this book perform everyday, spatialized micro-acts to contest the mutual containment of urbanites and nonhuman nature. Whether it is plant artist Vaughn Bell going for a city stroll in her personal biosphere, photographer Naima Green photographing Black urbanites in lush New York City parks, guerrilla gardeners launching seed bombs into abandoned city lots, or a satirical tweeter parodying BP's response to the 2010 *Deepwater Horizon* oil spill, the subjects in this book challenge deeply engrained Western directives to domesticate nonhuman nature. In examining how urban eco-artists perform alternate ecologies that celebrate the interconnectedness of marginalized human, vegetal, and aquatic life, Ryan suggests that small environmental performances can expose spatial injustice and increase spatial mobility.

Bringing a performance perspective to the environmental humanities, this interdisciplinary text offers readers stymied by the global climate crisis a way forward. It will appeal to a wide range of students and academics in performance, media studies, urban geography, and environmental studies.

Courtney B. Ryan is a Lecturer in the Program in Writing and Critical Inquiry, University at Albany, SUNY, USA.

"Courtney B. Ryan's piercing insights transform our relatedness to the everyday spaces around us, opening new understandings about how inequity is embedded into spatial relations, and how performance can partner with places both verdant and vulnerable to expose injustices and renew connections. Eloquent, passionate and particular, this book is a must read for those who seek to balance justice, beauty, and resilience through the arts. An important addition to ecodramaturgy and ecocriticism and the ways that place and privilege are intertwined."

Theresa May, *author of* Earth Matters on Stage: Ecology, Environment and American Theater *(Routledge, 2021), Professor, University of Oregon, USA*

"This is a fascinating, interdisciplinary study of how the control of the human and more-than-human world is spatially performed and resisted both 'in the dirt' of American backyards and 'online' in our Twitter feeds. Indeed, one of the pleasures of this book lies in the diversity of performances that Courtney B. Ryan assembles into a new archive of national acts of resistance to the logic of extraction driving climate change. She demonstrates that the often 'numbing' experience of the Anthropocene and climate change may be understood, addressed, and resisted through small, everyday acts. Ryan's engaging voice and the new cast of eco-performers she identifies are most welcome contributions to research in the environmental humanities."

Alicia Carroll, *Professor of English, Auburn University, USA*

ROUTLEDGE ENVIRONMENTAL HUMANITIES

Series editors: **Scott Slovic** (University of Idaho, USA), **Joni Adamson** (Arizona State University, USA) and **Yuki Masami** (Aoyama Gakuin University, Japan)

The *Routledge Environmental Humanities* series is an original and inspiring venture recognising that today's world agricultural and water crises, ocean pollution and resource depletion, global warming from greenhouse gases, urban sprawl, overpopulation, food insecurity and environmental justice are all *crises of culture*.

The reality of understanding and finding adaptive solutions to our present and future environmental challenges has shifted the epicenter of environmental studies away from an exclusively scientific and technological framework to one that depends on the human-focused disciplines and ideas of the humanities and allied social sciences.

We thus welcome book proposals from all humanities and social sciences disciplines for an inclusive and interdisciplinary series. We favour manuscripts aimed at an international readership and written in a lively and accessible style. The readership comprises scholars and students from the humanities and social sciences and thoughtful readers concerned about the human dimensions of environmental change.

For more information about this series, please visit: www.routledge.com/Routledge-Environmental-Humanities/book-series/REH

ECO-PERFORMANCE, ART, AND SPATIAL JUSTICE IN THE US

Courtney B. Ryan

LONDON AND NEW YORK

Designed cover image: Vaughn Bell, Portable Lawn, 2003

First published 2023
by Routledge
4 Park Square, Milton Park, Abingdon, Oxon OX14 4RN

and by Routledge
605 Third Avenue, New York, NY 10158

Routledge is an imprint of the Taylor & Francis Group, an informa business

British Library Cataloguing-in-Publication Data
A catalogue record for this book is available from the British Library

Library of Congress Cataloging-in-Publication Data
Names: Ryan, Courtney B., author.
Title: Eco-performance, art, and spatial justice in the US / Courtney B. Ryan.
Description: Abingdon, Oxon : Routledge, 2023. |
Series: Routledge environmental humanities |
Includes bibliographical references and index.
Identifiers: LCCN 2022042256 (print) | LCCN 2022042257 (ebook) |
ISBN 9781032067698 (hardback) | ISBN 9781032067704 (paperback) |
ISBN 9781003203766 (ebook)
Subjects: LCSH: City and town life in art--United States. |
Human ecology in art. | Arts, American--Themes, motives.
Classification: LCC NX650.C66 R93 2023 (print) |
LCC NX650.C66 (ebook) | DDC 700.973--dc23/eng/20221116
LC record available at https://lccn.loc.gov/2022042256
LC ebook record available at https://lccn.loc.gov/2022042257

ISBN: 978-1-032-06769-8 (hbk)
ISBN: 978-1-032-06770-4 (pbk)
ISBN: 978-1-003-20376-6 (ebk)

DOI: 10.4324/9781003203766

Typeset in Bembo
by Taylor & Francis Books

CONTENTS

FIGURES

ACKNOWLEDGEMENTS

This book has been a long time in the making, and, along the way, I have bene-fited from the support of so many colleagues, mentors, and loved ones.

Thank you to my undergraduate English professors, Jeana DelRosso and Gene Farrington, who hooked me on critical theory and inspired me to continue my edu-cation. Thank you to my PhD advisors, Shelley Salamensky and Elizabeth DeLough-rey, who encouraged and advised me long after my dissertation, from which this book has evolved, was complete. My dissertation was made possible through funding sup-port from the UCLA Department of Theater, Film and Television (TFT); the Center for the Study of Women; the Fred Thorp Fellowship; the Graduate Summer Research Mentorship; the Chancellor's Prize; and especially the Dissertation Year Fellowship. Special thanks to Lindsay Brandon Hunter, Tanya Brown, Areum Jeong, Linzi Juliano, Mary Martinez-Wenzl, Sean Metzger, Lisa Sloan, and the TFT support staff who helped me throughout the dissertating process.

I am grateful to my warm and wonderful colleagues in the Writing and Critical Inquiry Program at the University at Albany, SUNY, who supported me throughout the book writing process with feedback, encouragement, and—of course—faculty lounge chocolate. Special thanks go to Allison Craig, Sarah Giragosian, and Rae Muhlstock for generously and repeatedly reading my work. I am also thankful to my students for shaping and challenging my thinking, especially those in my inaugural Creative Arts and Environmental Crises course during the height of the pandemic: Luci Burnett, Maria Covey, Quialmeiry Carrasco Puntier, Katrina Siriban, Diana Slobodian, and Christine Sternbach. You inspire me.

Portions of this book were presented at many conferences over the years, and I am thankful for the opportunities to think through my ideas with others. Special thanks to the Ecology and Performance Working group at ASTR and the Environmental Humanities roundtables at MLA, both of which were incredibly fruitful to my writing process. I especially appreciated the kindness, accessibility, and scholarship of senior scholars like Alicia Carroll, Una Chaudhuri, William Germano, Petra Kuppers, Stephanie LeMenager, Theresa J. May, Vin Nardizzi, Kirsten Pullen, and Byron Santangelo.

Portions of chapter 1 were previously published in "Playing with Plants" in *Theatre Journal* 66.3 (2013) and portions of chapter 5 were previously published in "#BPCares: Sinking Oil, Spreadable Détournement" in *ISLE: Interdisciplinary Studies in Literature and the Environment* 26.4 (2019).

I am immensely appreciative of the anonymous reviewers of this book who gave me incisive and thought-provoking feedback, as well as to the responsive, helpful editors at Routledge: Rosie Anderson, Suzanne Arnold, Grace Harrison, and especially Matthew Shobbrook.

Many thanks to my eco-performance writing group who gave me productive feedback and kept me going: Kelli Shermeyer, Sarah Standing, Jonah Winn-Lenetsky, Lisa Woynarksi, and especially Angenette Spalink, my Zoom book buddy in the 11th hour. To Annika Speer, my dear friend and hype person since our first day at UCSB, thank you for your authenticity and humor. Thanks also to Katie Bell Barnett for the long walks and early feedback on the book proposal.

I am equally thankful to the many artists who gave me access to their work and their process: Vaughn Bell, Meghan Moe Beitiks, Naima Green, Julie Hébert, Marc Bamuthi Joseph, Mimi Poskitt, and Caridad Svich. Thanks also to Penny Jones at the Liz Christy Community Garden for allowing me to interview her.

I am indebted to my children's teachers at the Bethlehem Children's School, who kept teaching during a pandemic, and without whom this book would not be possible.

Thanks and love to my Mom and Dad, Cathy and John Ryan, who have always supported me and my dreams. And, most importantly, love and gratitude to my spouse, Emmet O'Hanlon, for always lending a sympathetic ear, and to our children, Quinn and Kieran, who remind me every day that life is for living.

INTRODUCTION

Toward a Spatialized Eco-Performance

8.a. Homeowners shall keep all shrubs, trees, hedges and plantings on the front and buffer yards and easements neatly trimmed and shall keep all such areas properly cultivated and free of trash, weeds and unsightly material…Weeds are defined as any undesired or uncultivated plant that grows in profusion (freely and abundantly), so as to crowd out a desired crop or disfigure a lawn or landscape. No wild or unplanted plants shall be allowed to grow; all must be removed as weeds.

Casas Adobe Terrace Homeowners Association Architectural and Landscape Standards and
Rules (CC&Rs Article IV, Section 1, Paragraph D), 2017

Homeowners in a Tucson, Arizona, neighborhood must abide by rules to "properly" cultivate their yards, as detailed in the above excerpt. Weeds, equated with "trash" and other "unsightly material," must be removed. Any "wild" plants that take root without human cultivation or consent are weeds that will "disfigure" the desired landscape with their excessive growth and abundance. Ironically, what really grows within these rules is an ableist fear of "unsightly" and disfigured plants taking over a planned, aesthetically normalized landscape. Categorical and absolute, the Casas Adobe standards and rules maintain a strict hierarchy in which plants cultivated by humans are desirable and plants that spring up on their own must be uprooted. Given the terrifying problems in the world right now—war, poverty, rising temperatures and sea level rise due to climate change, and the curtailment of civil rights, to name just a few—it may seem parochial to focus on something as minor as one upper middle-class homeowners association's petty rules regarding landscaping. But the pettiness is precisely the point. I begin with these bureaucratic standards to highlight the seemingly miniscule and tedious ways in which nonhuman nature[1] is micro-managed in everyday life.

While the massiveness of climate change in the Anthropocene, a term proposed by geologists to classify our current epoch in which humanity has a dominantly

DOI: 10.4324/9781003203766-1

negative impact on the earth, can invoke fear, this fear is rarely productive, tending to create a sense of overwhelming despair, grief, and inevitability.[2] Furthermore, the global ramifications of climate change also obscure its uneven effects on the Global South, on Black, Indigenous, and People of Color (BIPOC) communities, and on the poor. The totalizing language of disaster not only erases the ways in which certain people and places are disproportionately affected by climate change, but it also leaves little time to examine the driving forces behind climate change. And yet, it is important to situate this seemingly new sense of climate despair and anxiety within a Western framework. As eco-scholar and activist Kyle Powys Whyte (Potawatomi) argues, "Climate injustice, for Indigenous peoples, is less about the spectre of a new future and more like the experience of déjà vu," (2017, 88). Indigenous peoples, having experienced dispossession and genocide at the hands of colonialism, are now directly impacted by the disproportionate impacts of climate change and extractive capitalism—mining, drilling, deforesting at alarming rates to exact maximum profits. While the mounting effects of climate change may terrify some, Indigenous peoples have long grappled with the impacts of Western systems of power that subjugate the environment and minorities as inferior others. Anthropologist Zoe Todd (Métis) points out that Indigenous thinkers have, for millennia, argued for ecological interconnection (2016, 8) and eschewed hierarchical approaches to the environment (Allen, Laguna, 1992, 59), while it is only in recent decades that Western scholars have claimed to invent "new" understandings of ecological connectivity.

Among Western scholars in the sciences, this understanding is reflected in the turn to interdisciplinary task forces and direct action. Realizing, as sociologist David S. Meyer admits, "that the data won't carry the day" (as cited in Quackenbush 2022), some climate scientists have begun protesting government and corporate inaction. Meanwhile, among Western scholars in the humanities, appreciation for materiality and ecological interconnections have created figures like Donna Haraway's cyborgs (1991), companion species (2003), and "tentacular ones" (2016, 31) and concepts like Timothy Morton's "ecological thought" (2010) and "symbiotic real" (2017). However, despite millennia of often disregarded Indigenous thinking and the fairly recent ecological turn in Western scholarship, as well as biological evidence of trillions of microorganisms in the human body, in practice, the Western divide between humans and nonhuman nature remains deeply entrenched, a necessary justification for extractive capitalism. As decolonial theorist Macarena Gómez-Barris argues, extractive capitalism is rooted in colonialism. Focusing on what she calls "extractive zones"—Indigenous territories in South America that are disproportionately mined because of their biodiversity (2017, xvii–xx)—Gómez-Barris posits that "the extractive view sees territories as commodities, rendering land as for the taking, while also devalorizing the hidden worlds that form the nexus of human and nonhuman multiplicity" (2017, 5). Not only does extractive capitalism depend on an objectifying view of nonhuman nature and BIPOC communities, but it deepens this view with violent modes of extraction that leave wreckage in their wake.

While the extractive view renders the environment a resource, it also, like capitalism more broadly, hides its mode of production. For example, within the Global North, it is possible to one-click purchase just about anything—airfare, cell phones, fast fashion, novelty items—and remain wholly disconnected from the processes of production. I agree with David Harvey's assessment that despite many urban discontents—or I would argue because of them—"we somehow lack the stomach for systematic critique" (2012, 4). It is important to recognize that the "we" here is those, like myself, with the economic and racial privilege to opt out of critiquing systems of power that directly benefit us. And yet, the point stands that the onslaught of escalating environmental and social crises in an era of late-stage capitalism has created an overwhelming sense of outrage fatigue, climate grief, and what psychologist Paul Slovic and ecocritic Scott Slovic call a psychic numbness to quantitative information (2015, 7). Thus, while the vegetal micro-management in the Casas Adobe standards and rules is slight, inconsequential even, given the magnitude of climate change and extractive capitalism, its smallness makes it tangible in a way that climate change data and ecological entanglement writ large are not. I am interested in such bureaucratic micro-performances of environmental containment—and counter-performances that contest such containment—for their ability to expose, in concrete and digestible ways, deeply engrained Western directives and desires to contain and domesticate nonhuman nature. The Casas Adobe Terrace Homeowners Association (HOA) rules perform an exacting domestication that makes visible the often invisible forces of corporate and state environmental confinement. Thus, seemingly small performances by corporate and bureaucratic entities to visibly control nonhuman nature, whether it be through stringent gardening ordinances or oil leases, and by artists and activists to resist environmental micro-management, both expose the ways in which the control of marginalized human and nonhuman subjects is spatially performed.

Take, for example, Black gardener Ron Finley who, in 2010, was cited and subsequently subpoenaed for planting a vegetable garden on the parkway median outside his rental house in the food-insecure South Central Los Angeles.[3] The struggle between Finley and his city council, chronicled in Finley's highly viewed 2013 TED Talk, sparked outrage and challenged engrained private property laws, raising questions about how city space is cared for and by whom. The micro-performances of both the Los Angeles City Council, which issued the citation, and of Finley, who defied it, reveal the ways in which, in contrast to largely White[4] middle- and upper-class HOA owners[5] who can opt into their own surveillance, many BIPOC, queer, and poor communities are, alongside nonhuman nature, subjugated, confined, and micro-managed.[6] While views on urban and suburban landscape management are slowly changing in the US, with vegetable gardening gaining popularity during COVID-19 quarantines[7] and increasing interest in movements like No Mow May that give pollinators a chance to thrive, battles continue to be waged over who has the right to garden,[8] where people can garden,[9] and what a garden should look like. These localized battles hint at the much larger, uneven ways in which US corporate and state forces exert control over nonhuman life at home and in the Global South. I am in no way saying that an injustice in one particular place can be equated or applied to an injustice elsewhere, nor that they operate on the same scale with the same ecological consequences: a fine for gardening without permission in Los Angeles is not the equivalent of yet another oil spill in the Niger Delta, and I agree with Whyte that we must directly face "the very different ecological realities we all dwell in" (2018). However, I am saying that the view of nonhuman nature as an inferior and manageable other undergirds spatial injustices and that small acts that exert or resist such control can expose this view as manufactured and anti-ecological.

Just as small performances can highlight the micro-management of vegetal life and marginalized people, they can also expose the joint domestication of aquatic and human subjects. Take, for example, the micro-performances from the Twitter handle @LakeSuperior, an anonymously managed account. Written from the perspective of Lake Superior, the tweets are often anthropomorphically snarky; for instance, @LakeSuperior's bio reads: "I am the greatest lake of all time. G.L.O.A.T. (she/her)." But mixed in with self-aggrandizing tweets are news and science reports about the lake and photos of the water from followers of @LakeSuperior. Following the June 2022 overturn of Roe v. Wade in the US, which protected pregnant people's right to abortion, @LakeSuperior tweeted, "This lake vehemently stands with women having the right to choose" (as cited in Stein 2022). A follower, @sugarkane417, complained, "Yep, I follow @lakesuperior for political takes. Can't anything just be fun?" to which @LakeSuperior replied, "To begin, water is one of the most politicized sources in the world. I, sir, am water." In directly linking the control of uteruses to that of rivers, @LakeSuperior exposes, as ecofeminists have, the joint subjugation of women, queer people, and the environment.[10] Refusing to "just be fun" and tweet another photo of seemingly open waters, @LakeSuperior insists that the same state forces that restrict human rights also restrict the environment. In stressing that water is deeply politicized, @LakeSuperior hints at the often invisible ways in which water is constrained and made inaccessible by border walls, dams, mining, drilling, and urban runoff.[11] Even as Indigenous understandings of environmental personhood have led some states in the US, following countries like Bangladesh and New Zealand, to grant rivers legal rights, such laws remain contentious and difficult to enforce (Westerman 2019). While many Indigenous tribes in the US are located on rivers and are directly impacted by being in extractive zones,[12] people visiting rivers occasionally for recreational purposes may see them as apolitical "fun." Thus, @LakeSuperior's tweets both reveal the political contestation of seemingly open waters and the mutuality of human and nonhuman injustices.

Such moments of exposure are important interventions into the unrelenting domestication and containment of urban and suburban vegetal and aquatic life, revealing that even when environmental micro-management is presented as progress, maintenance, or sustainability, it is almost always a question of power. This micro-management reinforces a human/nonhuman hierarchy, and the inaccessibility and privatization of land and water places limits on who is entitled to healthy, green environments. What eco-theater scholar Theresa J. May has called the "shared vulnerability" of people and ecosystems (2017, 1) often is concealed beneath technocratic attempts to contain, manage, and subdue the environment—attempts that only intensify when disasters like hurricanes and tornadoes strike, momentarily exposing this shared vulnerability. Micro-performances that exact environmental control—such as the HOA rules—and that resist it—such as Ron Finley's community garden or @LakeSuperior's tweets—expose the ways in which, from city ordinances and fines for gardening on public property to river dams, vegetal and aquatic life is controlled and kept on the periphery of human action. They reveal the connections between seemingly small acts of environmental micro-management and extractive capitalism, privatization, and the erosion of civil liberties.

Thus, in this book, my primary aim is to consider how technocratic environmental containment in the US manifests itself spatially and performatively. How has vegetal and aquatic domestication rooted itself into the bedrock of urban life? How is this domestication normalized and reinforced by performance, whether that be the daily ritual of "turfgrass subjects" watering their lawns (Robbins and Sharp 2006) or the containment efforts of oil companies following major oil spills? To engage with these questions, I analyze a variety of cultural works that, like cracks in the concrete, temporarily break through the normative slabs of extractive capitalism, exposing moments when environmental containment fails. I argue that, while the onslaught of mounting environmental and social crises can be numbing, small, tactile micro-performances can briefly cut through the noise, exposing state and corporate micro-management and revealing flickers of tenuous interconnectivity between humans and nonhuman nature. Many of the works I focus on are created by eco-performers who, often with subversive humor, directly challenge environmental domestication through their art or draw attention to failed attempts to confine nonhuman nature. Whether it be guerrilla gardeners, planting on land that is not their own, or comedians sending parodic tweets mocking BP's failure to contain the 2010 BP oil spill in the Gulf of Mexico, all the eco-performers commit small, everyday acts of resistance that contest structures of spatial injustice and center on marginalized vegetal and aquatic subjects. By focusing on performances in which vegetal and aquatic life exceeds its imposed limits or confines, I seek to create small cracks in the concrete of environmental domestication and explore the complexities and challenges of human and nonhuman interactions.

In the following sections, I place my work within its two central frameworks: spatial justice and eco-performance. In this sense, the book reflects the interdisciplinarity popularized by the environmental humanities,[13] which eschews the disciplinary departmentalization so common in academia in favor of working together across disciplines to discuss pressing environmental issues (DeLoughrey, Didur, and Carrigan 2015, 2). I also define and contextualize some of the key ideas informing my understanding of spatial justice, urban life, micro-performance, eco-performance, and what I am calling spatialized eco-performance.

It's All about Space: Toward Spatial Justice

In situating this book within spatial studies, I seek to keep spatiality at the forefront of my analysis. Central to my argument are the views that, firstly, there are no neutral spaces, and, secondly, corporate and state control, extraction, and micro-management are exerted unevenly across different geographies. I focus primarily on US eco-performance from the 1970s until today, selecting vivid examples of spatialized eco-performance drawn from the visual arts, social media, photography, theater, film, and activism. Although it may seem counterintuitive to concentrate on the US given that the worst environmental destruction is taking place in the Global South, I do so in part because the US, is, as postcolonial ecocritics Cara Cilano and Elizabeth DeLoughrey suggest, best situated to critique its global exploitation of people and nonhuman nature (2007, 80). Second only to China on carbon emissions, the US must examine its extractive and consumptive practices, and I suggest that looking inward can be a productive starting place for such scrutiny. The tactile, small eco-performances in my archive show how spatial injustices are embedded in the daily lives of BIPOC and nonhuman nature within the US and how such injustices function within larger patterns of global extractive capitalism. Based on my field research in New York, Los Angeles, and Baton Rouge, many of the works I examine take place in urban centers. Densely packed and often diverse, cities are rife with chafing spatial injustices—inequities regarding how space is distributed, accessed, invested in, and surveilled. I consider how urban micro-performances, both those by city and corporate entities and those by resistant artists and activists, expose tedious, bureaucratic attempts to micro-manage marginalized nonhuman and human subjects. For example, in chapter 3, I examine micro-performances of guerrilla gardening, suggesting that the small act of tossing wildflower seeds on city property can expose the erosion of truly public spaces and challenge normative private property laws in the US.

In my views of spatial justice, I am influenced first and foremost by French Marxist philosopher Henri Lefebvre, foundational to urban geography today for his argument that space is not an abstract container but is socially produced ([1974] 1991). Over 50 years ago, he recognized the increasing "symbolic weight" of nature, its abstraction as background décor rather than material being, and worried that nature would become "lost to *thought*" (1991, 30–1, emphasis in original). In other words, the view of nature as intangible as opposed to material would allow its destruction. Time has proven Lefebvre's fears warranted, and the capitalistic abstraction of nonhuman nature increasingly serves as a cloak for environmental domestication and extractive capitalism. Urban geographers like Edward Soja, who has written on spatial injustices in Los Angeles, and David Harvey have both built on Marx and Lefebvre, expanding on Lefebvre's argument that people have a "right to the city" (1968) and examining how spatial injustices are unevenly embedded in city planning, operations, and daily life.[14] I agree with Harvey that, although the "right to the city" has at times been co-opted by private interests, Lefebvre intended it as "a common rather than an individual right," and, as such, it can be exercised to transform the city and urbanites alike (2008). Similarly, Soja builds on Lefebvre by suggesting that, since "space is socially produced," it can also be changed socially (2009). However, he warns that it is much easier to spot individual instances of spatial injustice than it is to recognize the underlying patterns that produce "unjust geographies;" thus, he advocates for a "critical spatial perspective" that explicitly considers the spatial causality of justice and injustice (2009). A critical spatial perspective is one which not only highlights the ways in which spatial injustice may exist in any city planning decision, whether it be where to pave highways or where to plant trees, but also the ways in which these seemingly isolated instances of injustice are connected to and consequences of geographically embedded, multilayered injustices. For example, as I discuss in more detail in chapter 2, a grocery store closing in a Black, food-insecure neighborhood is never just about one company's individual decision but is connected to a host of historic and ongoing spatial injustices like housing and supermarket redlining: discriminating against neighborhoods of color by labeling them "hazardous" investments. Thus, just as there are no apolitical or asocial spaces, neither are there any racially neutral geographies (Reese 2019, 3).

While the view of space as apolitical and race-neutral is not unique to the US, it is uniquely built into the country's foundation, and it is worth considering this history to understand how its legacies continue today. As legal scholar Jedediah Purdy argues, historically in the US, nature has been cast as being anti-political even as it has been ideologically wielded to justify genocide and slavery (2015, 20–7). He posits that the US has constructed four interrelated versions of nonhuman nature: providential, Romantic, utilitarian, and ecological (7–8). In the providential period, nature was seen as a gift from God to settler colonialists, and private property laws were created to erase Indigenous rights to the land (8–9). This was followed by a Romantic period in which nature was glorified as untouched and pure even as it was consumed as a vacation site (123), one, as environmental sociologist Dorceta E. Taylor stresses, designated only for urban, White, male elites (2016). Then, led by Theodore Roosevelt and others, a utilitarian understanding of nature took hold, which embraced conservationism but sought to manage nonhuman nature and people of color through technocratic administration (Purdy 2015, 179–80). While an ecological perspective of nature, in which everything is interconnected, rose to prominence following World War II, Purdy notes its connection to earlier strains of thought, particularly in its continued exclusion of people of color and some aspects of nonhuman nature (206). These four imaginings of nonhuman nature are linear but also simultaneous (27). The effects of these environmental imaginaries have been forged into land and sea, where nonhuman nature, especially in Indigenous territories, is domesticated, managed, treated, mined, parceled. These ideologies have shaped and continue to shape the ways in which nonhuman nature is privatized, regulated, and micro-managed both within the US and by the US globally. As Whiteness studies scholar George Lipsitz argues, racist practices like racial zoning and housing redlining can be traced back to the myth of "pure" land on which the American frontier was founded (2011, 30).

Thus, in assembling the cultural works in this book, I sought out performances that, rather than highlight singular examples of injustice, expose underlying, historic processes of spatial production. While I also engage with the related field of environmental justice, which focuses on how BIPOC communities have been disproportionately impacted by environmental hazards and pollutants, spatial justice is the throughline in this book. In emphasizing spatiality, I aim not only to show how injustice is geographically embedded into daily life but also how spatial mobility—the movement and flow of people, nonhuman life, and goods—is impacted. While sociologists tend to focus on the spatial mobility of people,[15] I find the concept generative for its potential, as cultural anthropologist Raúl Acosta writes, to include "the capacities, imaginaries, localities, materialities, effects, and reverberations of movements by humans, things, and other living beings" (2021, 538). The micro-performances in my archive are spatially mobile in that they cross literal and figurative boundaries, bringing vegetal, aquatic, and BIPOC life into spaces from which they have been deliberately excluded. For example, chapter 1 focuses on plant artists Vaughn Bell and Meghan Moe Beitiks, both of whom challenge the urban marginalization of plant life by bringing vegetal companions with them on their jaunts through the city—whether it be as a personal biosphere, a shopping cart tree, or a jogging buddy. I suggest that this transplantment of urban vegetal life from the windowsill, the pot, and other designated margins of city life into the center of human action exposes the ways in which vegetal life has been contained and micro-managed while also offering a more expansive, spatially mobile vision of urban vegetation. Meanwhile, in chapter 2, Marc Bamuthi Joseph's choreopoem *red, black, & GREEN: a blues* (2011) considers Black environmental life across four different cities—Harlem, Chicago, Oakland, and Houston—staging the various cityscapes as four sides of a house that come apart, shift, and return together in different configurations, revealing the multiscalar dimensions of spatial injustice. As diverse as these two performances and the rest of my archive are, they all share an emphasis on shifting spatial meanings and spatial mobility. Collectively, these small performances expose and resist spatial demarcations, challenging the spatial norms and limits placed on urban human and nonhuman subjects.

And yet, one potential critique of my focus on spatialized micro-performances is that I run the risk of displacing global extractive capitalism with an overemphasis on the local. This is a legitimate concern, especially given the tendency within US environmentalism to focus on local issues. Many eco-scholars have wrestled with this tension between local immediacy and the global networks of capital. For example, ecocritic Ursula K. Heise, troubled by the emphasis placed on localism in US eco-discourse (2008, 9), argues that localized scholarship must be grounded "in a thorough cultural and scientific understanding of the global" (2008, 59). Similarly, as ecocritic Stacy Alaimo argues, "the immediacy of phenomenology…does not enable transcorporeal mappings of networks of risk, harm, culpability and responsibility within which ordinary Western citizens and consumers find themselves" (2016, 2). These cautionary critiques of localism are particularly relevant to eco-performance, because just as its emphasis on embodied, place-based experiences can highlight ecological interconnectivity, it can also reinscribe insular understandings of the environment and the self that fail to consider how one's own actions and positionality affect countless others. Thus, as eco-theater scholars Wendy Arons and Theresa J. May suggest, it is crucial for eco-theater to make "connections between theories of globalization and those that recognize the importance of local and regional identities as represented" through performance (2012, 5). And that is why spatiality and spatial mobility are so central to this book; a critically spatial perspective is not limited to one specific site or performance but rather, like tree rings, extends outward to reveal uneven spatial injustices and ecological interdependencies.

While Heise (2008, 11), along with theater scholar Marcela Fuentes (2013, 32), imagine digitally zooming in and out of spatial perspectives, I find tree rings to be an apt metaphor both for their tactile materiality and for their uneven development. For example, although the growth rings that annually form on trees begin at the tree's center, their common axis may in fact begin at an off-center point. This speaks to the ways in which, while one may begin with one's own ecological reality, this reality is not necessarily the center of ecological thought. Similarly, the concentric rings that gradually form on a tree trunk are often uneven, their diametric growth dependent on environmental factors such as the climate and surrounding plants. Thus, while the tree's growth begins at a common point and extends outward, its pattern is determined by external forces. This might speak to the ways in which localized, micro-performances do not just enact spatial meaning but are enacted upon by existing global, regional, and local forces of containment, extraction, and exploitation. Finally, a tree's pith rays, like fine ribbons or tissues that begin near the tree's core, vertically cut across the concentric circles to transport food throughout the tree. These arboreal characteristics of uneven horizontal and vertical spatiality relate to the eco-performances in this book, which not only shape but are also shaped by other ecological realities and spatial injustices. Take, for example, the 2010 BP oil spill, which I discuss in-depth in chapter 5. An epic corporate and state containment failure that played out on an international stage, the spill and its news coverage exposed the spatially uneven consequences of petrocapitalism. While the spill in the Gulf of Mexico received ample attention, hundreds of spills that take place in the Niger Delta every year go unnoticed in the Global North, revealing what ecocritic Rob Nixon calls "slow violence," attritional, invisible violence in the Global South (2011, 2).

Alaimo suggests that, if local performances are mediated and contextualized within a broader understanding of scientific knowledges, they can actually open one up to "the larger material world" (2016, 2–4). I agree with Alaimo here and would add that contextualized and multiscalar micro-performances can, in small but meaningful ways, expose much larger forces of extractive capitalism and micromanagement, revealing the ways in which every environmental act has multiple, unseen ecological consequences. Focusing on micro-performances that center on marginalized human, vegetal, and aquatic subjects, I argue that, while spatial micromanagement and restrictions on spatial mobility may have local roots, they are connected to regional and global spatial injustices that can be exposed through performance.

Cracks in the Concrete: Spatialized Eco-Performance

I have been bandying about the words "performance," "micro-performance," and "eco-performance" with abandon, so now I want to define how I am using these terms and situate my work within a broader theater and performance context. While I have created the term "spatialized eco-performance" to highlight the spatial dimensions of performance—regardless of whether it takes place onstage, online, or in a river—eco-performance is already profoundly spatialized because of its emphasis on embodiment and place. As May writes, "Always an immediate, communal and material encounter among embodied performer, audience and place, theatre is ecological even as it is representational" (2005, 86). This is particularly the case in eco-performance, which often relates to a specific environment or environmental issue. Indeed, my focus on vegetal and water-based nonhuman nature both onstage and off is reflective of a larger move within eco-performance to consider the performance of nonhuman sites literally and figuratively. Take, for example, the Palgrave series Performing Landscapes, which includes *Performing Mountains* (Pitches 2020), *Performing Ruins* (Murray 2020), and *Performing Farmscapes* (Haedicke 2021). Given the established relationship between performance and place, my term "spatialized eco-performance" may seem redundant or jargony. But I find it useful for several reasons related to theater and performance's past and present.

First, it is important to understand how, historically, theater has participated in colonialism and imperialism. As foundational eco-theater scholar Una Chaudhuri suggests, Western theater, particularly naturalism and realism, has been profoundly "anti-ecological," reinforcing industrialism's bifurcation between nature and culture by treating the former as a backdrop for human action (1994, 26). Building on this work, May examines US anti-ecological theater in-depth, tracing ideologies like frontierism, settler colonialism, Manifest Destiny, and extractive capitalism within US theater from the nineteenth century to today (2021). She argues that frontier mythology still pervades theater, culture, and politics, and, thus, theater must examine its role in propagating such narratives (2021, 7–8). While Chaudhuri encourages Western theater to create a new, ecologically oriented practice "that refuses the universalization and metaphoricalization of nature" (1994, 24), May urges readers to pay heed to US theater's complicity in setter colonialism and neocolonialism and to tell untold "stories that actively practice compassion and demand justice" (2021, 4). Elsewhere, May and her co-author Wendy Arons have expanded on Chaudhuri's turn to the literal, arguing that performance must strive to appreciate ecology in a material sense (Arons and May 2012, 3). In this vein, they advance the idea of "ecodramaturgy," a term first coined by May (2010, 6): "Ecodramaturgy is theater and performance making that puts ecological reciprocity and community at the center of its theatrical and thematic intent" (Arons and May 2012, 4). It grapples with the challenges of staging the nonhuman world, which spans vaster times and places than most theater, often human-centered, allows.

In large part, I developed my concept of spatialized eco-performance in response to the historic and ongoing tendency within theater to abstract and marginalize nonhuman life. In emphasizing the spatiality of eco-performance, I aim not only to highlight the spaces in which performances take place, but also the ways in which, building on Soja, underlying processes of spatial (in)justice shape and are shaped by performance. I am not looking to reassert director Peter Brook's empty space, in which any space can be a "bare stage" (1968, 9), nor am I looking to return to theater scholar Bonnie Marranca's "ecologies of theater," which, as Chaudhuri, Arons, and May stress, is only metaphorically ecological (Chaudhuri 1994, 27; Arons and May 2012, 3). Rather, I articulate a spatialized eco-performance in direct contrast to the realism of traditional theater, in which the stage's four walls constitute the space, while also not insisting that spatialized eco-performance be site-specific in the traditional sense (performed in a particular location rather than on a stage). I suggest there is value in considering the socially produced spatiality embedded in any performance, be it in-person or digital, as well as in considering how micro-performances can expose underlying processes of spatial micro-management, surveillance, and inequity. While I also employ concepts of materiality and embodiment,[16] both key ideas in performance studies[17] and eco-theater, what connects the micro-performances in my archive is a shared emphasis on spatial mobility and engrained spatial injustices.

Just as I use the term "spatialized eco-performance" to highlight spatiality in performance, I prefer the term "eco-performance" to emphasize the multiple material and metaphorical modes in which performances on and within the environment can operate. Although ecodramaturgy and eco-theater can encompass a variety of performance genres, text-based dramaturgy and site-specific theater tend to dominate the field. While some of the performances in my archive are site-specific, I deliberately include digital, filmic, and cultural performances as well to show how eco-performance can make spatial meaning around a specific site even when the site itself is inaccessible. Like theater historian Scott Magelssen, who has studied simulated experiences (2014) and the performance of flight (2020), I often focus on "theater with a 'lower-case t,'" case studies that make meaning through theatrical tools but are not traditional Theater (2020, 7). Take, for instance, my analysis of guerrilla gardening in chapter 3 and of satirical tweets by @BPGlobal mocking BP's cover-up of its 2010 oil spill in chapter 5. Each operates in a different space: in the dirt and online. And, yet, as disparate as guerilla gardening and the BP tweets may appear, both deploy subversive humor to challenge environmental containment, the former by physically transgressing boundaries between private and public space and the latter by poking fun at corporate inability to contain ecological damage.

Like the HOA rules with which I began, throwing seed bombs or tweeting are micro-performances, as are most of the cultural works in my archive. In part, I emphasize small, everyday acts of micro-management and resistance, as I have already said, in direct contrast to the overwhelming magnitude of climate change and ecological disaster narratives. But my secondary reason for selecting small performances is to focus on, as communications and performance scholar Bryant Keith Alexander defines it, performance as "an act of doing" (2006). Performance is often seen as being everywhere, since, as Richard Schechner argues, "anything and everything can be studied 'as' performance" ([2002] 2013, 1). This ubiquity, combined with an emphasis on transgression through liminality—being on the border or margins of social institutions—can, as performance theorist Jon McKenzie argues, create a "liminal-norm," whereby "resistance itself becomes normative" (2001, 50). McKenzie demonstrates his point by considering how corporate culture also depends on performance, in the form of performance reviews, suggesting that both corporate culture and performance studies contain the imperative to *Perform or Else* (2001, 6). Not only can the overemphasis on liminal transgression create performance norms, but it can also oversell performance as a transformative cure-all for social ills. As eco-theater scholar Carl Lavery argues, theater and performance studies tends to make "largely positive—perhaps even hyperbolic—claims for theatre's capacity to bring about behaviour change, more often than not through some ecstatic or enchanted immersion in 'environment'" (2016, 229). Even more troubling is the fact that only those who participate in the performance are directly affected by it, thereby limiting the scope of any behavioral change it might foster.

Thus, I agree with Lavery that theater and performance must consider its limitations, its place as a weak, modest art that cannot save the world but can "make the world problematic, multiple, and complex" (2016, 234). Similarly, eco-theater scholar Lisa Woynarski suggests that eco-performance should embrace nuance and uncertainty rather than adhere to "reductive simplifications" that put forward clear-cut problems and solutions (2020, 7). In focusing on more accessible, quotidian micro-performances, like walking in a city park or tweeting, I seek to avoid grand proclamations of what theater and performance can solve or do. I am influenced by feminist philosopher Rosi Braidotti, who writes, "The pursuit of practices of hope, rooted in the ordinary micro-practices of everyday life, is a simple strategy to hold, sustain and map out sustainable transformations" (2006, 137). Like Alaimo (2016), I am not quite convinced that Braidotti's micro-practices of hope can create "sustainable transformations" (2006, 137), tending to agree with ecocritic Nicole Seymour that climate despair and hope are "often merely different sides of the same coin," both of which insist on neat, definitive answers about the future (2018, 3–4). Nonetheless, I suggest that small, spatialized doings can expose normalized spatial injustices. While many of the micro-performances in my archive gesture toward alternative ways of interacting with nonhuman nature and environmentalism, they often do so in slight, uncertain, and even contradictory ways. For example, in *red, black, & GREEN: a blues*, Haitian-American spoken word artist Marc Bamuthi Joseph must contend with his own desire to "go green" within an environmental movement that has yet to go Black (2013).

While the cultural works in my archive are all spatialized micro-performances or quotidian practices, many of them are also quite absurd and playful. In this sense, they reflect, as Seymour argues in her celebration of "bad environmentalism," the absurdities and ironies of the peculiar times in which we live (2018, 1). The eco-performers in this book play with the absurdity of attempting to separate people from place. They play with a hubris that tries to contain nonhuman nature, redirect roots, stem tides, and drill deeper. They play with nonhuman nature. For example, Meghan Moe Beitiks gets in a water fight with a cactus (2011) while Vaughn Bell takes her plant for a walk (2009). By satirizing small acts of environmental domestication, like the Casas Adobe Terrace HOA rules, the artists and activists in this book expose underlying spatial injustices toward BIPOC and nonhuman life. And, yet, even as they, to varying degrees, gesture toward alternate ecologies by challenging spatial acts of micro-management and marginalization, they do so in tentative, playful, and nuanced ways. As Morton points out, "Knowing more about interconnectedness results in more uncertainty" (2010, 59)—uncertainty of what interconnection means and how it operates in everyday life. While the artists and activists in this book denormalize spatial micro-management and interact with nonhuman nature, they do not pretend to know the ecological other wholly and completely. Instead, they play with the environment: digging into the soil, skimming the water, and imagining vegetal and oceanic lives.

Digging and Diving In

In this book, I am concerned with exposing environmental containment through micro-performance practices between humans and plants, water, and oil. The first half of the book centers on the spatial demarcations that have been made between urbanites and plants. It celebrates performance tactics that undermine such divisions and, at times, offer tenuous, potential modes of human and nonhuman interaction. Chapters 4 and 5 maintain the book's focus on undermining environmental confinement by broadening its scope to include waterscapes. This elemental shift is important, because, as DeLoughrey argues and as the previously mentioned @LakeSuperior exchange suggests, among non-Indigenous people in the West, the ocean continues to be perceived as an unmarked "wilderness or frontier," despite the recent development of a burgeoning critical ocean studies (2019, 134). Whereas the marginalization of plants in the city reflects man's domination of "nature," oceanic containment, contestation, and contamination remain hidden beneath romantic notions of pure wilderness. Given that the "most visible sign of planetary change is sea-level rise" (DeLoughrey 2019, 134), it is crucial to consider how environmental containment is maintained and disrupted on both land and water.

By focusing on vegetal and aquatic containment and cracks—moments when confinement fails—I highlight the ecological permeability belied by containment and by myths of uncharted waters. Some of these cracks are performative interventions, as when guerrilla gardeners illicitly plant on land that does not belong to them. Others are the effects of exploitation, as when 4.9 million barrels of oil spilled into the Gulf Mexico during the 2010 BP oil spill. In both cases, neatly marked divisions between human places and environmental spaces become laughably inaccurate and imagining other ways of interacting with nonhuman nature becomes possible. The micro-performances in my archive may appear insignificant or slight; after all, what can a single seed or a single tweet really do? And, yet, seemingly inconsequential exchanges between marginalized human and nonhuman subjects can contest and delegitimize deeply engrained spatial demarcations and injustices.

This is first seen in chapter 1, "In A Plant Time and Place: Plant Art in the City," which considers the marginalized containment of plants in US cities, where they often are treated as background décor to human action rather than as vital to life. I argue that the work of performance artists Vaughn Bell and Meghan Moe Beitiks highlights playful performance practices that subvert constructed divides between people and plants through small moments of human and vegetal interaction. For example, Bell (2006) invites people to wear plant biospheres on their heads, so they can inhabit plants' homes, while Beitiks (2010) goes jogging with an English Ivy, exchanging gases with it as they go. Through such micro-performances, Bell and Beitiks transplant vegetal life from the background of human action to the center. Performing what I call "transplantment," the artists traverse spatial demarcations between humans and plants and highlight vegetal experiences and traits. They critique the marginalization of plants and imagine an alternate ecology, in which plants inhabit the same spaces as urbanites. At the same time, I also suggest that Bell and Beitiks both reveal how plants and plant care tend to be associated with women, particularly with White women.

Chapter 2, "'I Speak to Him of Seeds:' Centering Black Experiences of Green Spaces," employs an environmental justice framework to consider the ways in which Black urbanites have been systematically excluded from green spaces, as well as the stereotype that urban Black neighborhoods are "concrete wastelands" devoid of plant life. I begin by analyzing Naima Green's photographic series *Jewels from the Hinterland* (2013–), which features prominent Black artists, activists, and professionals in city gardens. I argue that Green subverts White narratives of urban decay and environmental disinterest within Black communities through her quiet, everyday portraits. I then examine Marc Bamuthi Joseph's choreopoem *red, black, & GREEN: a blues* (2013), set in Harlem, Chicago, Oakland, and Houston, particularly the piece's ability to formulate ecological practices that celebrate Black life and improvise with limited land. Taken together, Green's and Joseph's works play with misrepresentations of Black relationships to nonhuman nature and celebrate Black urbanites' experiences of plants.

In chapter 3, "'Plant Some Shit:' Guerrilla Gardening as Tactical Performance," I maintain my focus on vegetal and human micro-management in US cities but expand my scope by considering eco-activism as a performative and subversive act. I analyze guerrilla gardening within the US, tracing the movement from the early 1970s in New York City to today. Throughout, I examine how the playful, vegetal micro-performances of guerrilla gardeners, from the Green Guerillas in Lower Manhattan in 1973 to Ron Finley in South Los Angeles today, unevenly challenge capitalistic demarcations between private and public land. I suggest that, whether they plant in a vacant lot, a median strip, or a pothole, the eco-activists in this chapter assert their right to the city. Analyzing the rhetoric and performance styles of various guerrilla gardeners, I argue that White gardeners have more spatial mobility than BIPOC gardeners and can take more dramatic license, leaning into the illicit aspects of guerrilla gardening without fearing for their lives. Contextualizing the international emphasis on guerrilla gardening as a subversive movement, I consider how guerrilla gardening performance varies based on gardeners' geography, racial identity, and overall purpose.

Together, the first three chapters focus on small eco-performances that are also micro-practices of traversing the city street, the park, and the vacant lot. To varying degrees, all the works in these chapters expose spatial divisions between urbanites and vegetal life through their performance of everyday practices that resist micro-management and interact with vegetal life in small, concrete ways. At the same time, their interactions are not universal or always successful: the relationships in chapter 1 between plant artists and vegetal life are highly mediated; the relationships in chapter 2 between Black urbanites and land are often complicated; while the relationships between guerrilla gardeners and plants can be fleeting when gardeners must throw their seeds and go. In this sense, the micro-practices in this section engage with plant life in uneven and ambivalent ways, often raising more questions than they answer. While the book shifts to waterscapes in chapters 4 and 5, it continues to expose the spatially unjust micro-management of marginalized people and nonhuman life. However, what makes this section unique is not only its focus on corporate and state aquatic containment but also on environmental narratives that seek to restore bodies of water to a mythical, pure state. I suggest that, while the aquatic containment efforts of extractive capitalism exacerbate spatial injustices, the notion of liberating water by returning it to some nonexistent natural state is no less damaging. In contrast to the previous section, in which I explore vegetal art and spatial mobility across many US cities, in this section I focus on two particular bodies of water in order to show how containment and ecological restoration narratives contest and bolster one another: what is wild must be contained and what is contained must be liberated.

Chapter 4, "'Touch the Water': Performing the Los Angeles River," centers on the containment of the 51-mile-long Los Angeles (LA) River, which was encased in concrete by the Army Corps of Engineers in 1959. I dedicate the entire chapter to LA River performances, because the river's hotly contested concrete channelization and rapidly shifting spatial narratives make it an ideal site from which to explore environmental containment and the many people affected by it. I show how, in the nineteenth century, the Tongva people were uprooted from the river and forced into servitude by their Spanish colonizers, while today, Latinx communities along the river are either disproportionately exposed to environmental hazards or are being displaced by gentrification. I examine the contradictory political performers around the river, including the environmental activists who want to "free the river from her concrete corset" (Hébert 2009, 2), the politicians who want to revitalize it, the Army Corps of Engineers which wants to contain it, and Hollywood directors who want to make it the scene of drag races, body dumps, and alien invasions. Throughout the chapter, I consider how the river's concrete channelization has created contesting containment narratives and ruptures between people and place, a theme explored in two very different performances. The first, the film *Chinatown* (1974), focuses on corruption in water management and places the properties of water in the film center stage. The second performance, Cornerstone Theater Company's *Touch the Water: A River Play* (2009), critiques the channelization and attempts to reconnect the river to Tongva and Latinx peoples. Despite their stylistic differences, both eco-performances trouble the river's domestication by playing with water and the shifting spatial narratives that surround it. With ambivalence and uncertainty, they contest both environmental containment and the myth of a return to an ecologically pristine state.

My focus on containment and ecological restoration narratives continues in chapter 5, "Performing Ecological Irresolution in the 2010 BP Oil Spill," which centers on (mis)representations of the 2010 disaster, the largest spill in US history at that time. Just as I focus on the particular site of the LA River in chapter 4 in order to explore the many containment and restoration narratives that surround it, I examine the BP oil spill in order to consider how myths of environmental disaster, containment, and resolution are produced. I argue that BP's hypervisible attempt to contain the ongoing oil leak in the Gulf of Mexico created a monolithic narrative of disaster management, whereby the spill seemed to be resolved when the leak was plugged. In contrast to this spectacular resolution, micro eco-performances like satirical tweets from @BPGlobalPR playfully subvert narratival closure, highlighting the environmental irresolution that still surrounds the spill and other unresolved spills, like those in the Niger Delta. Similarly, Look Left Look Right's play *NOLA* (2012) and Caridad Svich's play *The Way of Water* (2013) highlight irresolution by focusing on polyvocality and on the spill's widespread, interspecies toxicity. In contrast to BP's monolithic narrative of disaster resolution, both plays reveal the long-term, ongoing effects of the spill and make connections to other industrial disasters. Ultimately, I argue that spatially situated micro-performances of resistance and disruption can undercut narratives of environmental containment and resolution. Together, chapters 4 and 5 deploy playful and disruptive eco-performance practices to subvert the myths of aquatic containment and restoration.

In "The Fable of Managed Earth," biologist David Ehrenfeld urges ecologists and environmentalists to let go of the techno-optimism of a "gardened planet, in which all nature is tamed, preserved, and managed for its own good by enlightened, sophisticated humans" (2014, 85). And yet, within the West, colonizing Mars seems more conceivable than finding a way out of extractive capitalism. While the spatialized eco-performances in these chapters do not purport to solve this problem, they do poke fun at corporate and state attempts to micro-manage BIPOC, vegetal, and aquatic life. They expose and revel in moments of containment failure—when tree roots crack the sidewalk or when an ocean wave sloshes over an oil containment boom—and create disruptures through quotidian micro-practices like walking with plants, gardening on someone else's land, or tweeting. In an age of perpetual crisis, the works in this book gesture to tenuous but boundless possibilities for alternative ecological modes of being and doing.

Notes

1 Many eco-scholars have rejected the word "nature" as an entirely humanist construction. While alternative terms have been proposed by eco-scholars like Donna Haraway and Timothy Morton, I elect to use "nonhuman nature" interchangeably with "nonhuman life," because, as geographer Noel Castree points out, "there's no compelling evidence that 'nature' has lost its semantic importance as a key signifier in both expert and lay discourse" (2016, 151).

2 While climate grief is not a new idea, a recent interdisciplinary survey of 10,000 young people aged 16–25 from ten different countries found that 75% of young people found the future frightening and 59% were extremely worried about climate change (Hickman and Marks et al. 2021).

3 The United States Department of Agriculture Economic Research Service provides an interactive Food Access Research Atlas to track low-income and low-access areas throughout the US.

4 I capitalize the racial category of Whiteness throughout the book, in addition to other categories like Black, Brown, and Indigenous, to emphasize, as sociologist Eve L. Ewing argues, that "Whiteness is not only an absence" (2020).

5 Although homeownership in HOA communities continues to grow, with nearly 60% of all new single-family homes being built in HOAs, racial homogeneity is higher in HOAs than in non-HOAs: nearly 75% of all HOA homeowners are White, while 73% of non-HOA homeowners are White (Clarke and Freedman 2019, 7–8).

6 Take, for example, Jamaican-American Hermine Ricketts who, in 2013, was forced to destroy her front yard vegetable garden, which she and her White spouse had tended for 17 years in Miami Shores, Florida, or pay a $50 fine for each day the garden remained (Wamsley 2019). Six years later, after a drawn-out legal battle, a Florida law went into effect nullifying local bans on gardens, and Ricketts could finally plant again (Wamsley 2019).

7 Many news stories have celebrated "victory gardens" as part of the "war" on COVID-19. See, for example, D'Amelio 2020 and Davis 2020.

8 Take, for example, the three White women in a dilapidated Detroit neighborhood who called the police on Black gardener Marc Peeples dozens of times. Stalking charges were brought against Marc Peeples for, as his lawyer put it, "gardening while Black," but the charges were ultimately dismissed by the judge as false and racist (Burch 2018).

9 The visibility of front yard gardens means that they are often contested, regardless of whether the gardener lives in an HOA or non-HOA house or is a renter or homeowner. See Kurutz (2012) for US-wide examples of gardening citations and fines, which have led gardeners to resist the "war on gardening."

10 Ecofeminists like Dianna Fuss (1989), Carolyn Merchant (1980), and Val Plumwood (1993) and queer eco-scholars like Catriona Sandilands (1999) have been at the forefront of this work.

11 For more on specific threats to US rivers, see American River's Most Endangered Rivers of 2022 report.

12 Indigenous peoples are often forced to be at the forefront of environmental protest efforts because extractive capitalism affects their livelihood and way of life. For example, in 2021, the Menominee Tribe of Wisconsin fended off yet another attempt to dig an open pit mine on the Menominee River (Bowe 2021).

13 For more on the environmental humanities, see, for example, DeLoughrey, Didur, and Carrigan (2015), Oppermann and Iovino (2017), and Adamson and Davis (2017). Although the environmental humanities appears to be a new field, with new journals, conferences, and academic departments still emerging around it, Adamson and Davis point out that the term itself dates back to 2001 while its theoretical roots date back to "some of the earliest cosmological narratives" (2017, 5).

14 As Soja points out, while Harvey is influenced by Lefebvre, he does not employ the term "spatial justice" and his Marxism is often more concerned with justice itself than with its spatiality (2009).

15 See Ettore Recchi and Aurore Flipo's "Spatial Mobility in Social Theory" (2019) for the history of the concept of spatial mobility in sociology.

16 See, for example, Diana Taylor's groundbreaking book *The Archive and the Repertoire*, which argues for embodied memories and practices (2003).

17 Performance studies as a field originated at New York University and Northwestern University in the 1960s and was seen as a way for performance to break away from more traditional theater. It is highly interdisciplinary, because it offers a lens through which to examine identity, culture, politics, and everyday life. However, many theater and performance scholars today use "theater" and "performance" interchangeably.

References

Acosta, Raúl. 2021. "Mobility." *The SAGE Handbook of Cultural Anthropology*, edited by Lene Pederson and Lisa Cliggett, 537–553. London: Sage Publications.

Adamson, Joni and Michael Davis, eds. 2017. "Introduction." In *Humanities for the Environment: Integrating Knowledge, Forging New Constellations of Practice*, edited by Joni Adamson and Michael Davis, 3–19. New York: Routledge.

Alaimo, Stacy. 2016. *Exposed: Environmental Pleasures and Politics in Posthuman Times*. Minneapolis: University of Minnesota Press.

Alexander, Bryant Keith. 2006. "Performance and Pedagogy." In *The Sage Handbook of Performance Studies*, edited by D. Soyini Madison and Judith Hamera, 253–260. London: Sage.

Allen, Paula Gunn. 1992. *The Sacred Hoop: Recovering the Feminine in American Indian Traditions*. Boston: Beacon Press.

"America's Most Endangered Rivers of 2022." *American Rivers*. https://tinyurl.com/yeskxbup.

Arons, Wendy and Theresa J. May, eds. 2012. "Introduction." In *Readings in Performance and Ecology*, edited by Wendy Arons and Theresa J. May, 3–12. New York: Palgrave Macmillan.

Beitiks, Meghan Moe. 2010. *Yielding Air*. Performance. November 20. Oakland, CA. https://tinyurl.com/4rt5cnpm.

Beitiks, Meghan Moe. 2011. *Water Fight with a Cactus*. Performance. Oakland, CA. https://tinyurl.com/yc4u23w5.

Bell, Vaughn. 2006. *Biosphere Built for Two*. Exhibit. SOIL Gallery, Seattle, WA. https://tinyurl.com/3d8e8mw7.

Bell, Vaughn. 2009. *Landscape for Walking*. Edith Russ House for New Media, Oldenberg, Germany. https://tinyurl.com/295uffhp.

Bowe, Rebecca. 2021. "Tribe Fends Off Dangerous Open Pit Mine Plan." *Earthjustice*, May 14. https://tinyurl.com/u97xd8m4.

Braidotti, Rosi. 2006. *Transpositions: On Nomadic Ethics*. Malden, MA: Polity Press.

Brook, Peter. 1968. *The Empty Space*. New York: Scribner.

Burch, Audra D.S. 2018. "How 'Gardening While Black' Almost Landed This Detroit Man in Jail." *New York Times*, October 26. https://tinyurl.com/h9kdyzec.

Casas Adobes Terrace Homeowners Association. 2017. "Architectural and Landscaping Standards and Rules." https://tinyurl.com/5cdtkeu6.

Castree, Noel. 2016. "Nature." *Keywords for Environmental Studies*, edited by Joni Adamson, William A.Gleason, and David N. Pellow, 151–155. New York: NYU Press.

Chaudhuri, Una. 1994. "'There Must Be a Lot of Fish in That Lake': Toward an Ecological Theater." *Theater* 25 (1): 23–31.

Chinatown. 1974. Dir. Roman Polanski. Perf. Jack Nicholson and Faye Dunaway. *Paramount Pictures*.

Cilano, Cara and Elizabeth DeLoughrey. 2007. "Against Authenticity: Global Knowledges and Postcolonial Ecocriticism." *Interdisciplinary Studies in Literature and Environment* 14 (1): 71–87.

Clarke, Wyatt and Matthew Freedman. 2019. "*The rise and effects of homeowners associations.*" *Journal of Urban Economics* 112: 1–15.

D'Amelio, John. 2020. "'Victory Gardens' for the war against COVID-19." *CBS News*, April 5. https://tinyurl.com/yck2jm9x.

Davis, Chelsea. 2020. "Everything To Know About Starting Your COVID-19 Victory Garden." *Forbes*, April 16. https://tinyurl.com/2uh229wc.

DeLoughrey, Elizabeth M. 2019. *Allegories of the Anthropocene*. Durham, NC: Duke University Press.

DeLoughrey, Elizabeth, Jill Didur, and Anthony Carrigan, eds. 2015. "Introduction: A Postcolonial Environmental Humanities." In *Global Ecologies and the Environmental Humanities*, edited by Elizabeth DeLoughrey, Jill Didur, and Anthony Carrigan, 1–32. New York: Routledge.

Ehrenfeld, David. 2014. "The Fable of Managed Earth." In *Keeping the Wild: The Domestication of Earth*, edited by George Wuerthner, Eileen Crist, and Tom Butler, 85–108. San Francisco: Foundation for Deep Ecology.

Ewing, Eve L. 2020. "I'm a Black Scholar Who Studies Race. Here's Why I Capitalize 'White.'" *Zora*, July 2. https://tinyurl.com/p8k7w9zv.

Fuentes, Marcela A. 2013. "Zooming In and Out: Tactical Media Performance in Transnational Contexts." In *Performance, Politics, and Activism*, edited by John Rouse and Peter Lichtenfels, 32–55. New York: Palgrave McMillan.

Fuss, Diana. 1989. *Essentially Speaking*. London: Routledge, 1989.

Gómez-Barris, Macarena. 2017. *The Extractive Zone: Social Ecologies and Decolonial Perspectives*. Durham, NC: Duke University Press.

Green, Naima. 2013. *Jewels from the Hinterland*. Photographs. http://www.naimagreen.com.

Haedicke, Susan C. 2021. *Performing Farmscapes*. Cham, Switzerland: Palgrave Macmillan.

Haraway, Donna. 1991. *Simians, Cyborgs, and Women: The Reinvention of Nature*. New York: Routledge.

Haraway, Donna. 2003. *The Companion Species Manifesto: Dogs, People, and Significant Otherness*. Chicago: Prickly Paradigm Press.

Haraway, Donna. 2016. *Staying with the Trouble: Making Kin in the Chthulucene*. Durham: Duke University Press.

Harvey, David. 2008. "The Right to the City." *New Left Review* 53. https://tinyurl.com/2p8kz5ay.

Harvey, David. 2012. *Rebel Cities: From the Right to the City to the Urban Revolution*. London: Verso.

Hébert, Julie. 2009. *Touch the Water: A River Play*. Dir. Juliette Carrillo. *Cornerstone Theater Company*. Los Angeles. May 28.

Heise, Ursula K. 2008. *Sense of Place and Sense of Planet: The Environmental Imagination of the Global*. Oxford: Oxford University Press.

Hickman, Caroline and Elizabeth Marks, et al. 2021. "Climate anxiety in children and young people and their beliefs about government responses to climate change: a global survey." *Lancet Planet Health* 5 (12): E863–873.

Kurutz, Steven. 2012. "The Battlefront in the Front Yard." *New York Times*, December 19. https://tinyurl.com/54trd2dm.

Lavery, Carl. 2016. "Introduction: Performance and Ecology—What Can Theatre Do?" *Green Letters: Studies in Ecocriticism* 20 (3): 229–236.

Lefebvre, Henri. 1968. *Le droit à la ville*. Paris: Anthopos.

Lefebvre, Henri. [1974] 1991. *The Production of Space*. Trans. Donald Nicholson-Smith. Malden, MA: Blackwell Publishing.

Lipsitz, George. 2011. *How Racism Takes Place*. Philadelphia: Temple University Press.

Magelssen, Scott. 2014. *Simming: Participatory Performance and the Making of Meaning*. Ann Arbor: University of Michigan Press.

Magelssen, Scott. 2020. *Performing Flight: From the Barnstormers to Space Tourism*. United States: University of Michigan Press.

May, Theresa J. 2005. "Greening the Theater: Taking Ecocriticism from Page to Stage." *Journal of Interdisciplinary Literary Studies* 7 (1): 84–103.

May, Theresa J. 2010. "Kneading Marie Clements' Burning Vision". *Canadian Theatre Review* 144: 5–12.

May, Theresa J. 2017. "Tú eres mi otro yo—Staying with the Trouble: Ecodramaturgy & the AnthropoScene." *The Journal of American Drama and Theatre* 29 (2): 1–18.

May, Theresa J. 2021. *Earth Matters On Stage: Ecology and Environment in North American Theater*. London: Routledge.

Merchant, Carolyn. 1980. *The Death of Nature: Women, Ecology, and the Scientific Revolution*. New York: HarperCollins Publishers.

Morton, Timothy. 2010. *The Ecological Thought*. Cambridge, MA: Harvard University Press.

Morton, Timothy. 2017. *Humankind: Solidarity with Non-Human People*. London: Verso.

Murray, Simon. 2020. *Performing Ruins*. Cham, Switzerland: Palgrave Macmillan.

Oppermann, Serpil and Serenella Iovino, eds. 2017. "Introduction: The Environmental Humanities and the Challenges of the Anthropocene." In *Environmental Humanities: Voices from the Anthropocene*, edited by Serpil Oppermann and Serenella Iovino, 1–22. New York: Rowman & Littlefield.

Pitches, Jonathan. 2020. *Performing Mountains*. London: Palgrave Macmillan.

Plumwood, Val. 1993. *Feminism and the Mastery of Nature*. New York: Taylor & Francis.

Purdy, Jedediah. 2015. *After Nature: A Politics for the Anthropocene*. Cambridge: Harvard University Press.

Quackenbush, Casey. 2022. "The climate scientists are not alright." *The Washington Post*. May 20. https://tinyurl.com/4rdaptry.

Recchi, Ettore and Aurore Flipo. 2019. "Spatial Mobility in Spatial Theory." *SocietàMutamento-Politica* 10 (20): 125–137.

red, black, & GREEN: a blues. 2013. Marc Bamuthi Joseph/The Living Word Project, dir. Michael John Garcés. Redcat, Los Angeles. January 31–February 3.

Reese, Ashanté M. 2019. *Black Food Geographies: Race, Self-Reliance, and Food Access in Washington D.C.* Chapel Hill, North Carolina: UNC Press.

Robbins, Paul and Julie Sharp. 2006. "Turfgrass Subjects: The Political Economy of Urban Monoculture." In *In the Nature of Cities: Urban Political Ecology and the Politics of Urban Metabolism*, edited by Nik Heynen, Maria Kaika, and Erik Swyngedouw, 110–128. New York: Routledge.

Sandilands, Catriona. 1999. "Raising Your Hand in the Council of All Beings: Ecofeminism and Citizenship." *Ethics and the Environment* 4 (2): 219–233.

Schechner, Richard. [2002] 2013. *Performance Studies: An Introduction*. New York: Routledge.

Seymour, Nicole. 2018. *Bad Environmentalism: Irony and Irreverence in the Ecological Age*. Minneapolis, MN: University of Minnesota Press.

Slovic, Scott and Paul Slovic. 2015. "Introduction: The Psychophysics of Brightness and the Value of Life." In *Numbers and Nerves: Information, Emotion, and Meaning in a World of Data*, edited by Scott Slovic and Paul Slovic, 1–22. Corvallis, OR: Oregon State University.

Soja, Edward. 2009. "The City and Spatial Justice." *Spatial Justice* 1. https://tinyurl.com/3sa u74v8.

Stein, Emma. 2022. "Lake Superior Twitter account reaches online fame for its take on Roe v. Wade decision." *Detroit Free Press*, June 29. https://tinyurl.com/nk8sx3ap.

Svich, Caridad. 2013. *The Way of Water*. NoPassport Press.

Taylor, Diana. 2003. *The Archive and the Repertoire: Performing Cultural Memory in the Americas*. Durham: Duke University Press.

Taylor, Dorceta E. 2016. *The Rise of the American Conservation Movement: Power, Privilege, and Environmental Protection*. Durham, NC: Duke University Press.

Todd, Zoe. 2016. "An Indigenous Feminist's Take On The Ontological Turn: 'Ontology' Is Just Another Word For Colonialism." *Journal of Historical Sociology* 29 (1): 4–22.

United States Department of Agriculture Economic Research Service. Food Access Research Atlas. Last updated October 31, 2019. https://tinyurl.com/2c8kfd6t.

Wamsley, Laurel. 2019. "After 6-Year Battle, Florida Couple Wins the Right to Plant Veggies in the Front Yard." *NPR*, July 2. https://tinyurl.com/2ajfnj2f.

Westerman, Ashley. 2019. "Should Rivers Have Same Legal Rights as Humans? A Growing Number of Voices Say Yes." *NPR*, August 3. https://tinyurl.com/5dkr82m5.

Whyte, Kyle Powys. 2017. "Our Ancestors' Dystopia Now: Indigenous Conservation and the Anthropocene." In *The Routledge Companion to the Environmental Humanities*, edited by Ursula K. Heise, Jon Christensen, and Michelle Niemann, 206–215. New York: Routledge.

Whyte, Kyle Powys. 2018. "White Allies, Let's Be Honest About Decolonization." *Yes!* April 3. https://tinyurl.com/2p9au48z.

Woynarski, Lisa. 2020. *Ecodramaturgies: Theatre, Performance, and Climate Change*. Cham, Switzerland: Palgrave Macmillan.

1

IN A PLANT TIME AND PLACE[1]

Plant Art in the City

Verdant grass grows in a shopping cart pushed down a residential street. A glass dome filled with moss rests on a human head. A cactus retains water during a water fight. A snake plant gets its own art show. These acts, some conceived by contemporary performance and installation artist Vaughn Bell (she/her) and some by Meghan "Moe" Beitiks (she/they), all involve interspecies performance between plants and people. While some of the pieces are staged in art museums, many of them take place in city streets: for Bell in Seattle, Washington, and for Beitiks in Boston, Massachusetts, and Oakland, California. Whether it is Bell "parking" her shopping cart tree in a parking lot to rest beneath its shade on a sunny day or Beitiks taking an English Ivy for a jog in downtown Oakland, these artists show that plants belong in all the places people are. This is a radical idea given the fact that vegetal subjugation is a linchpin of Western notions of human dominion (Merchant [1994] 2008, 16–17). As plant philosopher Michael Marder argues, within Western thought, plants have "populated the margin of the margin" (2013, 2).

However, this is slowly starting to change. In the last ten years, there has been a "plant turn" in Western thought across the humanities and the sciences (Myers 2017). The burgeoning field of critical plant studies,[2] building on previous turns to posthumanism and animal studies (Arlander 2020, 124), reexamines plant and human relationships from a variety of disciplines and perspectives. Like other "turns" in Western scholarship, plant studies is not new outside of Western systems of thought. However, it marks an important moment of critical self-examination of how plants have been "othered" throughout all aspects of Western life, and it begins to consider how plants perform in their own right: how they communicate with one another (Simard 2016) and remember (Gagliano et al. 2014). Interest in vegetal life and well-being has also made its way into popular culture, through international bestsellers like *The Hidden Life of Trees* (2015), PlantTok (TikTok videos about plants), and international movements to save the bees by planting

DOI: 10.4324/9781003203766-2

native gardens with pollen-rich flowers. And yet, despite these exciting changes, the marginalization of plants is often deeply embedded into city design and architecture. Although attempts to "bring nature into the city" intensified in Europe and North America in the twentieth century, as views on pollution, work, and leisure changed (Brantz and Dümpelmann 2011, 2), it was added after city infrastructure was already in place. As such, in many cities, plants continue to be an afterthought, meant to complement and improve human life without ever complicating it or challenging its spatialized superiority.

Take, for instance, the uniform trees that dot many a US sidewalk in thriving city centers. Often evenly spaced and identical in species and size, these trees tend to fade into the background as pedestrians or drivers hurry past. Thus, the very ubiquity and necessity of plants has caused them to be ignored and devalued. While uniform trees serve as a commonplace, picturesque background in middle- and upper-class city neighborhoods, they are scarce in inner city neighborhoods, where historic redlining is directly linked to tree inequity,[3] which I discuss in more depth in the following chapter. Whether sidelined or absent altogether, vegetal life in the city often remains in the background of human action. As Marder observes, "The absolute familiarity of plants coincides with their sheer strangeness, the incapacity of humans to recognize elements of ourselves in the form of vegetal being" (2013, 4). Such recognition is crucial, not only to appreciate plants in their own right, but also to recognize how vegetal marginalization and micro-management is tied to other urban spatial injustices like tree inequity.

Because of its ability to frame, center, and elevate subjects, performance can be a particularly useful tool for bringing plants out of the margins, a place they have resided in within Western thought for centuries. Indeed, as feminist scholar Prudence Gibson argues in *The Plant Contract* (2018),

> the aesthetic act—visual and performance art—could mediate difficult post-Edenic relations with plants, could ease viewers into a more humble relationship with the vegetal, and could change our perceptions of plants as 'other' and instead return humans to the vegetal world
>
> *(in Gibson and Sandilands 2021).*

Thus, in this chapter, I consider how vegetal-centric eco-performances and micro-practices can not only bring plants to the fore of human thought but also bring people into plant thinking. Plants move and grow at their own pace, a pace that may seem inexorably slow to humans, particularly to urbanites in bustling cities. However, as performance studies scholar Richard Schechner argues, performance is "marked, framed, or heightened behavior separated out from 'just living life'" ([2002] 2013, 35). Bell's and Beitiks's heightened behaviors draw attention to the ways in which plants historically have been viewed and treated, especially in cities. In this chapter, I apply Marder's plant theories to the artists' vegetal micro-performances, and—drawing on critical plant studies, animal studies, and eco-performance for theoretical support—I consider how plant performance can upset the normalization of plant domestication and create more meaningful relationships between plants and people.

While plants are receiving a lot of attention in various fields lately, they continue to be underexplored in theater and performance. Perhaps this is because staging the vegetal raises gnarly questions like: how can one perform with plants in a meaningful, mutual way in an art form that is historically humanist? Or, as artist Annette Arlander asks, "Could exploring ways of performing with plants mitigate the anthropocentrism of performance art?" (2020, 137). Although eco-theater scholars have not considered these questions in-depth regarding plants, they have examined the risks of anthropomorphism when staging animals,[4] and these ideas are useful when considering vegetal performance. For example, eco-theater scholar Una Chaudhuri notes that since animals "will not speak, they are ceaselessly spoken, cast into a variety of discursive registers, endlessly troped…forced to perform *us*" (2010, 511, emphasis in the original). Whereas Chaudhuri combats animal ventriloquism, eco-theater scholar Theresa J. May cautions against becoming so preoccupied with the "snarl of anthropomorphism" that we ignore animal representation altogether (2012). Both perspectives are useful to plant and people interactions: on the one hand, plant assimilation is all too likely, given that plants' means of expression are even more unfamiliar to humans than animals' means, and on the other hand, Western performance scholars and artists cannot continue to ignore plants in performance for fear of misrepresenting them.

And yet, the likelihood of misrepresenting plants may be greater than that of misrepresenting animals, especially since, within Western thought, communication is primarily appreciated through language. While some animals communicate to humans through sound and nonverbal expressions—a wagging tail, a peck, a purr—our ability to detect plant communications is still limited.[5] However, as Monica Gagliano, John C. Ryan, and Patrícia Vieira argue, plants have their own forms of communication, such as electrical signaling, hormones, and scents (2017, xviii). Thus, despite how challenging it might be to think beyond verbal communication, "we should continue trying to listen to what plants tell us in their own modes of expression" (xviii). One of the primary ways plants communicate themselves, according to Marder, is spatially (2013, 75). For instance, plants can express their well-being through the growth of healthy leaves, shoots, or buds and their unmet needs through withering petals and stunted growth. In theorizing "plant-thinking," Marder argues that even though plants are voiceless, they, just like humans, express themselves spatially (75). To the extent that they physically take up space, they are "spatialized materiality" (75). However, this spatialized materiality often goes unacknowledged by humans until plants take up more space than they have been allotted—when tree roots crack city sidewalks, for example—or when plants take up less space than intended—shrinking, shriveling, or otherwise marring the landscape. While such instances of uncontainable or unhealthy plants may succeed in drawing the attention of humans, performances between people and plants can highlight everyday plant materiality that would otherwise go unnoticed.

Bell and Beitiks are not the first artists to stage encounters between plants and people. Much contemporary plant art tends to either focus on how plants can perform of their own accord (Gibson and Sandilands 2021) or on the inter-dependence of people and plants. Take, for example, Ani Liu's *Laboratory of Long-ings* (2017), in which human sweat is harvested for plant consumption.[6] Bell's and Beitiks's work also focuses on vegetal and human interdependence, but what sets them apart is their emphasis on the spatial mobility of plants and their use of absurdism to simultaneously critique the marginalization of flora and foster new relationships with plants based on vegetal qualities of time and spatiality. Privileging the space and time of plants over that of people, Bell and Beitiks supplant human-centric ontologies and create new epistemologies for human and plant relations. Whether it is Bell wearing a moss biosphere on her head as she walks through Boston (2003) or Beitiks *Yielding Air* to an air-purifying English Ivy (2010), both artists take plants from their expected place—the garden, the pot, the windowsill—and reimagine them in motion.

Their performance pieces feature plants "out of place"—plants on the move throughout busy urbanscapes, plants still materially rooted in their soil but meta-phorically uprooted from fixed locations. Performing what I call "transplantment," these pieces quite literally traverse the spatial demarcations of private/public, nature/culture, and plant/animal/human. By transplantment, I do not mean that plants are uprooted from their homes and moved to new homes, which can be traumatizing for them. Rather, they and the homes they germinated in—be it a shopping cart or a dome—shift from the margins of human activity to the center. In motion or prepared for movement, the plants perform material crossings throughout the city that inspire theoretical crossings as well. Through the transplant-ment of plants and place, Bell and Beitiks both critique the taxonomic marginalization of plants and perform an alternate ecology in which plants and people are inter-embodied. Reimagining their socio-spatial relationship with plants, these artists signal an innovative engagement between urban plants and people and, with it, a new form of vegetal performance.

Since flora's spatialized materiality largely goes unacknowledged, what is needed is a spatial reorientation, and this is where transplantment, the movement of plants across space and "out of place," becomes crucial. Plant mobility has the potential to undermine spatial norms and to highlight the materiality of plants, thus emphasiz-ing plants' and humans' shared spatiality. As critical theorist Bill Brown argues, objects become things when they either stop working or get in the way of humans; such occurrences alter the relationship between object and subject (2001, 3–4). While plants are living beings, they have been taxonomically reduced to objects, but, through spatial reorientation, their materiality can be reasserted. For example, the sight of a human wearing a plant dome on her head and ambling down a busy street might be the contemporary equivalent of the flâneur walking his turtle. The sight is humorous because it is incongruous with the speed of modern life. Similarly, the sight of someone jogging downtown while holding a large ivy is also incongruous, because plants are associated with rootedness and being on the periphery of human action. What begins as amusement, though, may grow into a questioning of the vegetal status quo. Playing with plants in places designated for humans and bringing humans into places designated for plants, Bell and Beitiks trouble the spatial boundaries separating plants and people and celebrate vegetal materiality.

Thus, in this chapter, I utilize the work of Bell and Beitiks to imagine new spatialized practices for plant and human interconnection. I begin by analyzing Bell's work in order to interrogate the constructions of nature/culture and private/public, before considering how the performance of a spatialized transplantment can alter plant and people relations. I then compare Bell's and Beitiks's work, expanding on the potential modes and applications of transplantment. Lastly, through an examination of one of Beitiks's staged pieces, I consider the potential and possible limitations of performing plants. I argue that, given the intensifying effects of climate change, it is crucial that plants' central role in our global ecology be acknowledged, and I suggest that interspecies performance is one important strategy for creating such recognition. And so I turn to performance interactions between people and plants, carbon dioxide and oxygen.

Shopping-Cart Performances

While both Bell and Beitiks deploy comedy to explore and foster relations between plants and humans, I begin with the former because of her dual emphasis on deconstructing taxonomical hierarchies and recasting plants as central contributors to city life. Formerly based in Boston and now in Seattle, Bell, a White woman raised in a family of landscapers, grows her own work. In this sense, she undermines hierarchical taxonomies not only by staging the spatialized materiality of plants but also through the act of gardening. For example, her 2002–03 series *Portable Environments* includes several pieces, some of them featuring lawns and some trees, but all of them grown by Bell in shopping carts. While most of the pieces were eventually shown in a gallery,[7] many began as filmed performances in which the artist wheeled the shopping-cart plants throughout the city of Boston. In each piece, flora, in several feet of dirt, fills the cart entirely and strains against the metal, thus demonstrating that it was grown in the shopping cart rather than placed inside of it fully grown. The fusion of the stereotypically natural flora and the cultural, urbanized shopping cart blurs boundaries between nature and culture, even as the transplantment of *Portable Environments* contests the strict separation between public and private space. By planting decorative lawns and trees, representative of an urban longing for suburbia, in shopping carts, which are more likely to be seen abandoned on city streets than at stores, Bell pairs a symbol of rootedness with one of transience.

Transversing spatial demarcations of public and private streets with her *Portable Environments*, she speaks to a common problem in American cities: that of limited and unequal access to flora. As she pushes her shopping-cart plants down both relatively green and entirely barren streets, Bell and her portable environments call attention to the larger environment and its management. For instance, the strict organization of public greenery—be it around a park, street, public university, school, or courthouse—and its maintenance may only be conducted by official, approved gardeners.[8] Furthermore, while some city dwellers are fortunate enough to have their own private gardens, many others are not. Thus, their engagement with green spaces is limited to observation and aesthetic appreciation, assuming that they have ready access to public parks. Socio-environmental injustices tend to be compounded, however, whereby people with the least amount of personal land often also have the least amount of public land in their neighborhoods, further decreasing the odds of interspecies engagement between people and plants. As urban geographer Edward Soja insists, "[j]ustice and injustice are infused into the multiscalar geographies in which we live," and they create "lasting structures of unevenly distributed advantage and disadvantage" (2010, 20). Although there has been a surge in innovative gardening practices in the last decade,[9] spatialized and multilayered environmental injustices mean that working-class neighborhoods and neighborhoods of color are often cut off from flora and, with it, clean air.[10]

One of the *Portable Environments* that particularly highlights this spatialized injustice is *Portable Lawn* (2003). In the documented performance, Bell vigorously pushes a metal shopping cart uphill; the cart is filled with dirt out of which sprouts unruly grass (see Figure 1.1). Around half of the cart's perimeter, Bell has placed a three-inch white picket fence, through which some of the grass grows. The conventional fence gestures to the privatization of land, but also undermines it by only marking off half of the lawn. Most significant of all, however, is where Bell travels

FIGURE 1.1 Bell pushes a shopping cart filled with growing grass and half-enclosed by a white picket fence. Vaughn Bell, *Portable Lawn*, 2003. Courtesy of the artist.

with the *Portable Lawn*: through a Boston neighborhood with identical white houses, each with a uniform front yard featuring only trimmed grass and two shrubs. Each house's patch of grass is guarded by a matching two-foot fence. The black, arched, iron-grate fencing appears to be more of an aesthetic choice than a protective one, yet it nonetheless serves to mark the yards as private property. The houses' front lawns, like so many throughout the country, are nondescript and unremarkable; they are ubiquitous sights that have become part of a pernicious lawn monoculture. Bell's mobile lawn, with its tall, uneven blades of grass and visible roots, stands in stark contrast to the stationary lawns, with their stubby, homogenized grass and buried roots. With ironic absurdity, Bell juxtaposes her *Portable Lawn* with the houses' unportable lawns in order to question the seeming normalcy of the latter and to raise public awareness about an otherwise invisible monoculture.

This monoculture is so vast that were turf grass to be a crop, it would be the "single largest irrigated 'crop' in the U.S., occupying a total area three times larger than the surface of irrigated corn" (Milesi et al. 2005).[11] The pervasiveness of lawns, as well as the massive amounts of chemicals and water needed to keep them in monocultural condition, goes unquestioned; as geographers Paul Robbins and Julie Sharp argue, turf grass is "viewed as a cultural artifact, rather than a political or economic one" (2006, 112). Lawns are commonplace, so much so that they only attract attention when they are not well-maintained—when they are overgrown, sparse, or yellowing—or, in the case of *Portable Lawn*, when they are taken out of their usual context and location. Because lawns only receive attention when they are out of order, they are often viewed aesthetically rather than politically. Robbins and Sharp argue, however, that urban monoculture is part of a political economy through which homeowners become "turfgrass subjects," not only subject to the influence of global chemical companies and to the judgment of their neighbors, but also subject to the lawn itself, "whose essential ecology is high maintenance, fussy, and energy demanding" (122). Robbins and Sharp's goal here is not to anthropomorphize lawns but rather to problematize the monocultural insistence on lawns, regardless of how much water they consume or how unsuited they are to desert or Mediterranean climates.[12]

Not only does turf grass homogenization contribute to climate change, but it also creates barriers between green spaces and people. For example, the chemicals used to maintain the monochromatic purity of lawns also keep people from inter-acting with them in any meaningful way. Chemical flags and "Keep off the grass" signage discourage people from approaching lawns, let alone touching or smelling them. University and courthouse lawns are often delicately roped off like museum pieces, while many private lawns are fenced off, reinforcing the fact that they are on private property and that any public engagement with them will be deemed trespassing. If, however, the size and maintenance of one's lawn is meant to represent one's financial and geographical security, then Bell's work threatens such middle-class, largely White measurements of stability,[13] supplanting them with roaming plants. Transplanting that which is most meant to represent an established place, *Portable Lawn* exposes lawn monoculture and, with its half-fence, mocks the strict privatization of lawns.

With her portable environments, which appear where least expected, Bell exposes naturalized representations of flora that cast plants in background roles. The sight of her and her *Portable Environments* traversing the city directly upsets normative representations of gardens as fixed, stationary, and rooted. Presenting flora in unusual circumstances, the artist ruptures rather than restores binaries of nature/culture and public/private and, in that sense, her work may be reflective of what geographer Maria Kaika calls the "urban uncanny"—moments when the supposedly natural makes an unexpected appearance in domesticated spaces (2005, 51).[14] The urban uncanny in Bell's work pops up, for instance, when a tree in a shopping cart brushes a parking meter or when the artist waits to cross a busy intersection with her companion tree. *Portable Environments* is just that—its pieces travel across demarcated spaces of public and private, natural and cultural. The sight of Bell and *Portable Environments* traveling along Boston streets may initially seem absurd, since plants, and grass in particular, are symbols of suburban rootedness. And, yet, the sight may lead one to consider why Bell's shopping carts seem so bizarre and out of place. Insomuch as plants are typically defined by their lack of locomotion—their inability to move from one place to another—Bell grants her portable pieces a greater degree of physical agency.[15] While the plants still depend on the artist to move them, just as they depend on her for daily care, their mobility destabilizes accepted definitions of plants as fixed, rooted, and instituted.

Whereas humans imagine themselves moving from one place to another, Bell's shopping-cart plants transplant urban environments and are themselves environments. On the most practical level, Bell's performance recycles abandoned shopping carts, turning discarded signs of neglect into mobile homes for plants. In the face of increasing privatization of public space, Bell creates plant art that both critiques the micro-management and privatization of green spaces and places plants in the center of human action. As ecofeminist Catriona Sandilands observes: "The loss of a public realm for ecological discussion signals the loss of the place where we might come to understand ourselves as ecological citizens rather than as managerial subjects or disciplined objects" (1999, 222). The shopping-cart pieces not only signal a loss of an ecological commons—a space in which flora and fauna can interact—but they also create transitory environments for ecological exchange between plants and people.

Transplanting Taxonomies

Bell's *Portable Environments* is not the artist's only series to both deconstruct and reimagine human and plant relations. However, whereas *Portable Environments* transplants flora across public and private space, the gallery installation *Personal Landscapes* (2005–06) transplants flora from the vegetal plane to the animal plane.[16] The piece features leashed plants, ranging in size from miniature to small, attached to dolly wheels. The leashed plants look as though they are awaiting walks, thereby linking their domestication to that of pets typically walked by humans. Like *Portable*

Environments, Personal Landscapes mocks the ways in which culture and nature have been historically represented as separate, oppositional entities. However, the piece also destabilizes the human/animal/plant triad and its ranked taxonomy; thus, it builds on *Portable Environments*, suggesting not only that plants can transplant fixed spatial boundaries, but that they can also transplant nominalistic boundaries. Even as they undermine the commodification of plants (and, subsequently, animals), Bell's leashed pieces also figure as what Donna Haraway calls "companion species" (2007, 7), gesturing toward a performative exchange between people and plants.

Personal Landscapes consists of plants in wheeled trays made of wood or porcelain (see Figure 1.2). Although Bell has, at times, taken the plants for city walks and invited gallery visitors to do likewise, this particular artistic iteration only *implies* mobility, capturing the plants in a pre-movement moment. Nonetheless, the performance of caring for the plants and the careful framing of the plant art are performances all their own, evidenced by the precise staging of the piece. For instance, *Personal Landscapes* features five transportable plants: the three largest are leashed closest to the gallery wall while the two smaller plants, which are no more than four inches by two inches, trail behind. The largest tray contains diverse cacti surrounded by desert stones, and, unlike the smaller pieces, it has large wheels that extend beyond the plant's base, not unlike monster wheels. The deep tire tread, combined with the metal frame and chain-link leash, suggests a sturdy, mobile plant that is prepared for all kinds of terrains.

FIGURE 1.2 Five plants grow in individual containers that have wheels and are leashed to the gallery wall. Vaughn Bell, *Personal Landscapes*, 2006. Photo courtesy of Richard Nicol.

In contrast, the four other plants' wheels are neatly tucked underneath their trays and their leashes are made of colorful cloth. For instance, the middle box contains tall grass and has a vibrant purple leash while two smaller boxes of grass with hot pink leashes trail behind it. The final plant, a mixture of crag and moss, is shaped like a shaggy Yorkshire terrier alertly awaiting its walk.

On the one hand, the title of the piece, *Personal Landscapes*, suggests a parody of humanist attempts to classify and dominate nature. Although the term "landscape" has been helpful in acknowledging human construction of land, it has contrarily strengthened the divide between humans and land, prioritizing intellectual conceptualization over material engagement. As ecofeminist Val Plumwood argues, "[t]o describe the land as a 'landscape' is to privilege the visual over other, more rounded and embodied ways of knowing the land" (2006, 123). It is to suggest that land can be surveyed and encompassed, and adding the word "personal" to the term "landscape" goes even further, insinuating that land can be owned, appropriated, privatized. Inviting "virtual and idealist approaches to the land" (123), landscape terminology[17] often abstracts the very materiality it seeks to contextualize.[18] Combined with the leashes, Bell's title gently mocks human ownership and dominion of land.

On the other hand, the phrase "personal landscapes" can refer not only to private ownership of land, but also to private, or intimate, experiences of it. As Bell herself says:

> I guess what I'm really interested in is landscape but not just landscape as a concept, that's something in the distance, but as a physical reality that humans are intimately connected to. I'm interested in the way the work can sort of reinforce that connection or make us aware of that connection in a different way
>
> *(KQED 2009).*

Personal Landscapes stages an alternate connection between people and plants, one in which the latter, for better or for worse, are compared to animals. If the leashes alone do not make this analogy evident, the crag and moss plant in the shape of a terrier certainly does. By directly placing plants in the role of companion animals, Bell not only stages an interspecies landscape, but also subverts the human/animal/plant hierarchy. However, just as the term "landscape" is both problematic and productive, so too is the comparison of plants to animals.

Because plants have been so marginalized, their comparison to animals is, in one sense, a promotion. Of course, this is not to say that plants are in any way inferior to animals, or humans for that matter, but rather that they have been taxonomically and practically treated as such. Meanwhile, human regard for companion animals has only intensified in the last century, to the point that pets are integral members of families. Indeed, the immense popularity of companion animals in New York City has led Roberta Olson and Kathleen Hulser to call the city a "petropolis" (2003, 133–43). Urban canine and feline companions in particular have increasingly been treated like humans—given organic food, traditionally human names, and luxurious stays at pet hotels (Nast 2006, 894).[19] Bell's evocative *Personal Landscapes* considers what it might be like if plants were treated as lovingly as companion animals. What if humans rushed home from work to play with their plants, to take them for neighborhood walks, to feed them only organic food? How might this performance of care bring plants from the periphery of human thought to the center? For instance, the three grass plants in *Personal Landscapes* may be interpreted as a broad sketch of kinship, a grouping of the same flora in varying sizes. The miniature trays of unruly lawn, in contrast to the larger tray, imply an ecological vulnerability and a greater need for personal attention and care. Likewise, beyond linking the domestication of plants to that of animals, the dog-shaped crag and moss can foster the same awareness and concern for minerals and flora that are typically only bestowed on household animals.

And yet, by linking plant and animal care, Bell also highlights the species' mutual subjugation. Animal studies has considered the anthropomorphism and commodification of animals for quite some time, and many of its findings apply to the "pet" plants in *Personal Landscapes*. For example, of all the animals that humans encounter, a staggering 98 percent are not companion animals, but farmed animals intended for human consumption (Wolfson and Sullivan 2004, 206). Thus, even as canines and felines receive increasingly more protective rights, most animals continue to go entirely unprotected. Linking plants to animals, then, does not necessarily afford them more ethical consideration. Similarly, just because companion animals are pampered does not automatically mean that they have more agency than marginalized plants; in fact, it may mean quite the opposite. As much as the term "companion animal" suggests an egalitarian relationship between humans and animals, the leashes in *Personal Landscapes* expose the underbelly of pet domestication. Each leash is a different color and size and seems to match the qualities of each plant: the delicately thin pink leashes are attached to miniature boxes of fine grass; the thicker purple leash is attached to the larger box of grass; the heavy, chain-link leash is attached to the tray of rugged cacti; and the black leash is attached to the black-and-brown moss-terrier. By complementing the flora with coordinating leashes, symbolic of the plants' domestication, Bell comically undermines the infantilization of both companion plants and animals. As Chaudhuri cautions, "the anthropomorphic and infantilizing mass-cultural discourse on animals" casts animals as "just like us, only cuter" (2010, 512). Therefore, while treating animals and, in Bell's pieces, plants like miniature humans may result in better care for both, it also refuses to acknowledge nonhumans on their own terms as simultaneously connected to and distinct from humans.

At the same time, the fact that each plant is housed in a wheeled mechanism seems reminiscent of Haraway's cyborgs, "hybrid[s] of machine and organism" (1991, 117). More recently, Haraway has turned to "companion species," of which cyborgs are "junior siblings" (2003, 11). Unlike the term "companion animal," the term "companion species" is heterogeneous enough to include flora, fauna, and minerals, and, like the cyborg, it offers the potential for ongoing interspecies hybridity. As Haraway writes, "The [interspecies] partners do not precede the meeting; species of all kinds, living and not, are consequent on a subject- and object-shaping dance of encounters" (2007, 4). By combining plant, animal, machine, and mineral, Bell subverts hierarchical, hermetic categorizations, insisting instead on multiple, ongoing interspecies relationalities. Exceeding taxonomical boundaries, Bell's plant art is made up of multiple organic and inorganic substances that cannot be limited to one fixed category but instead transplant normative species' divisions, blurring the lines between where one species ends and another begins. Thus, *Personal Landscapes* not only playfully mocks human appropriation and domestication of plants, but also stages a new interspecies hybridity that undermines the fixity of the human/animal/plant triad.

While all of Bell's work simultaneously subverts plant norms and performs new interspecies interactions, I have thus far largely focused on the former to first undermine existing practices before imagining new ones. Now, however, I turn to embodied interspecies practices, for, as eco-theater scholar Wendy Arons points out, "[w]hat 'nature' is, and how we relate to it, may be discursively constructed, but no matter how we apprehend that nature, there are in fact real ecological systems that are affected by material action (or non-action)" by humans (2010, 150). In the performances previously analyzed, all of the plants have apparatuses that assist their mobility, but also physically separate them from people; the shopping-cart handles and the leashes allow humans to push and pull wheeled plants, but they create distance between the two as well. In the following Bell performances, however, human and plant are more materially merged. In the first, which is a series of plant biospheres, people are transplanted instead of plants; human heads are surrounded by glass domes filled with various flora. This inverted transplantment places flora center stage, quite literally encompassing humans and facilitating an up-close and personal interspecies sensorial exchange. In the next and last Bell piece, *Garment for Flora–Fauna Relationship* (2006), flora is transplanted to the human body, suggesting a strategy for extended material exchange between plants and people. Together, these pieces stage innovative alternate ecologies and embodied practices for interspecies interaction.

Biospheres for Plant and People Permeability

If Bell's mobile plants act as portable companions, her biospheres create alternate ecologies in which plants and humans are on the same material plane. Such ecologies are crucial, given that cultural studies' spatial shift in the last few decades has tended to focus on the comings and goings of humans in space, rather than on nonhuman nature within space. In terms of theater studies in particular, Chaudhuri notes an overemphasis on humans' "ecological transit," their moves to and from environments with which they are "utterly and irremediably at odds" (1995, 82). How plants shift and move is rarely of any consequence except inasmuch as they inconvenience or uproot humans. So busy are most humans passing through their environments—with which they are irrevocably connected—that, even though nonhuman nature can speak, it is uncommon for humans to stand still long enough to listen (May 2005, 96).

In response to such postmodern haste, Bell has designed several biospheres, some of which include *Portable Personal Biosphere* (2003–04), *Biosphere Built for Two* (2006a, see Figure 1.3), *Metropolis* (2012), and *Village Green* (2008–). Each biosphere houses a variety of moss and, in the larger pieces, ferns. All the biospheres are made of clear glass, but *Portable Personal Biosphere* is spherically shaped and has one hole in its base for a human head, while the others are rectangularly shaped and have between two and four holes for heads. The larger pieces, too cumbersome for mobility, are hung from gallery ceilings so that visitors can stand with their heads inside the biosphere and their bodies outside. Bell's biospheres allow just enough space for people to peek their heads in; there is little room for head-turning, let alone for arms. Made stationary by all of the pieces (with the exception of the *Portable Personal Biosphere*), human visitors to the biospheres have nowhere to go; surrounded by flora that they might otherwise never notice, they have little choice but to fully acknowledge the plants that now loom large at their eye level.

FIGURE 1.3 A house-shaped, glass terrarium with plants and two people's heads inside. Vaughn Bell, *Biosphere Built for Two*, 2006. Photo courtesy of the artist.

In the biospheres, the encompassing moss is magnified as the human body is transplanted, stilled, and minimized.

Unlike Biosphere 2, the prodigious glass ark completed in 1991, Bell's biospheres are not made to human scale, but to moss scale. The Biosphere 2 project began because of an interest in human preservation and, as eco-theater scholar Baz Kershaw points out, it "has been seen as a metaphor for human survival against all the odds produced by the human animal" (2007, 318). By shaping her biospheres for moss rather than people, Bell privileges the former over the latter. Whereas Biosphere 2 was created as a place for humans to study and classify diverse organisms and environments, Bell's pieces are places for plants; humans are welcome to visit, but the biospheres are not able to wholly or permanently accommodate them. As Bell writes in her "real estate" description of *Biosphere for Two*: "Inhabitants: moss of various species, humans at times."[20] The human heads are temporarily transplanted to the realm of the plants, which physically and ideologically take center stage.

Typical of Bell's work, the biospheres convey a double meaning: on the one hand, they are facetiously commodified, advertised as vacation getaways; on the other hand, they are miniature worlds that imagine a greener and more intimate engagement with flora. As Bell describes it:

> The Personal Biosphere is the answer for anyone who feels the ill effects of urban living. Many long for the sweet smells of nature and greenery while living amidst concrete and diesel fumes. With this amazing new device you can have the smells of nature with you everywhere. As you walk, even down a busy sidewalk, you will have the sensation that you are looking out over a green horizon
>
> (2003–04).

Even as she employs the playful tone of a salesperson, mocking human desire to miniaturize and possess nature, Bell also envisions a more egalitarian relationship between vegetal life and people. Spatially inverting the plants' position, she places them on humans' visual level rather than at ground level. Enclosed in the biospheres, human visitors become more physically attuned to the varieties of moss and their specific environment—the moss's dips and swells and the beads of moisture that gradually form on the glass as plants and people exchange gases. These subtle environmental changes, detected by senses that are temporarily fixed in place rather than traveling to and fro, reveal the undeniable ways in which "place and person are permeable" (May 2005, 94). With their heads surrounded by plants, visitors to the biospheres are sensorially attuned and turned to the plants' materiality.

This figurative and literal turn to plants resonates with Haraway's definition of nature as both a *topos*—a "place," or rather a "commonplace"—and a *tropos*—a "trope" or "turn" (1992, 67). It is a *topos* in that it is a discursive place where participants may find common ground with which "to rebuild public cultures," but it is also a *tropos*, a "figure, construction, artifact, movement, displacement" (67). In that *tropos* means to "turn," Haraway argues that humans and nonhumans alike must turn toward the earth to articulate new, expanded understandings of nature, creating commonplaces that can lead to otherworlds. Bell's biospheres are places unto themselves, tropes of larger ecologies; they create miniature environments in which plants are central and, in the case of *Portable Personal Biosphere*, also traverse other environments. It is in these biospheres where, ironically, humans cannot turn their heads away from plants and must instead turn toward new conceptions of them. In particular, the shared biospheres like *Metropolis*, which can accommodate four human heads at once, offer a commonplace for new performance practices between humans and flora. Physically forced to stop turning away from flora, human biosphere participants are temporarily transplanted from human time and place to plant time and place; with the human and plant hierarchy momentarily displaced, they can begin to physically sense a more egalitarian Otherworld.

Toward an Interspecies Performance

I have explored plants as mobile environments, companion species, and sensorial ecologies, and now I turn to embodied performance in Bell's *Garment for Flora–Fauna Relationship* (2006b, see Figure 1.4). Like the artist's biospheres, it stages an inter-embodied relationship whereby plant and person are physically joined; however, unlike the biospheres, which can only temporarily house human heads, *Garment* allows for an extended interspecies exchange. A dress with a pouch at the chest for a bonsai plant and a side pouch for a water spritzer, *Garment* allows its wearer to exchange gases with a plant: the latter uses the wearer's carbon dioxide for photosynthesis[21] while the former inhales the oxygen released during photosynthesis. While people are dependent on trees and plants for oxygen, Western culture has often disregarded this relationship, but the garment puts the two species in close enough proximity that they can quite literally exchange gases. The interaction is not only material, though, but also metaphorical, in that the relationship is a microcosmic metonym for the macrocosmic gaseous exchange in which nearly all living organisms participate. Necessitating a material engagement between flora and fauna, *Garment* upsets taxonomical hierarchies by performing a relationship between humans and plants based on reciprocity rather than subjugation.

At the same time, though, while *Garment* offers a prime example of materialized interspecies exchange, its embodiment is also highly gendered.[22] Bell, an integral half of the performance piece, wears a dusty rose smock over jeans, and the plant rests in a pouch just above the artist's uterus. Thus, even as the piece fosters interspecies interdependency, it relies on notions of motherhood and maternal care to bolster the exchange. However, such associations are inevitable given the plant's general vicinity, the artist's own gender, and the piece's emphasis on nurture. As ecofeminist Carolyn Merchant argues, the representation of both women and nature as "naturally" nurturing caregivers on the one hand and wild, uncontrollably "natural" forces on the other persisted up until the Scientific Revolution,

FIGURE 1.4 Bell is watering a bonsai plant growing in her dress. Vaughn Bell, *Garment for Flora–Fauna Relationship*, 2006. Photo courtesy of the artist.

when man sought to master nature through mechanization (1980, 1–2). "Subdued by the machine," earth could now be reduced from an organism to a resource to be drained, pumped, cracked, quarried, and fracked far more than had been possible before the Scientific Revolution (2–3).

In harkening back to a pre-modern era in which women and nature are both represented as maternal caregivers, Bell successfully reasserts earth's materiality, its ontology as organism rather than scientific object, but, at the same time, she also reasserts an essentialized view of women and nature. This conundrum is a frequent one for ecofeminists, many of whom want to reestablish respect for the environment as a living organism without reinscribing the essentialist dominion and conflation of women and nature. In considering how women may care about the environment without reinforcing their patriarchal image as naturally maternalistic and caring, Sandilands argues that "it is vital that the ethics of care be raised as a potential part of a common world to which all actors might find relation" (1999, 226). In other words, rather than women de-essentializing their association with nature by disregarding the environment entirely, *all* people must foster a sense of "ecological citizenship," (225) whereby we "consider ourselves accountable to others whom we may not know," be they human, animal, or environmental others (231). Although *Garment* stresses accountability to flora dependents, as well as recognition of human dependency on plants, it lacks a diverse "ecological citizenship." By not depicting a variety of bodies in the garment, the piece reaffirms women's—especially White women's—naturalized role as caregivers, while also casting the plant as an infantilized dependent.

However, since Bell's work is always both a material exchange and a cultural critique, *Garment* parodies both the stereotype of women as natural caregivers and the stereotype of plants as infants wholly dependent on humans. Indeed, the choice of a bonsai, a miniature tree heavily managed and restricted to provide aesthetic pleasure to humans, undercuts the piece's titular suggestion of egalitarian exchange. As the artist explains,

> Bonsai are cute. These altered, manipulated trees are miniaturized in such a way as to make them humanly controlled, captives to aesthetics. At the same time, their cultivation is a kind of worship, or at least fetishizing, of natural forms and natural processes
>
> *(2006b).*

Bell marks this fetishization with the inclusion of what she calls "a baby bonsai carrier:" the dress's pouch that holds the plant. The "baby bonsai carrier" parodies the miniaturization of plants and takes the infantilizing impulse to uterine extremes. In this sense, *Garment* is akin to *Personal Landscapes* and other Bell pieces in its satire of vegetative dominion. Highlighting the irony of a worship of "natural forms" that leads horticulturalists to fussily manipulate bonsai, Bell asks viewers to consider the limits of plant micro-management. At what point does the bonsai become more of an aesthetic object for human enjoyment than a living organism?

At the same time, by placing plant and person in one garment, Bell resists the bonsai's normative representation as *objet'd'art*. What may begin as a gendered or infantilized relationship can grow into a more egalitarian exchange as the two species learn to share an intimate space—a human body—and to negotiate how they will move and sit together. The human must adapt herself to accommodate the presence, needs, and characteristics of the plant. Daily variables like access to sunlight and weather conditions all play a role in such a determination, but, unlike most gardeners, the artist may feel the plant's dampness or dryness against her own skin. Thus, she acquires an embodied and experiential knowledge of the plant rather than just an intellectual knowledge. As feminist theorist María Puig de la Bellacasa suggests, "Ways of knowing/caring reaffect objectified worlds, restage things in ways that generate possibility for other ways of relating and living, connect things that were not supposed to be connecting across the bifurcation of consciousness" (2017, 65). In other words, the act of caring has the potential to bridge binaries and offer alternate ways of coexisting in the world. In the case of *Garment for Flora–Fauna Relationship*, Bell's long-term, embodied care for the bonsai fosters a physical and psychological connection between plant and person at odds with the cultural marginalization and containment of plants, especially bonsai.

While the piece may draw on a long history of conflating women and nature as maternal caregivers, it also suggests that, through an extended, close interaction with plants, humans may eventually take on some characteristics of flora rather than only impose their own. Likewise, the bonsai is also altered by the experience, growing and releasing oxygen at different rates than it would elsewhere. As Bell writes,

> This garment enables the wearer to come closer to nature by breathing, eating, and traveling with the bonsai. At the same time, in an odd reversal the baby bonsai carrier forces the wearer to adapt their body to the tree's needs, in order to keep it alive
>
> *(2006b).*

Given enough time, the garment gradually changes both its inhabitants as they learn to coexist. The plant is wrapped in the same cloth that Bell herself is in, and it rests close to her diaphragm, which expands and contracts with every inhale and exhale. Even if she wanted to, Bell cannot forget the plant and its needs, just as, with every breath, she cannot forget that plants enable her own ability to breathe. As ecocritic Stacy Alaimo writes, science and environmental ethics are changed by the awareness that "'the environment' is not located somewhere out there, but is always the very substance of ourselves" (2010, 4). *Garment* creates such awareness, quite literally materializing plant and human interconnectivity. Through an ongoing exchange, plant and person negotiate space, air, and movement, and both are changed by the experience. Thus, through eco-performances like *Garment*, which create spaces of exchange between humans and plants, notions of human dominion are not only deconstructed, but also *supplanted* by the recognition of mutual dependence.

Bell and Beitiks at Play

Thus far, I have focused on Bell's work, which simultaneously critiques plant marginalization and fosters plant and human relationships. In order to expand the applications of transplantment, though, I turn now to plant performance artist Meghan "Moe" Beitiks, whose work seeks to remedy flora marginalization by setting plants front and center. The two artists have much in common: both are White; both have Master of Fine Arts degrees—Bell in Interrelated Media and Beitiks in Live Art—; and both utilize humor to strengthen interspecies interdependency between plants and people, particularly in cityscapes. However, although both artists' work is highly performative, Beitiks's pieces, particularly *The Plant is Present* (2011a), directly consider the responsibilities and significance of performance to transplantment. In this sense, Beitiks's work not only complements Bell's plant art but also allows for further consideration of the different modes and potentiality for transplantment within theater and performance studies.

The artists' subtly divergent comedic styles also highlight different aspects of transplantment: where Bell deploys irony, Beitiks deploys goofy playfulness. Where the former's absurdity is often linked to landscape scale—miniaturized trees and "pets"—the latter's absurdity is frequently linked to situational humor and performance interactions. While both artists play with the cultural boundaries that marginalize plants and cross those boundaries through interspecies interactions, Beitiks brings plants and their unique, individual qualities center stage. Whether she jogs with a plant, challenges it to a water fight, or helps it stage its own solo show, Beitiks seeks to highlight plants' biological characteristics through uncharacteristic play. Take, for instance, Beitiks's light and silly *Water Fight with a Cactus* performed in Oakland (2011b). Dressed like a gun-slinging Annie Oakley, the artist calls forth the American frontier mythos of rugged, human individualism and dominion over the land (May 2021). Armed with biodegradable bags of water, Beitiks starts a water fight with the cactus at high noon, staging a battle of "Water Retention vs. Water Retention. Prickly Pear vs. Prickly Personality" (2011b). In the end, of course, the cactus must win the showdown, given that it is designed to hold water and to withstand the heat, whereas Beitiks is not. This fanciful performance demonstrates the artist's interest in imagining unusual and unlikely interactions between plants and people. On the one hand, the piece is a goofy, aberrant improvisation, something the artist might have drummed up on one particularly slow-moving morning, but, on the other hand, it is a pear cactus showcase, merely using the water fight to highlight the plant's biological strength and endurance. While Beitiks initially stages the showdown as a meeting of two equals, she soon admits that, when it comes to desert climates and water retention, the cactus is far her superior. Whereas Bell draws on taxonomical histories of plant miniaturization and compartmentalization to playfully subvert them, here Beitiks restages and subverts frontier narratives of human dominion of the Wild West.

Despite the subtle differences between Bell and Beitiks, both artists are concerned with material and metaphorical transplantment, with changing the way people visually and mentally think of plants and, most of all, the way they experience them. Both artists also negotiate urban spaces, deploying creative strategies to uproot plants from the background of a bustling city and to incorporate them into the center of the action. For example, in *Landscape for Walking* (2009), Bell, as well as visitors to the Edith Russ House for New Media in Oldenburg, Germany, takes long walks through the city with a verdant walking stick. A lush, wavy fern atop a four-foot wooden pole, the walking stick allows participants to bring a plant companion on their city walk. Similarly, in *Yielding Air* (2010), Beitiks jogs with a potted English Ivy in downtown Oakland; dodging traffic at a busy intersection for 30 minutes, artist and plant both bounce to and fro from the high-impact movement. The pace of the two pieces could not be more different: Bell takes a leisurely, calming walk with a plant, whereas Beitiks takes an intense jog; the former gently holds her walking stick, allowing it to assist her movement, whereas the latter clutches the potted ivy, its tendrils trailing behind the artist as they move. As with her biospheres, Bell emphasizes the walking stick's soothing and calming effect, its ability to stimulate peaceful exchanges between harried urbanites and plants. Meanwhile, as with the cactus water fight, Beitiks goofily imagines plants engaging in unlikely activities that highlight their biological strengths; jogging with the English Ivy in congested traffic, the artist stresses the plant's detoxifying properties.

Despite the rhythmic differences between the two pieces, both materially transplant flora from the urban periphery to the center. Photos and videos of the performances are not only remarkable for what is highlighted—the artists and their companion plants—but also for what is missing from the frame: vegetation. Although Oldenburg and Oakland have little in common, the two cities, like most others, largely use flora to complement existing infrastructure; particularly in downtown areas, streets and high towers are the priority and, as an afterthought, some greenery may be added to soften the otherwise monochromatic severity. Privileging plant centrality and importance, both artists insist that their plant companions are every bit as mobile and integral to the city as they themselves are. In casting the plants as walking or jogging companions, the artists refuse to keep them sidelined and to perpetuate their representation as "a veritable symbol of stupor and immobility" (Marder 2013, 118). Not coincidentally, Bell and Beitiks both feature plants with remarkable air-purifying capabilities, thereby emphasizing the plants' functional and aesthetic contribution to urban environments. In different cities and at different paces, the two artists, as well as museum visitors in Bell's piece, perform extended interactions with plants, incorporating them into their daily activities to the point that they influence the way the artists move, feel, and think. Thus, what may begin as a vegetative relocation—transplanting plants from the urban periphery by integrating them into human activities—gradually alters the human participants and observers most of all, as they begin to reimagine plants' purpose, potential, and place in the city.

The Plant is Present

If Bell reimagines plants through tropes of landscape and scale, Beitiks reimagines them through tropes of theater and performance. This is crucial not only because there is a shortage of contemporary theater artists who work with ecological themes (Arons and May 2012, 1), but also because, in presenting plant and human interaction on a physical stage, Beitiks stages the meeting itself, as well as the larger consideration of vegetal performance. In that "performance is always a doing and a thing done," it is both immediate and completed, site-specific and framed by the countless performances that have preceded it (Diamond 1996, 1). However, since performance interpretation does not entirely depend on prior experience, there is still "the possibility of materializing something that exceeds our knowledge, that alters the shape of sites and imagines other as yet unsuspected modes of being" (2). With Beitiks's work, these "unsuspected modes of being" may not only include human behaviors and attitudes toward plants but also plants themselves as unsuspected—or rather humanly disregarded—beings in their own right. This is particularly evident in Beitiks's 2011 piece *The Plant is Present*, which deploys the theatrical stage as a device to challenge the innumerable humanist performances that precede it and to supplant the human actor with a vegetative one. In order for the plant to take center stage, though, the human performer must first be unseated. Thus, in *The Plant is Present*, Beitiks parodically replaces performance artist Marina Abromavić, who became a household name with her piece *The Artist is Present*, with a houseplant.

From March 14 through May 31, 2010, Marina Abromavić performed *The Artist is Present* in the Museum of Modern Art (MoMA). The artist sat silently for 736.5 hours in the museum atrium while visitors waited to sit across from her and look her in the eyes. The piece was only one part of MoMA's retrospective on Abromavić's 40-year career, yet it was the first to garner the performance artist such popular attention and acclaim. Lady Gaga attended the retrospective, Facebook pages and blogs were dedicated to the new piece, an HBO documentary was made, and since then the performance artist has collaborated with Lady Gaga, Jay-Z, and other popular artists.

In contrast, *The Plant is Present* was performed for two nights in 2011 at the School of the Art Institute of Chicago (SAIC), where visitors were welcome to sit opposite the plant for as long as they liked and to write about the experience afterward. To reach the plant, visitors had to pass through the exhibition entrance, which featured the title of the piece, a blown-up photo of the performer, along with its scientific name, *Sansevieria Trifasciata*, more commonly known as a snake plant. Adjacent to the doors was a four-paragraph blurb about the plant and its career improving air quality by absorbing toxins. Once visitors stepped through the exhibition's double doors, they were outside in the chilly November air, and there was a slightly raised platform set on the patchy grass. The small stage had just enough room for two chairs to face one another, and, in one of them, was the snake plant dressed in a black t-shirt, skirt, and shoes, its stiff, vertical leaves extending nearly four feet out of the shirt. Near each corner of the platform, bright stage lights put the plant and its potential visitors under the spotlight.

Both Beitiks's stage set-up and exhibition entrance echo *The Artist is Present*, and Beitiks's close adherence to Abromavić's performance serves to put the two pieces in conversation with each other. For example, the entrance signage to *The Plant is Present*, while smaller in scale than *The Artist is Present* signage (which takes up an entire gallery wall), achieves the same effect, marking the exhibit and its performer as noteworthy. Furthermore, although Beitiks did not receive permission to use the Rodchenko font featured in the Abromavić performance, she chose a highly similar font; likewise, the description of the snake plant as an "epic performer" with a long "career" converting toxins into oxygen stylistically matches MoMA's description of Abromavić's career, while also praising the unique achievements of the *Sansevieria Trifasciata*.

The Plant is Present continues to gesture to *The Artist is Present* in its stage set-up. Although the latter uses white tape rather than a raised platform to establish the performance space, both methods serve to mark off the area as important and to set the stage's occupants off from the observers invited to surround the square performance perimeter. Similarly, although the MoMA piece uses more lights and diffusers than the SAIC piece, both position the lighting in the four corners of the stage, intensely illuminating the chairs and their occupants. Thus, even as the two pieces allow for one-on-one connections between the two chairs' occupants, they also use bright lights and audience scrutiny to reflect on the actual performance of the interaction. In the case of *The Plant is Present*, this not only means that there may be individual connectivity with the snake plant, but also group consideration of what it means to share a moment with a plant. The industrial lighting plays a dual role in this consideration: first, it highlights that the plant is the star of the show, the one people have come to see. By placing the snake plant under the spotlight, Beitiks not only ensures that the plant is present but also that it is the sole performer rather than a background prop to a human's show. Second, the bright lighting, as well as *The Plant is Present*'s surface similarity to *The Artist is Present*, highlights people and plant relations in contrast to interpersonal relations. What does it mean and what can it mean to commune with a plant? The acts of looking, returning a gaze, and being looked at—all present in Abromavić's performance—suddenly take on different meanings when one of the parties is a plant.

By insisting that sitting across from a snake plant is as worthwhile as sitting across from any human, Beitiks foregrounds vegetal life and uses stage devices to encourage contemplation of shared plant–human communication, as well as actual communication. Indeed, many participants note that the intense lighting, the stage, and the intimate seating for two made them feel self-conscious at first; one writes, "I felt uneasy and then at ease. The rain created a strange intimate moment between myself and this living breathing being that I often sometimes forget is living and breathing. I'm walking away with a calm" (Beitiks 2011a). For this person, the shared experience of getting wet out in the rain with a plant reminds them of the commonality between them and the *Sansevieria Trifasciata*. Similarly for others, the initial discomfort of sitting alone across from a plant and being seen doing so eventually gives way to small observations about the plant and their own reactions to it; the simple task of spending one-on-one time with vegetal life allows for consideration of what the activity and the plant itself signify. Staging an alternate performance time, Beitiks gives participants the freedom to sit with the snake plant for as long as they wish. Temporarily normalizing human and plant sit-downs, the performance encourages an extended engagement with flora, rather than the passing glance plants typically receive as humans hurry past them. As Marder suggests, "plant life" has its own unique pace and movement, "which we customarily disregard, since it is too subtle for our cognitive and perceptual apparatuses to register in an everyday setting" and since our own tempo is so rapid (2013, 21). Granted an extended audience with the snake plant, stationary visitors may slow their own human tempo and consider plant time and rhythm.

However, although Beitiks's piece encourages human participants to spend time with the snake plant, it cannot determine how they interact with it. The varied responses to the experience reveal that there is still much more work to be done if plants are to be seen as anything other than fixed, unresponsive objects. For instance, several people project their own thoughts and feelings on to the plant, noting its ability to silently listen to them (Beitiks 2011a). Such responses maintain a subject/object relationship, in that the plant is cast as a fixture or prop for humans to reflect further on themselves rather than to engage with the plant. It is hard to imagine that any of the plant's particularities—its species, size, coloring, or characteristics—affect those human observers determined to see the plant as a prop to their own sense of self. At the same time, though, even a failed interaction—one that emphasizes human thought instead of considering plant thought—can be productive if the human participant takes notice of the plant, observing its specific spatiality rather than ignoring it. For instance, as one participant writes, "The swaying of the leaves felt like the plant was nodding to the conversation we had in my mind" (Beitiks 2011a). Although the participant interprets the plant's movement as tacit agreement, they nonetheless pay attention to its shape and movement. As philosopher Jane Bennett suggests in her exploration of vegetal sympathy, "Perceived resemblances in shape can trigger the thought that there also exist some shared *capacities* across the differences between plant and animal" (2017, 102). Thus, in searching for points of similarity or connection with the plant, participants might come to recognize shared abilities and affiliations.

While Beitiks's piece may seem absurd at first with its playful substitution of a plant for Abromavić, it, much like Bell's work, ultimately asks *why* such a substitution is seen as absurd and what the extent of plant–human interaction can be. While responses like, "The plant + I are no longer on speaking terms," maintain the piece's humor, they also reveal a resistance to even attempt to interact with the plant on a vegetal plane (Beitiks 2011a). Far more interesting are the responses which reflect an effort, even a failed one, to materially engage with the snake plant. While humans cannot comprehend plants through language, they can do so through spatiality: how does a plant move in the wind and rain? Does it grow toward the sun? In staging the snake plant, Beitiks provides a space for the consideration of such questions and a reflection on human and plant relations past and present.

Women and Nature

While Beitiks provides a space for alternate plant–human interaction by spotlighting the *Sansevieria Trifasciata* and by allowing participants unlimited time with the plant, the artist, like Bell, raises questions about the ways in which women and nature have been essentialized. However, whereas Bell's *Garment for Flora–Fauna Relationship* casts the human artist as a nurturing mother, Beitiks's piece casts the plant artist as a human female. To make a direct parallel between Abromavić and the snake plant, Beitiks attires the latter in a black skirt, shirt, and shoes, much like the outfit worn by the performer during *The Artist is Present*. Although this extends the piece's primary comparison, it may overshadow the plant's performance with Abromavić's and force the plant to play the role of human female instead of plant. As ecofeminists have shown, women and nature already have a long history of shared subjugation. Throughout Western history, to be "human"—White, Western, and male—meant to be rational, objective, and public, whereas to be other-than-human—female, of color, non-Western—meant to be irrational, subjective, emotional, domestic, and embodied (Sturgeon 1997, 8). Thus, those who are sexually or racially different have often been represented as "naturally" less than human.

The associations of White masculinity to culture and of women to nature persist still and are evident in both *The Artist is Present* and *The Plant is Present*. For instance, in the larger-than-life headshot used for the Abromavić retrospective, the artist holds a bouquet of flowers that grazes her chin, while tree branches frame her serenely set face. She looks into the distance, her windswept hair and the out-doorsy setting seeming to suggest an affinity with nature, despite the fact that the performance piece itself only features humans. While Beitiks's photo also frames the plant with tree branches, there is no flower bouquet; instead, there is a close-up of the snake plant's taut leaves, below which is a shorter blurb about the plant. Whereas the flowers in Abromavić's photo are props to make the artist herself seem more organic and akin to nature, the snake plant, already culturally recognized as "nature," needs no additional adornment.

In linking herself to nature, Abromavić draws on a long history of conflating women and people of color with nature. Subtly represented as one with nature in the exhibit introduction, Abromavić may then be seen as intuitive, mystical, or caring in her performance, not unlike "Mother Earth." Indeed, many participants in *The Artist is Present* were so moved by looking into Abromavić's eyes that they cried, inspiring the creation of the Tumblr blog "Marina Abromavić Made Me Cry." Although this response to the artist's piece is in large part due to her identity as a person and a performance artist, it is also undoubtedly influenced by the fact that she is a woman, and women are often essentialized as caring, understanding, and empathetic. The artist's headshot exacerbates rather than deconstructs this naturalization, suggesting that Abromavić is a mystical figure. In contrast, in keeping with Beitiks's goal to "act as a medium between nature and culture in the least mystical sense,"[23] the stark photo of the snake plant, accompanied by its scientific description, serves to demystify the plant, emphasizing its active role in cleaning the air rather than its representation as passive houseplant.

While Beitiks demystifies the snake plant in some ways, providing visitors with botanical specificities and individual time with the plant, they mystify it by attiring it as a human woman, reinforcing the constructed link between women and nature, just as Abromavić does in her photo. Despite the fact that plants may be male, female, asexual, or sexually fluid, they, like many animals, continue to be feminized. Indeed, the *Sansevieria Trifasciata* is typically propagated from cuttings rather than seeds, but this has not stopped it from derogatorily being called "mother-in-law's tongue" because of its sharp leaves, reinforcing both the perception of women as bristly and of plants as feminine. By dressing the snake plant as a woman, Beitiks not only anthropomorphizes it but strengthens the association of plants with femininity, causing most of the participants to gender their interaction with the plant. For instance, one claims, "She is SEXY and REAL" (Beitiks 2011a), thus only legitimating the *Sansevieria Trifasciata*'s realness—substance, materiality, and very ontology—through its sexiness, its degree of femininity. Another participant teases, "She was coming on to me, but I'm a faithful guy so I had to take leave" (2011a), cleverly playing with the verb "leave" and the noun "leaves," but also projecting the role of seductress onto the plant.

Although some of the other gendered responses are subtler, all of them conflate the plant, women, and femininity as one entity. As one participant observes, "It was very tranquil. It seemed like I was sitting with a woman. It was very peaceful and serene" (2011a). The goal of the piece may be to encourage plant–human interaction, but, because the engagement is already gendered by the plant's attire, the serenity some participants experience is tied to the dual essentialization of women and nature as natural, soothing, and soft. Arguably, Beitiks intends to expose the ways in which Abromavić and the *Sansevieria Trifasciata* are mutually gendered, or perhaps to create a human-like connection between participants and the plant by representing the latter as a human female. However, as the written responses to *The Plant is Present* reveal, imposing cultural gender constructions and sartorial conventions on plants may intensify their gendered objectification rather than foster an understanding of vegetal life.

Staging an Ecological Superstar

Despite the gendered anthropomorphism in the work, Beitiks's piece ultimately enables a snake plant to take center stage, asks thought-provoking questions, and encourages some degree of interspecies interaction. Every aspect of *The Plant is Present*, from the introductory material to the performance itself, forefronts the plant as an artist and professional in its own right. Describing the plant as a "botanical" and "epic" performer, Beitiks highlights its aesthetic and scientific accomplishments (2011c). As the artist writes in the piece's introduction, "Over the course of its career, it has gone for months without water, made fiber from its own body, and collaborated with NASA to remove toxins and pollutants from the very air we breathe" (2011c). Beitiks could just as easily use adjectives to describe the *Sansevieria Trifasciata*'s scientific properties, but instead she employs verbs to emphasize the plant's own actions and activity. In asking visitors to consider the plant as a lively performer with a crucial ecological role to play, Beitiks suggests that they appreciate its contribution and engage with the plant based on its actions rather than its culturally perceived inferiority in the human/animal/plant hierarchy. Thus, although *The Plant is Present* does not involve physical plant mobility as many of Bell's pieces do, it nonetheless transplants the *Sansevieria Trifasciata* from relative obscurity to stardom, from passive and peripheral window dressing to active and central ecological performer. For too long, explains Beitiks, the snake plant "has been stashed in dark corners, plunked into shop windows, and squished into lawn rows. Now we have the unique opportunity to fully appreciate the aesthetic value, artistic aura, and phenomenal performative work of this artist" (2011c). In assisting the snake plant to take the stage and thereby achieve prominence in a space reserved only for those who act and perform, Beitiks literally and figuratively elevates the houseplant from background extra to ecological superstar.

Perhaps most importantly, the snake plant's heightened visibility and accessibility allow for a greater appreciation of its qualities and a contemplation of its being. The theatrical stage, a unique and alternate space in which, for a brief time, anything and everything is possible, encourages dialogue, exchange, interaction. In theorizing radical performance, Kershaw argues that "performance can be most usefully described as an *ideological transaction* between a company of performers and the community of the audience," an ongoing, negotiated "transaction of meaning" (1992, 16–17). *The Plant is Present* not only begins a negotiation between the performers—the snake plant and its companion—but it also casts visitors as both participatory audience members and onstage performers. Playing a dual role, visitors individually perform their own interaction with the snake plant and negotiate the meaning of other audience members' engagement with the plant.

The experience of sharing the stage with a plant, of looking at and considering little else but the plant, allows for new ways of thinking through plant life. As transhumanist philosopher Richard M. Doyle posits, the cognitive awareness that humans are interconnected with their environment does not necessarily persuade people to change their environmental habits; rather, change "seems to hinge on an *experience* of this interconnection as well as an *understanding* of it" (2011, 7, emphasis in original). The experience of sitting across from the *Sansevieria Trifasciata* in the wind, cold, and—on the second night of the performance—rain, enables some participants to consider how their staged experience might extend beyond the performance space. For instance, one participant finds commonality with the plant based on their "shared vulnerability and strength" (Beitiks 2011a). Others find that, in closely observing the plant, they begin to take on its qualities rather than asserting their own; one imitates the plant's pose and smells its leaves while another experiences sympathy for the houseplant under harsh lights and in cold temperatures (Beitiks 2011a).

Finding commonality across difference, another participant observes, "The wind blows my hair and her; or its or she's leaves" (Beitiks 2011a). Not only does this statement suggest a shared movement but also an effort to know the plant rather than make assumptions about it: is it a she or an it? Does all of the plant sway in the wind or just the leaves? Indeed, those participants who observe the ways that the snake plant takes up space and moves within it may come far closer to communicating with it than those participants who speak at the plant or pretend it agrees with them. Since plants communicate spatially, small changes in size, shape, and movement convey their inner state. As Marder explains, "Plant-thinking [...] cannot but rely on material signification that bypasses conscious intentionality and coincides with the very phenomenality—the modes of appearance—of vegetal life" (2013, 75). Beitiks highlights these modes of appearance not only by providing an enlarged photo of the snake plant but also by creating a staged space for humans to observe plant phenomenality closely and to consider the possibilities, as well as the limits, of interspecies communication.

The very act of thinking about the plant—its needs, desires, movement, labor, and mode of communication—demonstrates "plant-thinking," what Marder calls "the promise and the name of an encounter…an invitation to abandon the familiar terrain of human and humanist thought and to meet vegetal life, if not in the place where it is, then at least halfway" (2013, 10). Of course, humans can never fully know or think like plants, and it is important to acknowledge this and, with it, plants' alterity. However, the effort to experience and understand plants on a material plane is crucial to fostering respect and protection for flora. Abromavić's performance was advertised and praised as a once in a lifetime experience, and, in recasting the performance artist with the air-purifying *Sansevieria Trifasciata*, Beitiks suggests that time spent with the snake plant is equally as life-changing. In fact, it may be more so if the performing snake plant can temporarily enable humans to reconsider plants and their ecological contributions to human life.

W(h)ither Transplantment?

One critique of both Bell's and Beitiks's pieces may be that, too often, they strive to incorporate plants into human activities—walking, jogging, fighting—rather than incorporating humans into plant activities and time. In striving to highlight vegetal life, the artists may be said at times to emphasize their own agency over that of plants. As Gibson and Sandilands warn,

> Unfortunately, the moment you frame a plant, or place a plant in a white cube, or perform a plant by connecting sensors and emitting a software screech within an art institution, you are aestheticising those plants, and there is a risk of diminishment
>
> *(2021, 8).*

While hypermediated performances can diminish vegetal life rather than illuminate it, plant art and aesthetics play an important role in disrupting hierarchical thinking. While a plant performs regardless of human intervention, our attention to that performance mediates it. Thus, there is no unmediated performance once humans are involved; there are only degrees of mediation. It is important to meet plants halfway by considering how they themselves perform. However, I would argue that mediations like Bell's shopping carts and Beitiks's stage both expose humanist assumptions about plant life and highlight vegetal materiality. While there is value in walking in the woods, there is also value in mediated plant art performances in art museums and city streets that bring plant life into the center of urban activities. Just as hypermediated plant art can obscure vegetal vitality, the insistence on unmediated vegetal performance can disregard plant art, like Bell's and Beitiks's, that seeks to challenge the marginalization of plant life and to create encounters between plants and people. As Gibson argues elsewhere, "Ascribing greater status to plant life is a political act, and art that draws attention to this shift in structures of legitimacy is also political" (2018, 5). In featuring plants and their unique characteristics in all aspects of urban life, Bell and Beitiks invite viewers to reevaluate the status and significance of vegetal life in Western culture.

Arguably, some of the pieces discussed here come closer to meeting plants halfway than others. Some, like Bell's biospheres and Beitiks's plant showcase, successfully highlight vegetative ecologies and encourage extended, intimate observations of and interactions with flora. Others, like Bell's fern walking stick and Beitiks's ivy jogging companion, may cast plants as sidekicks to human activity more than they forefront plant activity. Nonetheless, all of the artists' plant art stages an alternate ecology that transplants flora from the background of urbanscapes and human thought to the very center. For too long, plants, which sustain life, have been marginalized and taken for granted. Together, Bell and Beitiks denaturalize this normative state, performing comedic and spatialized modes of transplantment that foster relationships between people and plants.

Notes

1 My title is a nod to Jack Halberstam's *In A Queer Time and Place*, in which "queer time" and "queer space" challenge heteronormative, dominant institutions and cultural practices (2005, 1). I suggest that plants, as marginalized subjects, have potential to queer human norms of time and place.

2 For more on critical plant studies and its various branches, see Gibson and Sandilands (2021).

3 American Forests developed a Tree Equity Score for cities throughout the US: treeequityscore.org.

4 See, for instance: Chaudhuri (2007); Scott (2007); and Haraway (1992).

5 This is not to say that plants are mute; far from it. The emerging field of plant bioacoustics suggests that plants are constant communicators. For more on this, see Gagliano (2013).

6 For other examples of vegetal art, see John (2015).

7 Many of the pieces were shown in a 2003 exhibit, *Portable Garden*, at the Green Street Gallery in Boston.

8 Certainly, this is not to say that city plants should not be grown or maintained, but rather that they should be made more integral to city life and that their care should be shared.

9 For example, in the wake of the 2008 recession, community gardens sprang up in abandoned lots vacated during the height of the recession. Detroit, one of the cities hardest hit by the economic crisis, saw a huge growth in community gardens. For more on this, see Bittman (2011).

10 Environmental justice scholarship has worked to expose the underlying connections between environmental degradation and race and will be taken up more fully in the next chapter. For a fairly comprehensive overview of the movement and its more recent offshoot critical environmental justice studies, see Pellow (2018).

11 Michael T. Hernke and Rian J. Podein argue that although the majority of Americans have expressed interest in environmentally friendly lawn care, "aesthetic norms and the lobbying power of the lawn care industry" combine to maintain high pesticide usage in the US (2011, 228).

12 For more on turf grass homogenization across the urban US, see Groffman (2014).

13 The gap between White and Black homeownership is higher today than it was when "race-based discrimination against homebuyers was legal" (Choi 2020). In 2017, 71.9% of White Americans were homeowners, compared to 41.8% of Black Americans (Choi 2020).

14 Although Kaika is particularly concerned with water and the "urban uncanny"—for instance, the way in which a leaky toilet can bring the "outside" "inside"—the term might also apply to other material ruptures that expose the dichotomy between nature and culture.

15 The online versions of both The Free Dictionary and the Merriam-Webster dictionary describe plants as lacking locomotive movement. Although "locomotion" is often defined as the ability to move from place to place, it can also be defined as the "act" of moving.

16 *Personal Landscapes* appeared in an exhibition at the SOIL gallery in Seattle in January 2006 alongside *A Pack of Forests*. For more on the latter, see Ryan (2013).

17 It is important to note that Plumwood is most critical of cultural landscape studies, although she also finds the solitary term "landscape" problematic.

18 For instance, although Fuchs and Chaudhuri regard "landscape" as a useful mediation between theater and the world and between space and place, they also "acknowledge certain significant discontinuities and occlusions within the assumptions attached to the idea of landscape," and thus break up the term in their book's title, *Land/Scape/Theater* (2002, 2–3).

19 In light of the growing pet industry, Nast (2006) suggests that a new geographical discipline, "critical pet studies," is needed.

20 This description no longer appears on Bell's website, but the work itself is accessible still at https://tinyurl.com/2p927p2w.

21 Photosynthesis is the process whereby plants convert light energy into chemical energy; this energy is synthesized from carbon dioxide and water to create carbohydrate molecules that can be used or stored by plants.

22 I am grateful to Petra Kuppers for her insight on the piece's maternal aspects.

23 This quote is no longer on Beitiks's website.

References

Abramović, Marina. 2010. *The Artist is Present*. MoMA. https://tinyurl.com/958s6duj.

Alaimo, Stacy. 2010. *Bodily Natures: Science, Environment, and the Material Self*. Bloomington: Indiana University Press.

Arlander, Annette. 2020. "Performing with Plants in the Ob-scene Anthropocene." *Nordic Theatre Studies* 32 (1): 121–142.

Arons, Wendy. 2010. "Beyond the Nature/Culture Divide: Challenges from Ecocriticism and Evolutionary Biology for Theater Historiography." In *Theater Historiography: Critical Interventions*, edited by Henry Bial and Scott Magelssen, 148–161. Ann Arbor: University of Michigan Press.

Arons, Wendy and Theresa J. May, eds. 2012. "Introduction." In *Readings in Performance and Ecology*, edited by Wendy Arons and Theresa J. May, 3–12. New York: Palgrave Macmillan.

Beitiks, Meghan Moe. 2010. *Yielding Air*. Performance. November 20. Oakland, CA. https://tinyurl.com/4rt5cnpm.

Beitiks, Meghan Moe. 2011a. "Everyone Who Sat with The Plant, Day Two." *The Plant is Present*. School of the Art Institute, Chicago. New Blood Performance Festival. November 19–20. https://tinyurl.com/bdfdzr9a.

Beitiks, Meghan Moe. 2011b. *Water Fight with a Cactus*. Performance. Oakland, CA. https://tinyurl.com/yc4u23w5.

Beitiks, Meghan Moe. 2011c. *The Plant Was Present*. "Plant is Present Entrance." https://tinyurl.com/3nt7764h.

Bell, Vaughn. 2003. *Portable Environments*. Bakalar Gallery, Massachusetts College of Art and Design, Boston, MA. https://tinyurl.com/ezk2htym.

Bell, Vaughn. 2005–06. *Personal Landscapes*. SOIL Gallery, Seattle. https://tinyurl.com/mkryb9ba.

Bell, Vaughn. 2006a. *Biosphere Built for Two*. SOIL Gallery, Seattle, WA. https://tinyurl.com/2p927p2w.

Bell, Vaughn. 2006b. *Garment for Flora–Fauna Relationship*. "'Wasabi: Contemporary Art with a Japanese Kick!'", NAVE Gallery, Somerville, MA. March 9–April 13. https://tinyurl.com/3zxk9bdf.

Bell, Vaughn. 2008–. *Village Green*. https://tinyurl.com/yc7bxnkx.

Bell, Vaughn. 2009. *Landscape for Walking*. Edith Russ House for New Media, Oldenberg, Germany. Landscape 2.0. https://tinyurl.com/yh8zskba.

Bell, Vaughn. 2012. *Metropolis*. https://tinyurl.com/mxa9hjk6.

Bennett, Jane. 2017. "Vegetal Life and Onto-Sympathy." In *Entangled Worlds: Religion, Science, and New Materialisms*, edited by Catherine Keller and Mary-Jane Rubenstein, 89–107. New York: Fordham University Press.

Bittman, Mark. 2011. "Imagining Detroit." *The New York Times*. May 17. https://tinyurl.com/2p9fwhhw.

Brantz, Dorothee and Sonja Dümpelmann, eds. 2011. "Introduction." In *Greening the City: Urban Landscapes in the Twentieth Century*, edited by Dorothee Brantz and Sonja Dümpelmann, 1–16. Charlottesville: University of Virginia Press.

Brown, Bill. 2001. "Thing Theory." *Critical Inquiry* 28 (1): 1–22.

Chaudhuri, Una. 1995. *Staging Place: The Geography of Modern Drama*. Ann Arbor: University of Michigan Press.

Chaudhuri, Una. 2007. "De(Facing) the Animals: Zooësis and Performance." *TDR: The Drama Review* 51 (1): 8–20.

Chaudhuri, Una. 2010. "Animal Rites: Performing beyond the Human." In *Critical Theory and Performance*, ed. Janelle Reinelt and Joseph Roach, 506–520. Ann Arbor: University of Michigan Press.

Choi, Jung Hyun. 2020. "Breaking Down the White-Black Homeownership Gap." *Urban Institute*. February 21. https://tinyurl.com/3kxhzcus.

Diamond, Elin, ed. 1996. "Introduction." In *Performance and Cultural Politics*, edited by Elin Diamond, 1–14. New York: Routledge.

Doyle, Richard M. 2011. *Darwin's Pharmacy: Sex, Plants, and the Evolution of the Noösphere*. Seattle: University of Washington Press.

Fuchs, Elinor and Una Chaudhuri, eds. 2002. *Land/Scape/Theater*. Ann Arbor: University of Michigan Press.

Gagliano, Monica. 2013. "Green symphonies: a call for studies on acoustic communication in plants." *Behavioral Ecology* 24 (4): 789–796.

Gagliano, Monica, Michael Renton, Martial Depczynski, and Stefano Mancuso. 2014. "Experience Teaches Plants to Learn Faster and Forget Slower in Environments Where It Matters." *Oecologia* 175 (1): 63–72.

Gagliano, Monica, John C. Ryan, Patrícia Vierira, eds. 2017. "Introduction." In *The Language of Plants: Science, Philosophy, Literature*, edited by Monica Gagliano, John C. Ryan, and Patrícia Vierira. Minneapolis: University of Minnesota Press.

Gibson, Prudence. 2018. *The Plant Contract*. Leiden: Brill.

Gibson, Prudence and Catriona Sandilands. 2021. "Introduction: Plant Performance." *Performance Philosophy* 6 (2): 1–23.

Groffman, Peter M., et al. 2014. "Ecological homogenization of urban USA." *Frontiers in Ecology and the Environment* 12 (1): 74–81.

Halberstam, Jack. 2005. *In a Queer Time and Place: Transgender Bodies, Subcultural Lives*. New York: NYU Press.

Haraway, Donna. 1991. *Simians, Cyborgs, and Women: The Reinvention of Nature*. New York: Routledge.

Haraway, Donna. 1992. "Otherworldly Conversations; Terran Topics; Local Terms" In *Biopolitics: A Feminist and Ecological Reader in Biotechnology*, edited by Vandana Shiva and Ingunn Moster, 62–92. London: Zed Books.

Haraway, Donna. 2003. *The Companion Species Manifesto: Dogs, People, and Significant Otherness*. Chicago: Prickly Paradigm Press.

Haraway, Donna. 2007. *When Species Meet*. Minneapolis: University of Minnesota Press.

Hernke, M.T. and R.J. Podein. 2011. "Sustainability, Health, and Precautionary Perspectives on Lawn Pesticides and Alternatives." *Ecohealth* 8 (2): 223–232.

John, Charles Ryan. 2015. "Plant-Art: The Virtual and the Vegetal in Contemporary Performance and Installation Art." *Resilience: A Journal of the Environmental Humanities* 2(3): 40–57.

Kaika, Mara. 2005. *Cities of Flows: Modernity, Nature, and the City*. New York: Routledge.

Kershaw, Baz. 1992. *The Politics of Performance: Radical Theatre as Cultural Intervention*. New York: Routledge.

Kershaw, Baz. 2007. *Theatre Ecology: Environments and Performance Events*. Cambridge: Cambridge University Press.

KQED. 2009. "Landscaping." Gallery Crawl. https://tinyurl.com/2wxwtztj.

Liu, Ani. 2017. *Laboratory of Longing*. Mills Gallery, Boston Center for the Arts. October 6–7. https://tinyurl.com/2p9y3wuz.

Marder, Michael. 2013. *Plant-Thinking: A Philosophy of Vegetal Life*. New York: Columbia University Press.

May, Theresa J. 2005. "Greening the Theater: Taking Ecocriticism from Page to Stage." *Journal of Interdisciplinary Literary Studies* 7 (1): 84–103.

May, Theresa. 2012. "*Menageries of Blood: Animal Relations and Retaliations*." Earth Matters on Stage. Carnegie Mellon University. Pittsburgh, PA. May 31–June 2. Conference Presentation.

May, Theresa J. 2021. *Earth Matters on Stage: Ecology and Environment in North American Theater*. London: Routledge.

Merchant, Carolyn. 1980. *The Death of Nature: Women, Ecology, and the Scientific Revolution*. New York: HarperCollins Publishers.

Merchant, Carolyn. [1994] 2008. *Ecology*. 2nd ed. New York: Humanity Books.

Merriam-Webster. 2013. "Locomotion" and "Plant." *An Encyclopedia Britannica Company*.

Milesi, C, et. al. 2005. "*A Strategy for Mapping and Modeling the Ecological Effects of US Lawns*." *NASA Ames Research Center*. Moffett Field, CA.

Myers, Natasha. 2017. "From Anthropocene to Plantothropocene: Designing Gardens for Plant/People Involution." *History and Anthropology* 28 (30): 297–301.

Nast, Heidi J. 2006. "Critical Pet Studies?" *Antipode* 38 (5): 894–906.

Olson, Roberta J.M. and Kathleen Hulser. 2003. "Petropolis: A Social History of Urban Animal Companions." *Visual Studies* 18 (2): 133–143.

Pellow, David Naguib. 2018. *What is Critical Environmental Justice?* Cambridge, UK: Polity Press.

Plumwood, Val. 2006. "The Concept of a Cultural Landscape: Nature, Culture, and Agency in the Land." *Ethics & the Environment* 11 (2): 115–150.

Puig de la Bellacasa, María. 2017. *Matters of Care: Speculative Ethics in More Than Human Worlds*. Minneapolis: University of Minnesota Press.

Robbins, Paul and Julie Sharp. 2006. "Turfgrass Subjects: The Political Economy of Urban Monoculture." In *In the Nature of Cities: Urban Political Ecology and the Politics of Urban Metabolism*, edited by Nik Heynen, Maria Kaika, and Erik Swyngedouw, 110–128. New York: Routledge.

Ryan, Courtney B. 2013. "Playing with Plants." *Theatre Journal* 66 (3): 335–353.

Sandilands, Catriona. 1999. "Raising Your Hand in the Council of All Beings: Ecofeminism and Citizenship." *Ethics and the Environment* 4 (2): 219–233.

Schechner, Richard. [2002] 2013. *Performance Studies: An Introduction*. New York: Routledge.

Scott, Shelly R. 2007. "Conserving, Consuming, and Improving on Nature at Disney's Animal Kingdom." *Theatre Topics* 17 (2): 111–127.

Simard, Suzanne. 2016. "Leaf litter, expert Q&A." *Biohabitats* 15 (4).

Soja, W. Edward. 2010. *Seeking Spatial Justice*. Minneapolis: University of Minnesota Press.

Sturgeon, Noël. 1997. *Ecofeminist Natures: Race, Gender, Feminist Theory and Political Action*. New York: Routledge.

Wohlleben, Peter. 2015. *The Hidden Life of Trees: What They Feel, How They Communicate—Discoveries from a Secret World*. New York: Penguin Books.

Wolfson, Donald and Marianne Sullivan. 2004. "Foxes in the Hen House: Animals, Agribusiness, and the Law: A Modern American Fable." In *Animal Rights: Current Debates and New Directions*, edited by Cass R. Sustein and Martha C. Nussbaum, 205–233. New York: Oxford University Press.

2

"I SPEAK TO HIM OF SEEDS"

Centering Black Experiences of Green Spaces

In the nonfiction essay "My Mother's Garden" (2016), Kaitlyn Greenidge describes her experience as an African American scholarship student attending a largely White prep school in Boston in the 1990s. When Greenidge's class discusses welfare, the infamous stereotype of the "welfare queen," often caricatured as a Black, single mother who takes advantage of government services,[1] is an unspoken specter in their debates. This stereotype leads her White, upper-class peers to advocate for the dismantling of the welfare system. Ashamed to be seen as poor and longing to fit in, Greenidge rejects her mother's many invitations to help with the community garden that she and neighboring children are growing in front of their housing project. A few months after she starts the garden, Greenidge's mother is told by the town's housing authority that she must destroy it or be evicted. Left with no choice, her mother stops gardening and a maintenance worker covers the area in chemicals that kill the cherry tomatoes, cucumbers, and marigolds. Returning to school in the fall, Greenidge takes up a new daily ritual: every morning, as she passes a large vase of roses outside the fancy school office, she tears the tops off the largest blooms and crushes them until she smells of roses.

This small but meaningful act of defiance is, on the one hand, an immediate response to the destruction of her mother's garden. On the other hand, the garden's ruin is the culmination of countless other injustices, from Greenidge's classmates thinking they can decide an issue that does not directly affect them to the housing project enforcing stringent rules, such as banning computers and requiring renters to list academic scholarships as sources of income. In contrasting her mother's destroyed plot, now nothing but brown grass, to the flourishing roses at her prep school, Greenidge emphasizes the stark disparity between her lived experience and her classmates' experience. Whereas Greenidge's spatial mobility and activities are limited and surveilled, her rich, White classmates can thrive unfettered. As evidenced by the essay's title, which may reference Alice Walker's *In*

DOI: 10.4324/9781003203766-3

Search of Our Mothers' Gardens ([1967] 1983), the garden serves as the tipping point for Greenidge; it is the moment when she realizes that no amount of conformity or self-hatred can change the way her White classmates see her or the systemic racism that surrounds her. In trying to escape the racist stereotype of the "welfare queen," Greenidge eschews her mother's garden, afraid that gardening will make her seem poor. But, in actuality, it is gardening that allows for self-reliance, sustenance, and spatial mobility, all things that Greenidge's public housing, with its infantilizing rules, and her oppressively White prep school limit.

I begin with Greenidge's story because it reveals how seemingly disparate issues of anti-Blackness are interconnected: the trope of the "welfare queen" that haunts Greenidge as a teenager alienates her from gardening and serves as an unspoken rationale for regulating and limiting the spatial mobility and accessibility of public housing residents.[2] As anthropologist Ashanté M. Reese argues, highly visible forms of anti-Blackness like police shootings of unarmed Black people are often treated as separate from issues like food access and social services, and yet both "stem from shared roots that attempt to curtail Black mobility in and access to public space" and both lead to premature death (2019, 3). Such limitations create interconnected and compounded social, spatial, and environmental injustices that further dispossess African Americans of their access to land and affect Black experiences of the environment. While it is important to consider how seemingly disparate injustices are in fact interconnected, it is equally important to go "beyond an all-encompassing narrative of lack" (Reese 2019, 12). This common narrative can obscure the creativity and self-reliance many Black Americans practice in the face of social and environmental inequities.

Thus, in what follows, I consider how Black artists, faced with stereotypes and limitations placed on spatial mobility and access to green spaces, find creative ways to explore their complex relationships with the environment, particularly urban vegetation. Focusing first on Naima Green's photographic series *Jewels from the Hinterland* (2013–), which features portraits of Black and Brown people in city parks, I suggest that Green's work is a response to White environmentalism that has long ignored Black experiences of the outdoors. I argue that Green's work refutes the marginalization of both Black urbanites and vegetal life by revealing complex, multidimensional Black experiences of plants. I then turn to Marc Bamuthi Joseph's multimedia performance piece *red, black, & GREEN: a blues* (2012–13),[3] which reflects on Joseph's experience mounting what he calls "Life is Living" festivals in Black communities in Oakland, Harlem, Houston, and Chicago. A rumination on what "going green" can mean to people who experience anti-Blackness in every facet of life, *red, black, & GREEN: a blues (rbGb)* highlights the ways in which social, spatial, and environmental injustices are deeply entwined. Like *Jewels from the Hinterland*, it contests one-dimensional representations of Black experiences of the environment. While *Jewels from the Hinterland* highlights Black subjects at ease in green spaces, *rbGb* celebrates the art of, as the popular African American saying goes, "making a way out of no way." Although *rbGb* is a stage production and *Jewels from the Hinterland* is a photographic series, what connects them is their creative response to the spatial and representational limits imposed by systemic racism. In different ways, both pieces create spatial mobility and reclaim space to explore multivalent Black experiences of the environment.

Reclaiming Black Spaces and Black Environmental Identities

It is easy enough to say that representation matters and that artists who focus on Black experiences of the environment, like Green and Joseph, are doing important work. However, in order to understand the complexities and challenges involved in this work, or in any Black environmental project, one must look at the legacies of slavery and the history of environmentalism in the US. It is not a coincidence that environmental consciousness came to the fore in the US at the same time that Native Americans were being dispossessed of their land and that African Americans were still enslaved. "Nature" and "wilderness" have been wielded by settler colonialists in the US for centuries as a means of justifying the forced removal of Native Americans, the enslavement of Black people, and the recasting of stolen land as pristine and untouched (May 2020; Taylor 2016; Purdy 2015; Cronon 1995). As environmental sociologist Dorceta E. Taylor argues, for environmentalists of the late nineteenth and twentieth centuries, protecting the environment was intrinsically connected to building the nation; "powerful elites" deployed wilderness ideologies as a form of "cultural nationalism" (Taylor 2016, 190). Environmentalism, treated as apolitical and asocial, was, in actuality, part of a national agenda to sanitize and preserve nature for the benefit of wealthy Whites, and this legacy continues to this day.

One major consequence of this legacy is the pernicious misconception that African Americans are disinterested in environmental issues (Finney 2014, 4; Blum 2002; Virden and Walker 1999). This misconception disregards the ways in which civil rights are environmental rights and conceals environmental legacies of excluding Black people from White spaces and organizations. The growth of White spaces at the expense of Black mobility has created what cultural geographer Carolyn Finney calls the "legacy of contradictions": at the same time that African Americans were enslaved and Native Americans were forcibly removed from land, White immigrants were given land through the Homestead Act of 1862, and, while Jim Crow laws limited the spatial mobility of Black people, John Muir championed wilderness preservation and Gifford Pinchot created the forestry profession (2020). This legacy of exclusion from environmental spaces has been reframed as one of Black indifference to the environment, fueling racist stereotypes and policies that not only further affect Black Americans' access to and experience of the outdoors, but also their access to social and educational institutions (Finney 2014, 2; Sibley 1995).

In many ways, the environmental justice movement of the late 1970s and early 1980s was a direct response to White environmentalism's refusal to consider the interconnections of social, cultural, racial, and environmental issues and the unfair exclusion of people of color from governmental decision-making processes that directly affect their communities. An offshoot of the civil rights movement, the

environmental justice movement initially focused on the disproportionate distribution of toxins and environmental hazards in poor communities of color and
the lack of access to clean water and healthy air. A key moment in the movement
came in 1982 when over 500 people were arrested for protesting a Polychlorinate
Biphenyl (PCB) landfill in the predominantly African American Warren County,
North Carolina. This led to another defining moment in 1987 with the publication of a report, *Toxic Wastes and Race in the United States*, sponsored by the United
Church of Christ Commission for Racial Justice (UCC-CRJ). Synthesizing several
national reports on the locations and harms of hazardous waste facilities, the report
showed that people of color are far more likely to suffer from toxic exposure than are
White people: 60 percent of Latinos and African Americans and roughly 50 percent of
Native Americans, Asians, and Pacific Islanders were found to live near "uncontrolled
toxic waste sites" ("Toxic Wastes" 1987, xiv; Adams, Evans, and Stein 2002, 4). The
report's findings led Reverend Benjamin Chavis, then director of the UCC-CRJ, to
create the term "environmental racism," defining it as

> racial discrimination in environmental policy-making and the enforcement of
> regulations and laws, the deliberate targeting of people of color communities
> for toxic waste facilities, the official sanctioning of the life-threatening pre-
> sence of poisons and pollutants in our communities, and history of excluding
> people of color from leadership in the environmental movement
> *(as cited in Adamson, Evan, and Stein 2002, 4).*

This term remains useful in conjunction with environmental in/justice because it
makes explicit the racism that motivates much environmental injustice in the US.

The report spurred multiracial activists to hold the First National People of
Color Environmental Leadership Summit in 1991 in Washington, DC. Attended
by over 300 community leaders from the US, Canada, South and Central America,
and the Marshall Islands, the summit created 17 "Principles of Environmental Justice"
(1991), a commitment to pursuing environmental justice politically, economically,
and socially. Significantly, the preamble to the principles states that the leaders' purpose is to "secure our political, economic and cultural liberation that has been denied
for over 500 years of colonization and oppression, resulting in the poisoning of our
communities and land and the genocide of our peoples." While the Environmental
Protection Agency (EPA), which formed the Office of Environmental Equity in 1992
in response to the movement,[4] expanded the definition of environmental justice to
include the fair treatment of all people regardless of race or class, it is crucial to
remember the movement's founding principles. For the Summit leaders, American
environmental injustice began when European colonizers stripped Native Americans
of their land, and it continued when they enslaved African Americans to tend that
stolen land.

The environmental justice movement takes a holistic approach to the environment, defining it not as pristine and remote "nature," but as the physical places
where people live, work, learn, eat, and play.[5] It insists that any environmental

action consider both ecocentric and anthropocentric concerns instead of privileging the former over the latter. For example, a landmark 1990 letter from the SouthWest Organizing Project (SWOP) to the self-designated "Group of Ten"[6] mainstream environmental organizations called on the groups to work with communities of color and to hire people of color rather than to presume to speak for them. SWOP also noted that representatives from the major organizations claimed that "only in the recent past have people of color begun to realize the impacts of environmental contamination," when, in actuality, they had "been involved in environmental struggles for many years" (Moore et al. 1990). Since the SWOP letter was released over 30 years ago, many mainstream environmental organizations have begun reconsidering their goals, practices, and lack of diversity (Durlin 2010), and, in response to the Black Lives Matter protests of 2020, some are beginning to reckon with their founders' racist legacies.[7] And, yet, people of color are still underrepresented at major US environmental organizations,[8] putting an unfair burden on staffers of color to be hypervisible in their representation of their communities. Furthermore, while the early environmental justice movement succeeded in galvanizing mainstream environmental organizations and government agencies like the EPA to reexamine their priorities and policies, it has not stopped environmental injustices from occurring and, as some evidence suggests, growing worse (Pulido 2017, 524; Bullard et al. 2007).

"Second-generation" environmental justice scholarship considers why environmental injustice might be worsening (Pulido 2017) and how the movement's early focus on distribution might be expanded to consider the intersections between race and other identities like gender and sexuality (Pellow 2016, 223; Buckingham and Kulcur 2010; Walker 2010). In theorizing what he and Robert Brulle call "Critical Environmental Justice Studies," environmental justice scholar David N. Pellow argues for a more intersectional and interdisciplinary approach to environmental justice struggles and for a multiscalar approach that considers how environmental harms travel and affect different parts of the world (Pellow 2016, 223–3). As geographer Gordon Walker argues, environmental justice is spatial and scalar and "well-being, vulnerability and environment are spatially intertwined" (2009, 615). Although environmental justice research has always been spatial, early research relied on a "flat, Cartesian" model of spatiality whereby various environmental hazards were unequally distributed across geographical boundaries (Walker 2009, 618). While 1980s environmental justice work was crucial for its ability to document and expose environmental racism, anti-Blackness permeates every aspect of society, and, thus, requires a multiscalar and multi-pronged approach that goes beyond fixed boundaries. This approach is at work in *rbGb*, for example, which grapples with the ways in which social and environmental injustices are interconnected and seep into every aspect of Black life.

At the same time, while the shift in focus from distributional models of environmental justice to interdisciplinary, multiscalar models is useful, it is important to remember that the principles of environmental justice long preceded the movement's solidification in the 1980s (Smith 2007, 5). As historian Kimberly K. Smith has shown in her reframing of Black political thought from the abolition movement through the Harlem Renaissance, the writing of Black thinkers like Fredrick Douglass, W.E.B. Du Bois, and Langston Hughes is as environmental is it as political (2007, 3). For these thinkers, "humans' relationship to the natural world is affected by the justice or injustice of their social arrangements" (Smith 2007, 11). In other words, their experience of the environment cannot be separated from their experience of social injustices, whether the injustices were those that curtailed their access to the environment or forced them to work the land. While the environmental justice movement of the 1980s documents environmental racism and critical environmental justice studies makes explicit the connections between social and environmental injustice, historically, environmental thought and social justice were intertwined for many African American writers and remain so today. For example, while living in Lynchburg, Virginia, the eco-poet Camille T. Dungy saw the trees around her both as a reminder of the American South's history of brutal racism and as a source of connection to her environment (2009, xx–xi). On the one hand, as Smith argues, the history of Black environmentalism is a battle against "forces of alienation and dispossession" (2007, 12). On the other hand, as bell hooks suggests, the environment can provide both an escape from constructed categories of race and soil for growing food and being self-reliant (2009, 7–8).

The enduring legacies not only of slavery, segregation, and dispossession but also of self-reliance mean that Black experiences of the environment are complex and multidimensional. And, yet, these experiences are rarely represented and even more rarely shown in nuanced ways (Finney 2014, 2). The exclusion of Black experiences of the environment from popular cultural representations and from the mainstream environmental movement has profound effects. As Finney argues, images and stories of people's relationship to the environment affect not only how environmental narratives are understood but also educational, personal, and national narratives (2014, 3). Whitewashed environmentalism in the US both erases Black experiences of the environment and perpetuates harmful stereotypes of environmental and civic disregard. It reinscribes frontier myths of pristine wildernesses and wide, open spaces on which the US was built. To highlight Black experiences of the environment, then, is not just to add more diversity to US environmentalism and popular culture representations of the environment; it is to contest the spatial narratives on which the country was founded and is now maintained. While the early environmental justice movement proves that neighborhoods of color are disproportionately affected by environmental hazards and critical environmental justice studies explores the multiscalar, intersectional aspects of environmental injustice, Black environmental art and performance contest racist spatial and representational limitations and center Black experiences of the environment.

"Feeling at Ease": *Jewels from the Hinterland*

Given how COVID-19 has ravaged African American communities, exposing embedded environmental and social injustices, it may seem slight, particularly for me as a White person, to explore the issue of representation of Black urbanites in green spaces. And, yet, just as the pandemic drove many Americans to explore the outdoors, it revealed persistent stereotypes about who belongs in green spaces and who is entitled to leisure time. Take, for example, the false police report that Amy Cooper, a White woman, made against Christian Cooper (no relation), a Black man, while he was birdwatching in Central Park in May 2020. Or the murder of Black jogger Ahmaud Arbery in Georgia in February 2020. Everyday occurrences like these support Finney's argument that "Racialization and representation are not passive processes; they also have the power to determine who actually participates in environment-related activities and who does not; which voices are heard in environmental debates and which voices are not" (2014, 3). Overwhelmingly White representations of urbanites in green spaces actively drown out Black and Brown experiences of nature, and this presents a dire threat to African Americans who are seen by White people as invading White spaces and engaging in White activities.

In response to this dominant narrative, Naima Green's ongoing series *Jewels from the Hinterland* (2013–) offers a vital counternarrative that centers Black experiences of the outdoors. The series now includes over 80 portraits of Black and Brown individuals in city parks. While many of the photos were taken in parks in and around New York City, the project has expanded to include other major US and international cities. What sets Green's series apart from other works of photography that focus on Black experiences of the environment is its emphasis on quietude and leisure. This is unique and contrasts with, for example, the work of British photographer Ingrid Pollard, which highlights the uneasiness and discomfort Black people experience in the English countryside, both because of Britain's colonial past, as explored in *Self Evident* (1995), and because of the stereotypical association of Black people with cities, as seen in *Pastoral Interlude* (1987–88). In contrast, Green is interested in showing Black and Brown individuals being comfortable in the outdoors. As she puts it, *Jewels from the Hinterland* is about "feeling at ease in natural green spaces, regions where black and brown urbanites are not 'supposed' to be at home: our hinterlands" (as cited in Mueller 2016). Rather than alienate her subjects from their environment, Green often creates a sense of oneness between the two. Whereas Pollard invokes the pastoral in her title to subvert it, Green seems to embrace the utopic hinterlands to reclaim the pastoral for Black subjects.

Take, for instance, Green's photo in which the subject, Lipton, is framed by a magnolia tree with light pink petals (see Figure 2.1). Lips slightly parted, he returns the camera's gaze with a restful, warm expression. The branches extend beyond the frame and form a bower around him, simultaneously suggesting a broad expanse and an intimate enclosure. Surrounded and still as he is, Lipton seems to be in tune with the tree. It is hard to say just how the tree affects Lipton and how he affects the tree, but they appear to be in communion. This 2015 photo taken in Prospect Park in Brooklyn is one of several in which Black and Brown subjects are in direct contact with plant life; whether they are sitting in a tree, laying in the grass,

FIGURE 2.1 A man is surrounded by a blooming magnolia tree in a park. Lipton, Prospect Park, from *Jewels from the Hinterland*, 2015. Courtesy Naima Green.

stroking a leaf, or walking through a meadow, many of the individuals seem to be immersed in their experience of the surrounding foliage. These images of peaceful, environmental immersion in city parks are subtly radical, because they contest popular culture representations of Black and Brown life as laden with scenes of urban decay and dilapidation.

Even though, as Taylor argues, Black people have been farming in the US for over four centuries, the long-lasting legacies of slavery—from sharecropping to being denied credit to only being allowed to farm "hazard-prone land" to systemic segregation and racism—drove Black farmers to cities during the Great Migration (2016, 1). Once in the cities, African Americans were prevented from buying homes in the suburbs due to federally promoted housing discrimination and "redlining," the practice of refusing mortgage loans to African Americans in "high-risk"—read Black—neighborhoods (Rothstein 2017). Instead of this ongoing history of dispossession and spatial immobility garnering the attention it deserves, it is often supplanted in the news media by hypervisible stereotypes that conflate Blackness with urban ruin. Take, for example, the word "ghetto," which in the US has come to mean low-income, crime-ridden African American neighborhoods (Richardson and Donley 2018; Anderson et al. 2012). The stereotype's association with violence and dilapidation looms so large in the news media and the cultural imaginary that it conceals the racist economic and political policies that create and maintain segregated spaces to begin with. This stereotype goes hand in hand with that of the "Urban African American," which environmental humanities scholar Nicole Seymour describes as a "racialized environmental affect" of "the emotions and dispositions expected of certain racial groups in terms of their relationships to environment" (2018, 151). The flattened figure of the "Urban African American" is represented as disinterested in and alienated from green spaces, while low-income, Black neighborhoods themselves are seen as concrete wastelands, barren of vegetal life.

Tired stereotypes of Black pathologies of violence are quietly rebutted in Green's series, which captures vital, varied relationships and connective possibilities between people of color and vegetal life. In contrast to the one-dimensional figure of the "Urban African American," Green's subjects offer a multitude of responses to plant life. Indeed, Green created the series because she wanted to see herself—and her experience of green spaces growing up—represented. But, beyond drawing attention to marginalized vegetal experiences, she suggests that there is no single, uniform way to engage with plants. Some of her subjects appear joyful or peaceful, suggesting that their vegetal environment has a positive effect on them. Some subjects seem guarded and others open; some disenchanted and others absorbed; some confident and others defiant. Importantly, then, in seeking to normalize Black and Brown experiences of green spaces, Green does not universalize any one subject's relationship with plants or seek to assimilate Black experiences with White experiences. The complexity of responses from Green's subjects illustrates Dungy's point that Black environmental writers do not see or write about the environment in the same way as White writers; the ongoing legacies of slavery create both connection to and alienation from vegetal life (2007, xxi–xxii). For example, while some of the subjects in *Jewels from the Hinterland* seem to be peacefully or leisurely interacting with plants, others interactions seem more pensive or fraught.

The variety of responses suggests that there is no singular or correct way of interacting with the environment. Similarly, the range of settings—from city parks to rooftop gardens—suggest that environments can include many different types of green spaces. As Dungy argues, White notions of the pastoral, of landscapes, and of meditations on nature need to expand to include Black and Brown experiences of the environment (2007, xxi–xxii). Similarly, Rue Mapp, who created the non-profit Outdoor Afro for outdoorsy African Americans, claims, "We are not out here to replicate what White people are doing in the outdoors" (as cited in Parks 2020). While Mapp wants to make representations of Black environmental experiences ordinary, she does not want to flatten or dilute those experiences into a narrowed, White understanding of being outdoors (Parks 2020). For Mapp, riding a bike down a city street or attending outdoor parties offer legitimate and meaningful ways of interacting with the environment (Parks 2020). While Green's primary goal, as she puts it, is to show "that black and brown people can exist comfortably and confidently in green spaces as places of leisure, as spaces that are calm and meditative spaces," (as cited in Meyerson 2016) her subjects' varied responses to these sites also show that Black and Brown relationships with vegetal life can be unique and multidimensional.

The multidimensionality in Green's series also extends to the vegetal life featured in every photo. Whether it is sunflowers on a Brooklyn rooftop garden, wild fields at West Harlem Piers Park, or climbing ivy at Riverside Park in Manhattan, the varied vegetation surrounds each subject and fills or expands beyond the frame. The expansiveness of the plants and the variety of locations question representations of cities as sites of urban decay. Just as Black and Brown urbanites' experiences of green spaces have been marginalized in popular culture, so too has urban vegetation, as explored in the first chapter. If plants have been subjugated to the margins of Western thought, as Michael Marder argues (2013, 2), urban vegetation tends to be viewed as minimal and contained, operating on the periphery of the bustling city. However, in focusing on the environmental experiences of marginalized Black and Brown urbanites, Green also highlights the rich, varied vegetal life that her subjects engage with, thereby connecting the diversity of Black and Brown interactions with plants to vegetal biodiversity and urban lushness. In capturing one subject luxuriating in a patch of biennial wormwood weeds, another sitting in an oak tree, or another standing in a field of pinegrass, Green connects the biodiversity of urban vegetal life to the complexity and variety of Black and Brown material interactions with plants. Just as she undercuts hegemonic, White representations of Black people as entirely disconnected from nature by featuring Black and Brown lived experiences of vegetal life, she also contests the stereotypical view of urban plants as contained, potted, and peripheral by featuring abundant, expansive, and varied vegetation.

By highlighting diverse Black and Brown experiences of biodiverse plants, Green explores the rich complexity of both. As nonfiction author Lauret Savoy writes in an argument for the need for more diverse environmental writing, "What is key is recognizing the biodiversity of self and others, and resisting any mono-identity or mono-culture of mind" (2008). In contrast to one-dimensional or nonexistent representations of Black experiences of green spaces in popular culture, Green offers an array of responses, and the biodiversity of featured vegetal life contributes to those responses. As queer ecologists have suggested, the alterity of vegetal life can serve to challenge homogenizing norms of race and gender. Queer ecologist Catriona Sandilands argues that plants "queer life" with their biodiversity and their range of states, shapes, growth patterns, and gender fluidity (2017, 422). Through their very existence, plants challenge narrow, limited identity categories; their vast proliferation and categorical possibilities evade identificatory containment and blur heteronormative and racist limitations. In queering life, vegetal biodiversity offers more expansive ways of knowing oneself and others. Indeed, Marder argues that since plants think spatially without a head or sense of self-identity, by attempting to understand them, albeit in a limited capacity, we "can grow past the fictious shells of *our* identity and *our* existential ontology" (2013, 10–13, emphasis in original). Mapp suggests something similar: "The trees do not know that you are Black, the birds don't know how much money is in your account, and the flowers are going to bloom no matter what your gender" (as cited in Parks 2020). In this sense, the non-cognition of plants can reveal the construction of identity, including identities of race and gender.

At the same time, I do not want to suggest that the non-cognition of plants erases the specificity of Black and Brown experiences of environments, but rather that it opens up a range of identificatory and relational possibilities. While the rich biodiversity in Green's series expands identificatory possibilities for Black and vegetal life, the project is a direct response to one-dimensional popular cultural representations of Black urbanites. In composing the title *Jewels from the Hinterland*, Green says that she defined "hinterland" as "an area lying beyond what's visible or what's known," places that have always been part of Green's life but that are "not really seen as universal from a public consciousness" (as cited in Meyerson 2016). By centering nuanced, complex Black and Brown experiences of vegetal spaces that are often made less accessible and less welcoming to African Americans, Green celebrates Black environmental belonging. This sense of empowered belonging is heightened by the tactile exchanges between human and vegetal subjects in the photos: surrounded, cushioned, or grazed by foliage, each subject directly engages with plants. The overall effect, across the 80 portraits, is quiet, soft, lush, and leisurely, a subtle challenge to stereotypes of hardened, Black city dwellers and emaciated plant life.

One might argue that, in largely featuring Black and Brown subjects at ease in green spaces, *Jewels from the Hinterland* belies the ways in which African Americans have been made to feel unwelcome when outdoors, or the ways in which their spatial mobility in and access to green spaces has been limited. However, as feminist theorist Tina Campt suggests in her study of historical vernacular photography, images might be engaged with

> as sites of *articulation* and *aspiration*; as personal and social statements that express how ordinary individuals envisioned their sense of self, their subjectivity, and their social status; and as objects that capture and preserve those articulations in the present as well as for the future
>
> *(2012, 7, emphasis in original).*

For Green and many of her subjects, the photographic series is an articulation of their lived experiences with and in green spaces, and each photograph captures an actual experience and a unique interaction with vegetal life. At the same time, the images are aspirational in that they create a visual space in which the subjects are preserved as they wish to be seen—as environmentally and spatially empowered— not as how they have been seen in White environmental representations.

By creating a subtle and nuanced sense of belonging in green spaces, Green offers a counternarrative to stereotypical representations of Black urban life. But *Jewels from the Hinterland* is remarkable not only because Green highlights woefully underrepresented urban Black and Brown experiences of vegetal life, as well as marginalized urban plant life itself, but also because she refuses a universalizing, mono-experience of vegetal engagement. The biodiversity of vegetal life and of Black and Brown interactions with plants contest narrowed, limiting, and categorical identities, representations, and experiences of plants and offer exciting possibilities for rethinking and expanding understandings of who belongs in green spaces and what engaging with vegetal life can mean.

red, black, & GREEN: a blues

Like *Jewels from the Hinterland*, the multimedia choreopoem[9] *red, black, & GREEN: a blues (rbGb)* focuses on the everyday, lived experiences of African American urbanites. Unlike Green's piece, which features Black and Brown people at home in lush, city gardens, *rbGb* is concerned with compounded environmental and social injustices that alienate African Americans from the mainstream environmental movement in the US. As I will show, the performance pushes back against White environmental understandings of sustainability and "going green" by asking what can grow out of racism, hardship, and packed city spaces. Celebrating Black life while also mourning its loss, as well as the racial injustices that cause it, the piece advocates for an ecological ethos that honors Black life and turns to the garden as a means of self-reliance.

rbGb, written by spoken word artist Marc Bamuthi Joseph and directed by Michael John Garcés, features Joseph; Traci Tolmaire, a dancer and singer; Yaw, a musician; and Tommy Shepherd (aka Emcee Soulati), a drummer and turntablist. The entirely reclaimed set was designed by installation and set designer Theaster Gates.[10] *rbGb* is loosely based on Joseph's and his collaborators' Life is Living festival, which celebrates art and environmental justice. The festival occurs annually in Oakland and often includes dance classes, graffiti exhibitions, poetry slams, food justice classes, and gardening demonstrations.[11] Its inspiration came to Joseph after he witnessed his students from the group Youth Speaks repeatedly compete in environmental poetry slams where they were the only African Americans present (Lee 2012). Realizing that someone needed to bring the eco-party to low-income Black communities rather than trying to bring entire communities to the event, Joseph created the Life is Living festival specifically for Black neighborhoods. While *rbGb* has toured throughout the US, the piece itself features the first four cities in which the festival took place: Harlem, Chicago, Oakland, and Houston. Highlighting the various environmental injustices in the four cities, the performance considers how African American communities can heal and thrive in spite of such injustice.

Early in the performance, Joseph's goal is to "green the ghetto" (2012, 72), but, as he spends more time getting to know residents and seeing the anti-Blackness that they contend with on a daily basis, he realizes that his initial purpose is misplaced. He must ask himself what he, as a well-educated, second-generation Haitian-American and an environmentalist, can do to make meaningful change. Grappling with his more privileged class position, Joseph, in front of a projection of dilapidated "project rowhouses in Houston," confesses, "Truth be told, it's been seven years since I lived/somewhere that someone else might call the hood/I occasionally put my finger over the date on my expired ghetto pass" (2012, 75). Watching Joseph navigate the messy complexities and intricacies of putting environmental justice into action, one realizes just how complicated such a task can be. Through his experience, of both staging the Life is Living festivals and reliving his journey in *rbGb*, he, and the audience along with him, discovers that any effective environmental justice effort must be multifaceted and holistic. Just as Joseph's festival focuses on the celebration of African American life, rather than on single-issue environmentalism, so too does *rbGb*, as it nonlinearly recounts the artist's experience bringing the festival to the four different cities.

In order to do this, *rbGb* draws on African Americans' extensive musical and civil rights heritage; indeed, the title *red, black, & GREEN: a blues* not only references Marcus Garvey's Pan African flag, but also the long history of blues music within African American culture. Through spoken word poetry, blues music, gospel music, hip hop, dance, ballet, and film footage of Life is Living festivals, *rbGb* both critiques the environmental injustices that have jeopardized the health and safety of impoverished Black communities and celebrates Black life. It asks what going "green" actually means, gradually problematizing the elitist concept and calling for a more holistic approach to and understanding of environmentalism. Celebrating an ecological ethos based on survival and self-reliance, *rbGb* exemplifies the African American concept of "making a way out of no way," or, in the words of social theorist Michel de Certeau, the "art of 'making do'" (1984, 30).

Home Is the Environment

rbGb not only celebrates an ecological ethos but also invites audiences to join in. As was my experience seeing the show in 2013, every performance begins with ushers welcoming the incoming audience onstage to witness the unfolding action up close. The house lights remain on for the first 20 minutes of the show, and audience members can circle the perimeter of a shotgun house[12] set center stage. A man sits in a rocking chair on what appears to be the "front" of the house, softly singing the hymn, "I've Got Peace like a River" in a rich, deep voice. He is accompanied by a woman from within the house. Inside the house's two paneless windows are three of the four performers: in one upstage left window, Joseph dances back and forth, momentarily filling the window frame before disappearing from view. Rapidly moving from side to side, he appears trapped in the house. Behind him, the sole female performer, Tolmaire, presses her hands to her ears, bobbing to music that only she can hear. She vigorously jerks her upper body but leaves her lower body firmly planted, as though stuck in place. Then, in a downstage right window, Joseph cuts watermelon and offers it to passing audience members. His kind, calm manner suggests that the fruit is proffered without insult or irony but, in the performance I saw, many audience members declined.

Suddenly, the audience is forced to step back as the performers pull apart the house, splitting it into four large pieces, each representative of a different city: Chicago, Houston, Harlem, and Oakland. Now the audience too can move inside the house, peering into its crevices and open spaces. The four performers fall into a vocal and physical call and response: Tolmaire calls out while Joseph dances to her lyric; then, Joseph responds with a lyric of his own that Tolmaire's body echoes. As the two sing and dance in tandem within the wide-open house, the other two performers take up percussion. Shepherd sits atop a chair on the "roof" of what was formerly the "back" porch; in rhythm with the vocals, he bangs against a reclaimed dustpan and trashcan, shaking the set piece with verve. Meanwhile, Yaw alternates between drumming on another set piece's steps and house frame.

The performers only break from their activity to push the pieces of the house farther and farther apart, until each section takes up a corner of the stage, and audience members, running out of space, gradually filter to their seats. Throughout the performance, the artists continually shift the house pieces, highlighting one and isolating another, bringing two or three pieces together to make different configurations. The tempo of this task always varies to match the energy of the performance at any moment. A mournful blues ballad may yield to a joyous hip hop number, a spirited march may be truncated by a quiet ritual. Through song and dance, the performers evoke the unique energy and rhythm of each city, and, after reliving their experiences in four disparate cities, they slowly reassemble the shotgun house. Significantly, though, the house is not in the exact formation it began in; the "back" is now in "front" and the "front" is now in "back," signaling not only a spatial rearrangement but a metaphorical rearrangement of "home."

"Home" in *rbGb* functions on a number of material and metaphorical levels. When the set piece is a whole unit, it stands in for the countless number of similarly nondescript African American homes in impoverished neighborhoods. It also speaks to the ways in which ecology, economy, and home are interrelated; as eco-theater scholar Theresa J. May points out, "ecology and economics both come from the same Greek *oikos*, meaning 'house' and connoting home or dwelling" (2006, 132). One's home is an integral part of one's environment and one's experience of place, something which the environmental justice movement has long attended to in contrast to the broader environmental movement in the US, which emphasizes "the great outdoors" as an escape from home. The fact that the shotgun house is the only set piece and is positioned at centerstage highlights its prominence not only in the performance but also in people's lives. When the performance starts, most of the performers are in the house, their choreography giving the impression of being stuck, trapped, or rooted in place. This speaks to the ways in which African Americans' economic and spatial mobility have been curtailed by racist housing policies, and it suggests that any consideration of the environment must begin with the places people live: their home environment.

When the shotgun house is one unit, it functions as both a material and metaphorical home, but, when the house is broken into four separate pieces, it represents four distinct US cities. Thus, not only does *rbGb* consider what environmentalism might mean for people of color locally, in their own homes, it also considers its meaning across cities and regional differences. The unique characteristics of Chicago, Houston, Harlem, and Oakland are represented in *rbGb* through music, dance, and spatiality. As set designer Theaster Gates explains,

> We've tried to figure out ways to tease out nuances and the differences between them [the cities]. We built the structures in compartments so that together they mimic a shotgun house that you might find in Houston. And then that shotgun house breaks apart into these sections where rooms become opportunities for sharing story or video or other acts of celebration
>
> *("Marc" 2012).*

Each section loosely represents a city, a color, a season: Chicago in red summer, Houston in black autumn, Harlem in green winter, and Oakland in blue spring. The colors are only implied with one small, colored light bulb on each house section, and by the seasons referenced by the ensemble in passing.

However, the most notable differences city to city are expressed through rhythm and story. For instance, the use of blues and ballet imbues Chicago with a slow, mournful pace, while the use of hip hop and fast-paced spoken word imbues Harlem with a driven, clipped pace. On the one hand, Joseph's nonlinear journey through the four cities causes their differences to overlap and converge, as one city rhythm quickly gives way to another, suggesting commonality across metropolitan difference. On the other hand, the four performers often split into the house's four quadrants before coming together again, implying a spatial simultaneity in which the action in each city is ongoing and concurrent. In stressing the unique paces and tones of the four cities, *rbGb* also highlights the particularities between environmental movements and communities of color in one American city and those in another, emphasizing the need for varied, disparate strategies to meet local socio-environmental needs.

"What Would Grow Here?": Joy and Mourning

Joseph has unique experiences in each city, all of which contribute to his evolving understanding of what environment and environmentalism can mean. In Oakland and Harlem, for instance, he finds himself overwhelmed by the exclusive and doctrinaire environmental groups he encounters, but, in Houston and Chicago, he is troubled by the ubiquitous poverty and violence he witnesses. Take, for example, an encounter Joseph has with a grief-stricken mother in Chicago:

> Me and my do-gooder friends are
> greening the ghetto
> > I ask a mother about environment
> > She responds in the language of
> disaster
> > > The culture of hazard
> > > Summer climax of climate
> > > 36 school kids gun blasted to the
> hereafter
>
> *(2012, 72).*

Throughout this scene, Joseph contrasts his narrowed understanding of environmentalism with a capital "E"—"going green" and recycling—with the mother's understanding: her climate is gun violence, her ecosystem is "black boy death" (2012, 74). While Joseph speaks, Tolmaire embodies the woman's loss, rocking back and forth, unmoored, without anything to steady her. Then, she leans on Joseph, pushing her body off of his with increasing force, her weight a physical resistance to the son's untimely death. Faced with the mother's raw sorrow, Joseph grows self-conscious about the narrowed environmental goals of his group, which seem woefully inadequate in the face of systemic racism and violence. The exchange leads Joseph to recognize that, "If you're brown, you can't go green until you hold a respect for black life" (2012, 3). Seeing the effects of gun violence up close, Joseph realizes that what is needed is a celebration of Black life and culture, an acknowledgement that, for many African Americans, survival is its own form of sustainability.

Witnessing environmental injustices meant to make people of color feel broken—from derelict parks to food insecurity to poor air quality—Joseph discovers that any effective, lasting environmentalism must be rooted in everyday life. At first, he wants to "[g]reen the ghetto" with "Mos def bustin in the park on a solar/powered stage" (2012, 72) but soon realizes that, in order to go forward, African American communities must go back; they must be able to grieve for those murdered and celebrate those who are still alive. Initially, Joseph's narrowed definition of environmentalism aligns with the broader environmental movement in the US, emphasizing what Black people can do to improve the environment with little attention to their precarious environments and endangered lives. Realizing that any environmentalism that fails to consider lived realities is disingenuous and impractical, Joseph proposes a "Life is Living" festival as a space to celebrate life and mourn its loss. As performance studies scholar Harvey Young argues, in response to writers' tendency to focus on either Black misery or Black joy, what is needed "is a pragmatic understanding not only of the ways in which the past shadows the present but also of how the joys and, perhaps, the *jouissance* of blackness, are tempered with pain" (2010, 6). Throughout the choreopoem, Joseph comes to discover that any attempt to "[g]reen the ghetto" (2012, 72) would just be papering over the actual, complex lived experiences of Black Americans. Instead, he proposes an ecological practice that, in response to racism, violence, and fragmentation, simultaneously mourns and celebrates African American lives and environments.

Recognizing the inextricable connection between pain and joy, Joseph turns to a primary source of both for many African Americans: the soil, which is a reminder of the legacies of slavery and systemic racism but also a source of self-reliance. Looking at the mother's picture of her son who was killed, he says

> Because the FIRST thing you notice is
> his skin
> If it were soil, his is the earth brown
> you'd want to sow in.

> A Chicago sun
> Hard times
> He does not blink
>
> So think of this brother brown
>   Now see this mother black
>   See how dark the day becomes when
> you bury the sun
>
> *(2012, 73).*

Likening the boy's skin to rich soil to sow in, Joseph suggests an embodied connection between the two, a connection that is extended by the repeated use of the word "sun" where "son" might appear. Particularly in performance, "son" might also be the "sun," and this homophonic interchangeability places the same value on each. Humans cannot live without the sun, just as the mother cannot live without her son. Both the sun and Black life sustain life and the loss of both is unfathomable. By interconnecting moments of loss with those of celebration, *rbGb* suggests that Black life and death are connected to the life of the soil, which has the potential to sustain life.

The relationality between Black life and death, between Black joy and sorrow, becomes a theme throughout *rbGb*, and home soil serves as the site of both. Describing a gardener and builder to the Chicago mother, Joseph says he, "Builds homes/Lotsa black boy souls in the wood/floors and steel beams" (2012, 74). The idea that Black homes and lives are built with and out of death highlights the permeability between renewal and death, growth and remains. Upon hearing about Joseph's gardening plans, the mother asks, "What would grow here?" (2012, 74), a question that haunts Joseph. What can grow "fertilized by native son blood under the/concrete…What strange fruit…?" (2012, 75). Potentially referencing Richard Wright's 1940 novel *Native Son*, in which a Chicago youth cannot escape the anti-Blackness that engulfs him, and Billie Holliday's 1939 song "Strange Fruit," written and composed by Abel Meeropol to protest lynchings in the American South, Joseph connects the violent racial injustices of the past and present to the land as both a site of horror and hope. Contemplating the lack of value placed on Black lives, particularly those of Black young men, Joseph turns to the earth, even though he cannot imagine what can possibly grow out of hatred, violence, and bloodshed.

In his own contemplation of an "aesthetics of the earth," philosopher Édouard Glissant acknowledges the seeming incongruity of loving land that reminds one of one's colonization and, in this case, one's enslavement and disenfranchisement (1997, 151; DeLoughrey and Handley 2011, 27–8). And, yet, Glissant contends that, if healing is to begin, a "passion for the land where one lives is a start, an action we must endlessly risk" (as cited in DeLoughrey and Handley 2011, 27). To risk loving a land and home "fertilized by native son blood under the/concrete" (Joseph 2012, 75) is indeed terrifying, painful, and unfathomable, and, as Joseph gradually realizes, even harder to tell others to do. Thus, rather than deliver pat, environmental didacticism to people he encounters in the four cities, or to the *rbGb* audience, Joseph acknowledges and commemorates African Americans' personal and collective losses and celebrates vibrant, self-reliant gardening practices, art forms, homes, and—most of all—lives. Incongruously, miraculously, the scene between the Chicago mother and Joseph gives way to a marching band celebration, the preachy eco-festival idea now supplanted by the "Life is Living" festival celebrating Black life. Like a trombone in a marching band, the choreopoem slides back and forth between celebratory gospel music and the blues, between joy and mourning.

"Fuck Green" or The Trouble with Going Green

One way in which Joseph comes to recognize the need to celebrate Black life and mourn its loss is through witnessing environmental and social injustices, like packed city spaces and gun violence. Another way is through his own encounters with wealthy environmentalists in Oakland and stringent ones in Harlem. For example, in the middle of the scene about the grieving mother from Chicago, Joseph intercuts it with a recollection of the first time he tried to fundraise in Oakland. He visits an economically privileged, "big eco-group," hoping it will agree to help fund his festival to "brown the green movement" (2012, 73–4). Instead of offering the artist financial assistance, group members "pray over tofu/for 10 minutes" and invite Joseph to "a composting sweat lodge to vision quest" the festival (2012, 74). Joseph's comical bemusement as he recounts the experience reveals a startling disconnection between his own understanding of "going green" and the eco-group's understanding. Juxtaposed with environmental injustices like food insecurity, poor air quality, and limited access to green spaces, the group's bourgeois environmentalism seems out of touch with the actual needs and realities of many low-income, African American communities. The jarring experience with the eco-group, sandwiched between the harrowing encounter with the grieving mother, leads Joseph to say, "fuck green/I wanna throw a joint to celebrate life ...Healthy living/Sustainable survival practices/Mourning..." (2012, 74). This rejection of "green" is a repudiation of a narrowed, capitalistic form of environmentalism, which Joseph comes to see as antithetical to Black life and ecological practices.

The more cities Joseph visits and the more people he meets, the more he begins to suspect the commodification and elitism embedded in "going green." For example, in Houston, Joseph goes to "spill" his "spiel about green" to Mr. Aaron, an elderly Black man, only to have Mr. Aaron point out, "Green is also the color of the BP logo/and all the money that spills over the city like a sleek leak" (2012, 79). In one cutting line, Mr. Aaron has captured the irony embedded in green capitalism. BP, like other oil companies, both creates environmental catastrophes, such as the 2010 oil spill, and presents itself as the solution to the very problems it creates (Ryan 2019; Hitchcock 2012). This circular production extends to all companies that tout themselves as being "green" in order to generate more revenue. As Marx famously argues, capitalism is "accumulation for accumulation's sake, production for production's sake" (1906, 652). This makes capitalism antithetical to any environmental ethos that seeks to preserve the earth. Indeed, many scholars have noted that there is a "metabolic rift" between environmentalism and capitalism; as political ecologist Ivan R. Scales puts it, there is "a growing spatial, ecological and social separation of societies from the ecosystems that support them" (2014, 478). Thus, even as the word "green" is invoked and wielded by corporations to signify consideration for the environment, green capital is an oxymoron that further distances consumers from actual ecologies. In pointing out that green is the color of the money that pours into Houston's oil industry and spills back out when companies like BP invite disaster, Mr. Aaron speaks to the duplicity and harmfulness often contained in the word "green."

In contrasting his initial views about greening Black communities with the lived experiences of Mr. Aaron and the Chicagoan mother, Joseph challenges and ultimately undermines the value of the word "green." His juxtaposition of the unfairly disenfranchised and the incredibly privileged suggests that rather than "brown the green movement" (2012, 74), he wants to entirely rethink the green movement and, with it, mainstream environmentalism in the US. This is first evident when Joseph intercuts his scene with the grieving mother from Chicago with his experience of the elitist eco-group in Oakland, and it resurfaces again when he directly contrasts the environmental and social injustice he sees in Harlem with the doctrinaire practices of the "green czar of Harlem" (2012, 84).

As the performers shift the house compartments to transition from Houston to Harlem, they quicken their pace and begin marching in a row center stage, their intense, rapid rhythm channeling and matching that of New York City. Taking on the city's frenetic rhythm, the artists also take on its residents' sense of claustrophobic chaos. They pop in and out of windows, over and onto steps. Joseph and Tolmaire dance while one performer drums on house steps and ceiling beams and another on wind chimes made of recycled lights. Their hasty physicality and rhythm, combined with their literal lack of breath, suggest that Harlem is confining, stifling, overwhelming. In a repeated chorus refrain, the performers chant

> What are we gonna do when
> there's nothing left to eat but
> money
> and regret
> And the fungus
> and the stench of a bitter future black
> bagging us in the night
> for The right to breathe clean
> …air?
>
> *(2012, 84)*

In imagining a near-future abundance of money but a shortage of food, Joseph devalues money, which cannot directly sustain life, and prioritizes food which can.

He stresses that simply fighting for the right to clean air, which should be a human right, can lead to governmental surveillance and retribution in the form of black bagging, the warrantless monitoring and sometimes invasion of the homes of people deemed a threat to national security. The juxtaposition between the FBI's long history of tracking Black activists, from the civil rights era[13] to Black Lives Matter protests today,[14] and the reasonable demands for clean air highlights how environmental injustice is often state-sanctioned. What is regulated is not the air quality of Black communities but the people fighting for clean air.

Throughout the scene, the performers' breathing intensifies, their synchronized gasps filling every pause in the choreopoem. Taken literally, the gasps speak to the shortage of clean air and oxygen-producing trees in many poor, African American communities. Indeed, there is increasing evidence to suggest that urban tree inequity is race-based (Watkins and Gerrish 2018) and causes a host of health issues (Kondo et al. 2018, 445). In addition, the breathing might also speak to the many Black lives cut short by police violence. *RbGb* specifically mentions Sean Bell, the 23-year-old who was killed by the police in Queens the night before his wedding. Since *rbGb* was produced, the breathing scene has gained new meaning with the 2014 murder of Eric Garner, who said "I can't breathe" 11 times while being choked to death by New York Police Department officers in Staten Island. "I can't breathe" became a rallying cry of the Black Lives Matter movement, and the slogan frequently appears on protest signs and T-shirts. While Garner's murder was the first to bring the phrase "I can't breathe" to national attention, subsequent killings of unarmed African Americans like George Floyd, who uttered the same words, have reinforced the resonance of the expression. In *rbGb*, the ragged breathing combined with phrases like "you won't/let/me/breathe" (2012, 85), much like the protest cry "I can't breathe," holds a multitude of meanings. There is a literal inability to breathe due to police brutality and air pollutants, and a metaphorical inability to breathe due to the "black/bagging," regulating, surveilling, and curtailing of Black spatial mobility.

Joseph finds he also cannot breathe when he visits the "green czar of Harlem" to see if he will contribute to his Life is Living festival (2012, 84). Before the guru will consider signing on to the project, he wants to know if Joseph's credentials meet his doctrinaire environmental standards. The three other performers act as the czar, interrogating Joseph about his environmental practices: "Are you inflating tires? Are you/driving less? You in a car co-op? skipping the/elevator? takin the stairs? You eating local/organic non packaged and fresh?" (2012, 84). Joseph is grilled about everything from whether he makes his own baby food to whether he changes his "furnace filters in the winter" (2012, 85). In a particularly comedic moment, the czar asks Joseph if he brings his own cup to Starbucks only to gleefully shout, "trick question fuck Starbucks!" (2012, 84). The nonstop interrogation demonstrates how difficult it is to meet socially imposed green standards, while the trick question suggests that there are many traps along the way, where doing the "right" thing is actually the "wrong" thing.

Completely overwhelmed, Joseph asks, "I say yo harlem czar, man I wanna go/green,/but how the fuck can I you won't/let/me/breathe…" (2012, 85). The question becomes a rhythmic refrain gradually taken up by all of the performers. Returning to a horizontal line, the group's marching, stamping, and emphasis on the word "breathe" echoes its earlier refrain; tonally and thematically connected, the two moments not only critique unequal access to clean air in Harlem and police brutality but also the czar's stiflingly restrictive environmentalism. In his dogmatic single-mindedness, the Harlem czar is emblematic of many mainstream environmentalists who have fixed, yet convoluted, rules and regulations that must be followed if one is to prove one's environmental knowledge and commitment. Tellingly, the czar is concerned solely with conservation—of energy, animals, trees, and other resources—and fails to consider how he might create more egalitarian access to and distribution of existing resources.

Rather than discuss Joseph's concerns about food insecurity and air quality, the czar wants to verify the artist's "green" credentials. This juxtaposition critiques doctrinaire environmentalism that privileges strict regulations and conservation practices over disenfranchised humans in the environment, as well as over personal, material connections with the earth. As hooks asks, "Can we embrace an ethos of sustainability that is not solely about the appropriate care of the world's resources, but is also about the creation of meaning—the making of lives that we feel are worth living?" (2009, 2). It is through making meaning of life, affirming life, and improving quality of life that an appreciation for the earth can be fostered. Thus, Joseph's Life is Living festival is a celebration of Black life, as much an opportunity to create and appreciate art and culture—music, poetry, graffiti—as it is a chance to highlight gardening practices and healthy living.

Although the Harlem scene is playful, it nonetheless exposes serious problems embedded in the majority of mainstream environmentalism: green guilt and an emphasis on individual responsibility over corporate and governmental responsibility. Green marketing is particularly adept at capitalizing on this guilt, insinuating that no matter what one does, it is never enough. The desire to "go green," and, more importantly, to *appear* to be "going green" often supplant the need to materially connect with the environment. Green capitalism relies on green consumers who can afford to pay more for eco-labeling that assuages their guilt over buying products. The higher price tag on products touted as environmentally friendly serves to authenticate their legitimacy, suggesting that green consumerism is really a green elitism that is far more about distinctions of class and race than it is about saving the environment.

While the Harlem czar is most concerned with Joseph's reduction in energy consumption by taking the stairs, turning down the thermostat, reusing containers, and other energy-saving measures, he also interrogates Joseph about eating "local/ organic" food and buying "toxic free products" (2012, 84–5), both of which are more expensive than commercially produced, conventional goods. The insistence on pricey, organic products, as well as labor-intensive activities like making one's own baby food, stands in stark contrast to and distracts from social and environmental injustices like police brutality, poor air quality, and food insecurity. As Scales argues, "Green consumption reassures consumers that they are 'doing good' simply through their choices as consumers. In doing so, it hides the need for significant political and economic change that can only occur through political engagement" (2014, 486). In other words, green consumption can become a substitute for taking the political action necessary to hold governments and corporations responsible both for their impact on the environment, which is far greater than any individual impact, and for their disproportionate impact on people of color.

Joseph finds that he is neither wealthy enough for Oakland's "green" group, nor hip enough for Harlem's "green" guru. Caught between his guilt for asking impoverished people to "go green" and his guilt for not being "green" enough himself, he demonstrates the need for ecological practices that speak directly to African American experiences that have not been co-opted by green capitalism. As he puts it,

> keep your standards higher but don't keep
> my people out
>   collective organizing we're uprising
> here and now
>   movement of a people means all the
> people cha
>   save the people save planet say it with
> me with now…
> (Joseph 2012, 85).

Saving the planet begins with environmental justice, fighting for equal access to clean air, healthy food, and green spaces. Environmentalism that fails to consider people beyond their greening efforts is doubly exclusive: it ignores the ways in which the environment and poor BIPOC are mutually exploited, and it enforces rigid environmental standards that financial and time constraints make impossible to meet.

Although Joseph may have begun his Life is Living project with the intention of teaching African American communities to go "green," he gradually realizes, after listening to individuals' stories and experiencing their neighborhoods, that "going green" can be limited and, at times, counterproductive (Thomas 2013, 574). What is needed instead is a flexible, inclusive, and improvisational understanding of sustainability and environmentalism. Celebrating Black lives rather than green mandates, Joseph suggests that whether African Americans are suffering from grief-stricken loss and poverty, or from a self-imposed environmental regulation overload, the remedy is still the same: a renewed, material connection to the earth. While such a connection is by no means a cure-all, especially for those particularly affected by environmental and social injustice, it nonetheless has restorative properties. A celebration of Black life and, with it, the life of the soil, cannot erase what has been lost, but it can ground such loss in ecological practices that simultaneously celebrate life and mourn its loss. Thus, in the next section, I turn to Joseph's emphasis on gardening as a means of creating more egalitarian access and personal connection to food.

"I Speak to Him of Seeds"

Joseph's ecological practice in *rbGb* is most clearly defined when the piece specifically turns to gardening, as it does in scenes set in Houston and Oakland. In the former, performers hum a bluesy melody while gardening: with laborious movements and bent backs, they push their weight onto imagined shovels and hunch over imagined plots. Meanwhile, Tolmaire snaps actual peas in rhythm with their movements. The deliberate specificity and heaviness of the choreography, alongside the steady sound of freshly snapped peas, imbue the vignette with a sense of ritual, not unlike an earlier scene in which a performer sprinkles "[l]ibation for gulf coast. Water to baptize ..." (2012, 81). In this sense, the acts of gardening and preparing a meal are given as much significance in *rbGb* as a healing and baptism ritual, since both are matters of life and death. As Joseph says, "black folk re-imagine green/or rather re-imagine life" (2012, 79). In shifting from the green of green capitalism to the green of a garden, *rbGb* places value on "sweat equity" over monetary assets (2012, 77). Reimagining Black life as its own form of sustainability, Joseph turns to life-sustaining practices like gardening, because "[g]reen goes fast but land lasts" (2012, 84). Making a distinction between green currencies—both capital and cultural—and gardening, Joseph suggests a metaphorical turn to the soil to mourn loss of life and a literal turn to it to sustain life.

And, yet, such a turn is not easy given the painful legacies of slavery and the ways in which the spatial mobility of Black people has been curtailed by housing discrimination. Joseph wryly observes as much when he says, "Black folk pack big culture in little spaces. Next to no land. On some environmental shit" (2012, 79). Operating within actual gaps and cracks, Joseph encourages working with whatever one has and planting wherever one can. Thus, *rbGb*'s ecological practice and ethos might be one of "making a way out of no way" or, in the vein of de Certeau, "making do" by finding "*ways of using* the constraining order of the place" one is in (1984, 30, emphasis in original). Whether it is music, dance, or gardening, *rbGb* takes a practical yet celebratory approach in its advocacy for environmental justice. Even as the choreopoem ultimately champions ecological practices like gardening and Black celebration of life, it also maintains a flexibility, openness, and adaptability that allow for divergent narratives of environmentalism. Through his experience staging the Life is Living festival, Joseph comes to not only advocate for material interactions with dirt but also personal understandings of environmentalism.

The idea of making a way out of no way, of making do, despite tremendous limitations comes up again when Joseph discusses the Black Panthers with his son in Oakland:

My son asks me about panthers
    I speak to him of seeds
    Of sometimes working in an orchard a
sapling's length
    Of never grown trees
    Of ever hard work
    Of uncompleted cycles
    Of hands in the dirt
    Of the paradox of cultivating some-
thing you will never see
                      (2012, 86).

With repetition and power stylistically akin to Langston Hughes, this moment calls to the past, present, and future—a past in which enslaved African Americans did not experience the fruit of their labor, where, shackled to the land, they were alienated from the land. It speaks to a present in which Black life is threatened and cut short by systemic racism, and it calls to a future hoped for but not yet seen—in which the 400-year fight for racial, social, and environmental justice is won. Joseph tells his son that they "have always managed to overcome" (2012, 86). Comparing fledgling civil rights to the seeds of a newly planted tree, Joseph suggests that the survival and promise of both is interconnected. The ecological practice in *rbGb*, then, is one of survival in narrow, unrealized spaces: survival of African Americans, survival of the land, and the ways in which those two survivals are interdependent.

Trees take years to grow, and Joseph promises his son that "forty years from now, we'll be here too" (2012, 86). This promise bears an abundance of faith, given the murdered young men the show discusses—the unnamed boy from Chicago, Sean Bell, Bobby Hutton—and the countless others it does not name. Recalling standing with his son in Oakland's Bobby Hutton Park[15] and struggling to explain to him the history of the Black Panther Party, why it was necessary and why many of its members were killed, Joseph utters the last lines of the choreopoem: "Next time we go to the park, I bet you'll still find panther blue seeds, If you look real close…" (2012, 87).

With these final, telling words, the performers begin recomposing the shotgun house, as Tolmaire sings, "If you want me to stay, stay, stay…" The rearrangement of the four compartments into a new order reflects the performers' own spatial and performative journey; by the end of the piece, their experiences of various neighborhoods and residents has challenged and reshaped their understanding of environmentalism. The shotgun house's rearrangement into a whole but altered unit also speaks to the four cities' shifting relations, the ways in which seemingly local environmental justice practices are regionally, nationally, and even globally interconnected. Indeed, in the final moments of *rbGb*, the performers disappear into the house, from which a solitary light illuminates, suggesting an ongoing environmental justice dialogue (Thomas 2013, 576). The four compartments, loosely representative of four cities, are moved throughout *rbGb* to suggest spatialized experiences of particular neighborhoods, but, in rejoining the disparate set pieces, the performers highlight the need for simultaneously local and global understandings of home and urban ecology. In *rbGb*, then, environmental justice begins and ends with the home and the earthly foundation on which home is built. It offers one possible ecological practice that, out of necessity, celebrates life and sustains life through the cultivation of home and land.

Taken together, *Jewels from the Hinterland* and *rbGb* celebrate Black vegetal joy. Where the latter wrestles with the complexities of trying to live an ecologically sustainable life in a country where Black life is unsustainable, the former offers a quiet but powerful visual narrative of Black bodies at leisure in nature. Like the viral trend on TikTok of Black men frolicking through fields, Green's series serves as a joyful counternarrative to White exclusions of Black bodies in environmentalism and green spaces. Meanwhile, Joseph playfully critiques "going green" and proposes an alternative: "going Black" by celebrating Black life. In both *rbGb* and *Jewels in the Hinterland*, life means living on one's own terms in relation to vegetal life. In the face of anti-Black spatial limitations, Green and Joseph perform spatial mobility, Green by featuring a diversity of Black, Brown, and vegetal subjects in parks across New York City and Joseph through his traveling Life is Living festival and the constant spatial reorientation of the metaphorical and material house in *rbGb*. While Green and Joseph may be performing in environmental hinterlands—spaces not yet fully charted or known—their spatial explorations of Black experiences in green spaces sow the seeds of environmental belonging and ecological interconnection.

Notes

1 The pernicious, racist stereotype of the "welfare queen" has led to the ongoing criminalization and stigmatization of poverty (Kohler-Hausmann 2007).
2 Greenidge notes in her essay that, in her housing project, most of the residents were White, suggesting that the housing project's regulations were motivated by class as much as race. However, in introducing the stereotype of the "welfare queen" in her essay, Greenidge seems focused on how Black bodies in particular are pathologized and monitored.
3 All quotations taken from *red, black, & GREEN: a blues* come from the 2012 publication of the script in the journal *Theater*, and all descriptions of the production come from my viewing of the show in January 2013 at Redcat in Los Angeles.
4 The name was changed from the Office of Environmental Equity to the Office of Environmental Justice in 1994.
5 A popular slogan of the early environmental justice movement in the US was "where we live, work, and play" (Gottlieb 2009, 7).
6 The Group of Ten includes Sierra Club, Natural Resources Defense Council, Environmental Defense Fund, National Audubon Society, The Wilderness Society, National Parks Conservation Association, Friends of the Earth, National Wildlife Federation, Earthjustice, and the Isaak Walton League.
7 For example, following the 2020 protests of the murder of George Floyd and the campaign to remove Confederate monuments in the US, both the Sierra Club and the Audubon Society publicly addressed their founders' racist histories.
8 According to diversity data from a 2020 report by Green 2.0, "an independent advocacy campaign to increase racial and ethnic diversity within the mainstream environmental movement," incremental progress has been made to add more people of color to staff

and boards, but many major organizations did not submit diversity data and environmental organizations remain largely White.

9 Choreopoems combine music, poetry, and dance. Ntozake Shange came up with the term to describe her 1975 theater piece, *For Colored Girls Who Have Considered Suicide/ When the Rainbow is Enuf.* Joseph pays homage to Shange both by calling his piece a choreopoem and by entitling the first section "The Colored Museum."

10 Theaster Gates also performed, alternating with Yaw. In the Redcat production, though, Yaw performed.

11 More information about the Life is Living festival and other projects is available at https:// lil20.youthspeaks.org.

12 Shotgun houses are long, narrow, rectangular homes common among African Americans in the South during the Reconstruction Era into the early twentieth century. Theaster Gates modeled his set design on a shotgun house that one might find in Houston.

13 The most famous example of the FBI tracking civil rights activists is Martin Luther King Jr., whom the FBI wiretapped and blackmailed.

14 During the George Floyd protests in the summer of 2020, the US Department of Homeland Security used drones, airplanes, and helicopters to surveille protestors in 15 cities (Kanno-Youngs 2020).

15 Although the park is "officially" named the DeFremery Park, it is locally known for the 17-year-old Black Panther killed by police officers in 1968.

References

Adamson, Joni, Mei Mei Evans, and Rachel Stein. 2002. "Introduction." In *Environmental Justice Reader: Politics, Poetics, & Pedagogy*, edited by Joni Adamson, Mei Mei Evans, and Rachel Stein, 3–14. Tucson: University of Arizona Press.

Anderson, Elijah et al. 2012. "The Iconic Ghetto." *The Annals of the American Academy of Political and Social Science* 642 (1): 8–24.

Blum, Elizabeth D. 2002. "Power, Danger, and Control: Slave Women's Perceptions of Wilderness in the Nineteenth Century." *Women's Studies* 31 (2): 247–265.

Buckingham, Susan and Rakibe Kulcur. 2010. "Gendered Geographies of Environmental Justice." In *Spaces of Environmental Justice*, edited by Ryan Holifield, Michael Porter, and Gordon Walker, 70–94. New York: Wiley-Blackwell.

Bullard, Robert, et al. 2007. *Toxic Wastes and Race at Twenty, 1987–2007.* Cleveland, Ohio: United Church of Christ.

Campt, Tina M. 2012. *Image Matters: Archive, Photography, and the African Diaspora in Europe.* Durham, North Carolina: Duke University Press.

Cronon, William. 1995. "The Trouble with Wilderness; or, Getting Back to the Wrong Nature." In *Uncommon Ground: Rethinking the Human Place in Nature*, edited by William Cronon, 69–90. New York: W.W. Norton & Co.

de Certeau, Michel. 1984. *The Practice of Everyday Life.* Trans. Steven Rendall. Berkeley: University of California Press.

DeLoughrey, Elizabeth and George B. Handley. 2011. "Introduction: Toward an Aesthetics of the Earth." In *Postcolonial Ecologies: Literatures of the Environment*, edited by Elizabeth DeLoughrey and George B. Handley, 3–42. Oxford: Oxford University Press.

Dungy, Camille T. 2009. "Introduction: The Nature of African American Poetry." In *Black Nature: Four Centuries of African American Nature Poetry*, edited by Camille T. Dungy, xix–xxxiv. Athens, Georgia: University of Georgia Press.

Durlin, Marty. 2010. "The Group of 10 Respond." *High Country News*, February 1. https:// www.hcn.org/issues/42.2/the-group-of-10-responds.

Finney, Carolyn. 2014. *Black Faces, White Spaces: Reimagining the Relationship of African Americans to the Great Outdoors*. Chapel Hill, North Carolina: University of North Carolina Press.

Finney, Carolyn. 2020. "Self-Evident." *Beside Magazine*, 8, June 14. https://tinyurl.com/4tjsve3n.

Glissant, Édouard. 1997. *Poetics of Relation*. Trans. Betsy Wing. Ann Arbor: University of Michigan.

Gottlieb, Robert. 2009. "Where We Live, Work, Play…and Eat: Expanding the Environmental Justice Agenda." *Environmental Justice* 2 (1): 7–8.

Green 2.0. "2020 NGO & Foundation Transparency Report Card." https://tinyurl.com/5dnprdvh.

Green, Naima. 2013–. *Jewels from the Hinterland*. Photograph series. Exhibited 2014. The Wall, Myers Media Art Studio. New York, New York. https://tinyurl.com/5w6j6rbj.

Greenidge, Kaitlyn. 2016. "My Mother's Garden." *New York Times*. March 26.

Hitchcock, Peter. 2012. "Everything's Gone Green: The Environment of BP's Narrative." *Imaginations: Journal of Cross-Cultural Image Studies* 3 (2): np.

hooks, bell. 2009. *Belonging: A Culture of Place*. London: Routledge.

Joseph, Marc Bamuthi. 2012. "*Red, Black, & GREEN: a blues*." *Theater* 42 (3): 69–87.

Kanno-Youngs, Zolan. 2020. "U.S. Watched George Floyd Protests in 15 Cities Using Aerial Surveillance." *New York Times*, June 19.

Kohler-Hausman, Julilly. 2007. "'The Crime of Survival': Fraud Prosecutions, Community Surveillance, and the Original 'Welfare Queen.'" *Journal of Social History* 41 (2): 329–354.

Kondo, Michelle C. et al. 2018. "Urban Green Space and Its Impact on Human Health." *International Journal of Environmental Research and Public Health* 15 (3): 445.

Lee, Felicia. 2012. "Socially Engaged Without Preaching." *New York Times*, October 26.

"Marc Bamuthi Joseph with Theaster Gates: red, black, & GREEN: a blues." 2012. Vimeo. MCA Chicago. https://tinyurl.com/43spyxr8.

Marder, Michael. 2013. *Plant-Thinking: A Philosophy of Vegetal Life*. New York: Columbia University Press.

Marx, Karl. 1906. *Capital: A Critique of Political Economy*. Trans. Samuel Moore and Edward Aveling. New York: The Modern Library.

May, Theresa J. 2006. "'Consequences Unforeseen…' in Raisin in the Sun and Caroline, Or Change." *Journal of Dramatic Theory and Criticism* 20 (2): 127–144.

May, Theresa J. 2021. *Earth Matters on Stage: Ecology and Environment in American Theater*. New York: Routledge.

Meyerson, Collier. 2016. "The essence of #BlackGirlMagic is in these photographs." *Fusion*, May 25. https://tinyurl.com/ym5f2c92.

Moore, Richard, et al. 1990. Letter from the Southwest Organizing Project to the National Wildlife Association, March 16. https://tinyurl.com/5n6vd543.

Mueller, Nora. 2016. "Naima Green's Beautiful Portraiture Is Changing Public Perception of Green Spaces." *Garden Collage Magazine*, September 10. https://tinyurl.com/5n8c9tmm.

Parks, Shoshi. 2020. "Nature as Resistance: Through her Oakland nonprofit Outdoor Afro, founder Rue Mapp takes Black empowerment outside." *7x7*, June 21. https://tinyurl.com/4u4waph7.

Pellow, David N. 2016. "Toward a Critical Environmental Justice Studies: Black Lives Matter as an Environmental Justice Challenge." *Du Bois Review* 13 (2): 221–236.

Pollard, Ingrid. 1988. *Pastoral Interlude*. Hand-tinted silver prints, 5–20x24 inches. https://tinyurl.com/4vx84kkz.

Pollard, Ingrid. 1995. *Self Evident*. Photograph series. Ikon Gallery. Birmingham, UK. https://tinyurl.com/bckry8wv.

"Principles of Environmental Justice." 1991. First National People of Color Environmental Leadership Summit, October 24–27. Washington D.C. https://tinyurl.com/2p9as9zh.

Pulido, Laura. 2017. "Geographies of Race and Ethnicity II: Environmental Racism, Racial Capitalism, and State-Sanctioned Violence." *Progress in Human Geography* 41 (4): 524–533.

Purdy, Jedediah. 2015. *After Nature: A Politics for the Anthropocene*. Cambridge: Harvard University Press.

red, black, & GREEN: a blues. 2013. Performance. Marc Bamuthi Joseph/The Living Word Project. Dir. Michael John Garcés. Redcat, Los Angeles. 31 January–3 February.

Reese, Ashanté M. 2019. *Black Food Geographies: Race, Self-Reliance, and Food Access in Washington D.C.* Chapel Hill, North Carolina: UNC Press.

Richardson, Shaun and Amy Donley. 2018. "'That's So Ghetto!' A Study of the Racial and Socioeconomic Implications of the Adjective Ghetto." *Theory in Action* 11 (4): 22–43.

Rothstein, Richard. 2017. *The Color of Law: A Forgotten History of How Our Government Segregated America*. New York: Liveright Publishing.

Ryan, Courtney B. 2019. "#BPCares: Sinking Oil, Spreadable Disrupture." *ISLE: Interdisciplinary Studies in Literature and the Environment* 26 (4): 882–900.

Sandilands, Catriona. 2017. "Fear of a Queer Plant?" *GLQ* 23 (3): 419–428.

Savoy, Lauret. 2008. "The Future of Environmental Essay: A Discourse." *Terrain.org* 22.

Scales, Ivan R. 2014. "Green Consumption, Ecolabelling and Capitalism's Environmental Limits." *Geography Compass* 8: 477–489.

Seymour, Nicole. 2018. *Bad Environmentalism: Irony and Irreverence in the Ecological Age*. Minneapolis, MN: University of Minnesota Press.

Sibley, David. 1995. *Geographies of Exclusion: Society and Difference in the West*. London: Routledge.

Smith, Kimberly K. 2007. *African American Environmental Thought: Foundations*. Lawrence, Kansas: University Press of Kansas.

Taylor, Dorceta E. 2016. *The Rise of the American Conservation Movement: Power, Privilege, and Environmental Protection*. Durham, NC: Duke University Press.

Thomas, Arden. 2013. Rev. of *red, black, & GREEN: a blues*, by Marc Bamuthi Joseph. *Theatre Journal* 65 (4): 546–574.

"Toxic Wastes and Race in the United States: A National Report on the Racial and Socio-Economic Characteristics of Communities with Hazardous Waste Sites." 1987. *Commission for Racial Justice: United Church of Christ*. https://tinyurl.com/mudax5ey.

Virden, R.J. and G.J. Walker. 1999. "Ethnic/Racial and Gender Variations among Meanings Given to, and Preferences for, the Natural Environment." *Leisure Sciences* 21 (3): 219–239.

Walker, Alice. [1967] 1983. *In Search of Our Mothers' Gardens: Womanist Prose*. Orlando, FL: Harcourt.

Walker, Gordon. 2009. "Beyond Distribution and Proximity: Exploring the Multiple Spatialities of Environmental Justice." *Antipode* 41 (4): 614–636.

Watkins, Shannon Lea and Ed Gerrish. 2018. "The Relationship between Urban Forests and Race: A Meta-Analysis." *Journal of Environmental Management* 209 (1): 152–168.

Young, Harvey. 2010. *Embodying Black Experience: Stillness, Critical Memory, and the Black Body*. Ann Arbor: University of Michigan Press.

3

"PLANT SOME SHIT"

Guerrilla Gardening as Tactical Performance

When much of city life came to a screeching halt at the start of the COVID-19 pandemic, many people in the US turned to gardening. So popular were TikTok videos on the subject that the hashtag PlantTok became its own category.[1] In particular, guerrilla gardening, what I would define as planting on land one does not own without express permission, experienced renewed attention. For example, TikTok sensation @sfinbloom, short for the guerrilla gardening group San Francisco in Bloom, gained popularity for sprinkling wildflower seeds out of shakers and water guns while skateboarding through the city. Many other TikTokers shared recipes for "seed bombs," which consist of compost, seeds, clay, water, and sometimes cayenne pepper as an insect repellant. Perhaps the most famous aspect of guerrilla gardening, seed bombs often are tossed by gardeners when they want to plant in inaccessible, fenced-off areas.[2] Like urban agriculture more broadly, it is difficult to assess just how popular guerrilla gardening is, because of its informal and sometimes covert nature, but it is practiced internationally and many formal gardening projects can be traced back to guerilla gardening (Hardman et al. 2018, 7; Scott et al. 2013).

Part of guerrilla gardening's ambiguity stems from the fact that the very definition of the activity varies based on who you ask. For example, on the Lower East Side in the 1970s, the Green Guerillas saw guerrilla and community gardening, in the words of member Amos Taylor, as "a form of civil disobedience. We were basically saying to the government, if you won't do it we will" (as cited in "Our History"). Meanwhile, Londoner Richard Reynolds, perhaps the world's most famous guerrilla gardener today, emphatically defines guerrilla gardening as "THE ILLICIT CULTIVATION OF SOMEONE ELSE'S LAND" (2008, 16, capitalization in original), while others, like Vancouver community ecologist David Tracey, are more flexible, defining it as "gardening public space with or without permission" (2007, 4). Ron Finley, a gardener from Los Angeles, has made the term gangsta gardener synonymous with guerrilla gardening and interprets gangsta

DOI: 10.4324/9781003203766-4

as "revolutionary" and "vital" but not illegal (Ron Finley Project 2022). Just as the definition of guerrilla gardening might vary depending on who you ask, so too might the location and style of gardening. Some guerrilla gardeners focus on neglected, city-owned medians, parkways, and sidewalks while others focus on rental properties. Some, like Reynolds, focus on ornamental plants while others, like Finley, primarily focus on vegetal plants. Thus, guerrilla gardeners are not a homogenous, radical entity but can include a range of people from those enthralled with the illicitness of the activity to those who simply do not realize that they need permission to garden on public land. (Adams and Hardman 2014, 1116; Hardman et al. 2018, 8).

Much attention has been paid to guerrilla gardening as an anticapitalist subculture contesting property laws (Tracey 2007; Reynolds 2008); a source of communal engagement (Adams and Hardman 2014, 1107); and a localized, situationally specific intervention (Adams and Hardman 2014, 1107–09; Crane, Viswanathan, and Whitelaw 2013, 76). While, as urban geographers David Adams and Michael Hardman note, there is a tendency among scholars and guerrilla gardeners to focus on the more subversive and illicit elements of guerrilla gardening (2014, 1106–07), these aspects of the movement have been examined from a political and sociological perspective rather than from a performance perspective. Furthermore, given that, as Adams and Hardman argue, guerrilla gardeners are influenced by their individual identities, geographies, and purpose (2014, 1107–09), it is useful to consider how such factors affect their performance of guerrilla gardening activism. How do diverse guerrilla gardeners perform and why? How does their use of theatricality, metaphor, and playfulness reflect particular cultural, racial, and class gardening identities? Like theater historian Scott Magelssen, who has studied simulated experiences and American flight as performance, in this chapter, I focus on "theater with a 'lower-case t,'" case studies that make meaning through theatrical tools but are not traditional Theater (2020, 7). I would argue that analyzing guerrilla gardening through a performance lens serves to highlight the site-specific, improvisational tactics different guerrilla gardeners deploy to create more green spaces and attract others to their cause. Furthermore, by examining guerrilla gardening as an embodied practice and performance that changes over time based on gardeners' unique identities and needs, it is possible to resist what Adams and Hardman see as the tendency to abstract or romanticize guerrilla gardening (2013, 1107). As performance studies scholar Diana Taylor argues, "[W]e learn and transmit knowledge through embodied action, through cultural agency, and by making choices. Performance…functions as an episteme, a way of knowing, not simply an object of analysis" (2003, xvi). As a site-specific, embodied way of knowing, performance is an ideal lens to examine the highly situational, diffuse, and changeable guerrilla gardening movement.

Unlike community gardens, which are typically authorized and thus longer-lasting, guerrilla gardens, if illicit, are often ephemeral, operating simultaneously as activism and performance. For example, the movement's creation of terms like "seed bombs," or "seed grenades," and its use of code names not only draw on military references but performance tactics as well. Deploying playfulness and hyperbole, guerrilla gardening can serve to highlight the unequal privatization of land, the mismanagement of city grounds, and the regulation of seemingly "public" spaces. The radical notion that land belongs to everyone and to no one is a challenge to dominant, capitalistic private property laws, particularly in the US where property laws were used to dispossess Indigenous peoples and enslave African Americans. Thus, guerrilla gardeners must deploy improvisational, creative tactics; as Michel de Certeau puts it, tactics "must vigilantly make use of the cracks that particular conjunctions open in the surveillance of the proprietary powers" (1984, 36). One tactic utilized by guerrilla gardeners is playing with language, particularly with vegetal or militaristic metaphors in their groups' names. Take, for instance, Trowels on the Prowl (TOP) in Chicago (Mahany and Cox 2008), which teamed up with Skokie Outlaws Improving the Landscape (SOIL) to create TOP-SOIL guerrilla gardening events. Meanwhile, in Dublin, Ireland, the Plant Bandits garden as part of the larger organization Extinction Rebellion (Coyle 2020). As these playful names suggest, even though guerrilla gardening is an activist movement rather than a traditional performance, it nonetheless employs tactical performance elements to achieve its gardening goals and to attract new members to its cause. As we shall see, guerrilla gardening's origins in the West are rooted in anti-military and performance activism.

Perhaps most importantly, focusing on guerrilla gardening as a performance draws attention to the actual embodied performers doing the gardening, who may have a varying degree of spatial mobility—the ability to move freely through different locations. For example, some geographers have argued that guerrilla gardening should be defined as an informal act rather than an illegal one, given that no known arrests have been made for guerrilla gardening (Hardman et al. 2018, 7; Adams, Hardman, and Larkham 2015). Similarly, criminologist Andrew Millie argues that guerrilla gardening, at least in the UK, is "normalised law-breaking" (2022). And, yet, it is important to consider the role that race likely plays in the debate between guerrilla gardening as informal or illegal, especially in the US where Black young adults are seven times more likely to be arrested than their White counterparts (Schleiden et al. 2020). Given the criminalization of Black people in the US, police and bureaucratic response to guerrilla gardening may depend on *who* is doing the gardening and where. The risks involved in guerrilla gardening are higher for people of color in the US than they are for their White counterparts, and, thus, how guerrilla gardeners define their activities may be influenced by their degree of privilege and spatial mobility.

Thus, in this chapter, I will be focusing on guerrilla gardening as both a form of activism and a performance, in which gardeners' performance is shaped by their specific identities and geographies. This inquiry is important because it raises questions about who has access to green spaces, who is entitled to engage in unlawful behavior, and what the vegetal and political significance of short-term gardening can be. As cultural studies scholar George McKay argues, the movement "can actually touch on a multitude of contemporary questions" about access to private and public space, "food production and consumption," and political empowerment (2011, 192). Examining significant, primarily US-based guerrilla gardeners from the 1970s until today, I suggest that performance tactics may be used by various guerrilla gardeners at times to highlight systems of oppression and environmental injustice and, at other times, to obscure them through decontextualized hyper-performances of illicitness. Since guerrilla gardening ideology can be intentionally ambiguous, I provide a brief history of the movement in the US before analyzing the performance tactics of three distinctive radical gardeners: Liz Christy in 1970s New York, Richard Reynolds in London,[3] and Ron Finley in Los Angeles. I have chosen these three gardeners not only because of their prominence in the guerrilla gardening movement but also because of the ways in which their distinct guerrilla gardening identities, geographies, and purposes propel them to draw on site-specific, improvisational performance tactics to achieve their goals.

From Guerrilla Garden to Historic Garden

Considering that guerrilla gardening can be the simple act of dropping or planting seeds on land that one does not own, its history is likely as long as that of gardening itself.[4] However, it was not until 1973 that the term "guerrilla gardening" was coined by the Green Guerillas[5] group, which was founded by artist Liz Christy after she became inspired by national greening efforts and by the first Earth Day in 1970 (Young 2021). After throwing seed grenades into abandoned lots around the Lower East Side of Manhattan, Liz Christy and her friends began guerrilla gardening in a vacant lot on Elizabeth Street, but the garden paradise was soon paved…to put up a parking lot (Ferguson 1999, 83). Undeterred, the Green Guerillas took over the nearby corner of Bowery and Houston, a city lot that had become the neighborhood dumpster, filled with broken refrigerators and six feet of trash (Brooks and Marten 2005). After a publicized battle with the city (Ferguson 1999, 83), the group was able to rent the space for one dollar a month (Loggins 2007). Unusual for a guerrilla gardening project, many of which are destroyed, the Green Guerillas' work still exists to this day; renamed the Liz Christy Community Garden (LCCG), it is the oldest community garden in New York City.

Now one of the 550 gardens in NYC Parks' GreenThumb Community Gardening program, the LCCG has evolved over the course of 50 years from a radical, illicit garden to a community garden with a generic Parks gate that is locked outside of the garden's limited operating hours. On the one hand, the homogenous fence around the garden's perimeter and the limited operating hours reassert the very boundaries of private and public space that the 1970s Green Guerillas upset, though the garden was fenced in even in the 1970s.[6] On the other hand, the fact that the garden has survived and been tended by volunteers for 50 years is in large part due to its ability to adapt to local needs. When the group first began as a fruit and vegetable garden, the Lower East Side was a dilapidated area in a bankrupt city, necessitating the Green Guerillas' illicit intervention; however, as the once working-class neighborhood gentrified, so too did the garden. In 2004, when the garden was in danger of being demolished to make way for luxury apartments, volunteers were able to save it by transferring the garden to NYC Parks (Jones 2022).[7]

Thus, while the LCCG has evolved from its radical origins, becoming a part of the official NYC Parks system has afforded it a longevity it likely could not have managed on its own. What began as much-needed vegetable and fruit patches has become much-needed, decades-old trees and biodiverse plants that create shade and oxygen in an area that is now otherwise highly developed. In my interview with longtime Liz Christy Garden member Penny Jones, she pointed out that, while food justice and food initiatives are important, "What people don't talk about is…that these older gardens are oxygen lungs for the neighborhoods, number one; they bring the temperature down and they bring the cost of air conditioning down in the surrounding buildings" (2022). Growing and maintaining trees takes years, and, while the early Green Guerillas played a crucial role in challenging the city's neglect of impoverished areas and providing communal food, the LCGG's ultimate evolution from a guerrilla garden to a long-term one speaks to a continual commitment to the plants and their growth. As a long-term performance, it also highlights the ways in which the "meanings of space are seen to be remade continually through performative enactments" (Adams and Hardman 2014, 1109).

Insomuch as guerrilla gardening is a challenge to capitalistic property laws, the Liz Christy Community Garden in its current form may seem like a shadow of its former self. And, yet, even in the 1970s, the Green Guerillas had to rent the lot from the city to avoid destruction, albeit for a dollar a month. While the group initially rebelled against property laws to create meaningful change, in order to build on that change they had to participate in a monetary transaction with the city. This reveals the ways in which transgression and its norms are interconnected. As sociologist Chris Jenks argues, "Transgressive behavior…does not deny limits or boundaries, rather it exceeds them and thus completes them" (2003, 7). In other words, transgression can only be recognized as such in contrast to known rules and is therefore a part of the rules. By guerrilla gardening on property that they did not rent or own, the early Green Guerillas exceeded the rules, and the rules were reasserted when their first garden was paved over and when they rented their second garden to preserve it. The decisions the Green Guerillas faced, to rent the garden in 1974 and to transfer it to NYC Parks in 2004, were ones that may have deradicalized the group but vitalized the garden. As McKay notes, there is an ideological split between activists who emphasize the "guerrilla" aspect of the movement and those who emphasize the gardening aspect (2011, 189). And, as we will see, there is a degree of truth to this, but I would argue that the split is more of a moving line. Because guerrilla gardening is highly situational and contextual, it can be adapted to suit different geographic and temporal needs. The longer a guerrilla gardening performance continues, the more likely it is to shift from the impromptu improvisations of guerrilla gardening to something more vegetally focused.

Although the Liz Christy Community Garden has traded its seed grenades in for vegetal continuity, it is in many ways still quietly transgressive. For example, on my visit to the garden in the spring of 2022, I was struck by the contrast between the garden and the surrounding area. Adjacent to a subway entrance, the LCCG has less than a couple of feet between it and one of the AvalonBay luxury high-rises that looms above much of its foliage (see Figure 3.1). Across the street, AvalonBay's other set of luxury apartments features a Whole Foods on the ground floor.

In contrast to the city grid, the garden features winding, curved lines, something Liz Christy initiated in the 1970s and which has been developed with the addition of circular wooden and stone paths (Jones 2022). When I visited, I saw graffiti scrawled on the NYC Parks signs (perhaps a fittingly illicit act for a once illicit garden) and heard countless horns and sirens. And, yet, inside the Picturesque style garden,[8] the lush foliage provides a respite from the noise and heat. Benches, alcoves, paths that lead nowhere invite one to sit, to pause, to go slow (see Figure 3.2).

Much like Vaughn Bell's biospheres in chapter 1 and Naima Green's photographs in chapter 2, the LCCG provides a leisurely space for vegetal and human connection. While the garden has official status on the National Registry of Historic Places, the fact that it continues to exist in any form, surrounding as it is by

FIGURE 3.1 The AvalonBay apartment complex looms over the garden's trees. Photograph by the author.

FIGURE 3.2 A path made of wooden stumps with the words "GO SLOW" on the first stump. Photograph by the author.

multi-million-dollar properties, speaks to the power of community organizing, first with guerrilla gardening tactics in the 1970s and later with letter writing and petitions in the early 2000s.

In contrast to the surrounding area, which is fast-paced, moneyed, and economically designed, the LCCG is meandering and funded by donations and sweat equity. Indeed, although the garden is locked when a member cannot be present, volunteers can earn keys to the garden and become members after working in it for 40 hours (Jones 2022). While the garden has limited operating hours for the general public and belongs to the NYC Parks, volunteers can gain a sense of ownership and autonomy through labor and stewardship. Furthermore, the Green Guerillas today is a sister organization of the LCCG and has expanded beyond the gentrified Lower East Side, providing seedlings, funding, and programming to currently disenfranchised neighborhoods in Harlem, Brooklyn, and the South Bronx ("Our Programs"). Thus, what began as a local guerrilla gardening intervention has gradually expanded across divergent New York City boroughs. This speaks to the ways in which short-term, illicit vegetal politics can morph into more sustainable vegetal practices. While I am primarily concerned with the performance tactics that guerrilla gardens deploy to politicize their agenda and to improvise with limited land, the Green Guerillas over time provide an apt example of how performance tactics and gardening practices can evolve to suit the current needs of the community. As Adams and Hardman suggest, the illicit and subversive elements of guerrilla gardening have received a great deal of attention, but what is less discussed are the ways in which guerrilla gardens can become sites of "communal gathering" (2014, 1107–09). The ability to maintain a garden without fear of its destruction allows communal ties to the garden and to fellow volunteers to deepen and grow.

Staging Little Wars

And yet, in many ways, it is the more overtly subversive performance tactics of guerrilla gardeners that visibly demonstrate that green spaces should be communal and accessible to everyone. For many guerrilla gardeners, any space—public or private—can be improved, and anyone with a few native seeds is capable of gardening. The accessibility of guerrilla gardening, combined with the thrill of transgressing spatial norms, attracts newcomers to the movement in a way that established community gardens cannot. For example, a 1973 Green Guerilla Fact Sheet (see Figure 3.3) offers "seed grenade" recipes and instructions for launching. Gardeners are advised to "assemble" either old glass Christmas ornaments or balloons and fill them with water, peat moss, fertilizer, and seeds. Then, gardeners should

> [c]hoose a lot that has a fence and is legally inaccessible. Calculate in advance how many grenades will be needed to cover the area. Check carefully before throwing. Observe all normal safety precautions. Suggested throwing techniques are: for Christmas ornaments—use an underhand throw; for the water balloons—use an overhand throw
>
> *(Green Guerillas Fact Sheet 1973).*

The sheet is a playful and improvisational amalgam of gardening and military terms. The list of ingredients, the grenade diagram, and the seed list—which explains when certain plants are most seasonable—all suggest a seriousness of task. At the same time, the militant language, such as "assemble the ingredients" rather than gather the ingredients, and "grenade membrane" rather than balloon or ornament (Green Guerillas Fact Sheet 1973), is rendered comical by its own hyperbole and its juxtaposition with the recommended throwing techniques. While the suggested use of ornaments and balloons, not to mention chemical fertilizers, reveals a historical lack of understanding about non-biodegradable materials, it nonetheless, along with the recommended throwing techniques, evokes an improvisational tone. As ironically ill-suited as balloons and ornaments are now known to be for gardening, their use is suggestive of what Michel de Certeau calls the art of "making do" through everyday practices (1984, 29). Deploying performance tactics that make use of what is available and take action in quite literal gaps

Green Guerillas Fact Sheet

417 LAFAYETTE STREET
NEW YORK, NEW YORK 10003
212/ 674-8124

TWO
SEED GRENADE RECIPES
OR
HOW TO HIDE ILLEGAL DUMPING SPACE

Assemble the following ingredients:

A. Old glass Christmas ornaments
   Small funnel
   Pelletized, time-release
    fertilizer
   Peatmoss "crumbs"
   Tissue
   Seeds - see below

B. Small balloons
   Funnel
   Pelletized, time-release
    fertilizer
   Peatmoss "crumbs"
   Seeds - see below
   sink faucet

Add seed and fertilizer to grenade membrane:

Add seeds and fertilizer
first, followed by moist peatmoss
"crumbs". Stuff the opening at the
top with a small piece of tissue.
Gently shake to mix thoroughly.

Add seeds and fertilizer first, followed
by moistened peatmoss "crumbs". Stretch
the mouth of the balloon over the faucet
mouth and carefully fill with water.
Tie off the opening. Gently shake to
mix thoroughly.

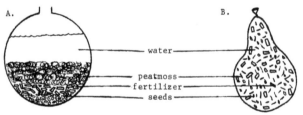

Instructions for use:

Choose a lot that has a fence and is legally inaccessible. Calculate
in advance how many grenades will be needed to cover the area. Check
carefully before throwing. Observe all normal safety precautions. Suggested
throwing techniques are: for Christmas ornaments - use an underhand throw;
for the water balloons - use an overhand throw.

Seed list

for early fall	for early spring	for late spring	for early summer
Soybeans	Batchelor Buttons	Cosmos	Sunflower
Clover	Dianthus	Portulaca	ornamental grass mix
Winter rye	Wildflower mix	Zinnia	Marigolds
Cleome	plain old grass	Nicotiana	Zinnia

FIGURE 3.3 Green Guerillas Fact Sheet. An instruction sheet illustrating the production
of seed grenades. Photo credit: Green Guerillas, 1973.

and cracks, the 1970s Green Guerillas upset boundaries of private and public space and made urban gardening more accessible. Through playful militancy, the group transgresses the norms of land ownership to create a communal gardening space.

And, yet, beneath the playfulness of the group's fact sheet lies a more serious purpose for applying militant terminology to gardening. The Green Guerillas' deployment of the term "guerrilla" in 1973, like the San Francisco Mime Troupe's deployment of it in 1965 for "guerrilla theater," was inspired by Ernesto "Che" Guevara's 1961 handbook *Guerrilla Warfare* (Doyle 2002; Reynolds 2008, 17).[9] Etymologically, the Spanish word "guerrilla" means "little war," and insomuch as radical gardeners are waging improvisational, localized wars against unequal, limited access to land, the term is useful. Just as R.G. Davis's guerrilla theater sought to provoke artists to lead a US countercultural revolution (Doyle 2002), guerrilla gardening intends to revolutionize the act and art of gardening, as well as to interrogate the privatization of land. As Adam Purple explains of his renowned Garden of Eden in Manhattan,[10] "The city was doing nothing with that land, they were ambushing it…Why would I bother getting permission from them? It's the people's turf. I made that garden for everybody" (as cited in Ferguson 1999, 87). Inspired by Guevara's call for agrarian reform and just, equitable distribution of land, guerrilla theater and guerrilla gardening both reimagine public space and subvert privatized space. In 1967, for instance, Davis explained that guerrilla theater must destroy the entire structure of private property, something exemplified by the San Francisco Mime Troupe's reclamation of public parks for its theater productions (Doyle 2002). Similarly, guerrilla gardening is a material performance that can expose inequitable land distribution and create more egalitarian access to green space. Thus, the term "guerrilla" is useful in contesting the privatization of land and emphasizing the ways in which, as Tracey writes, "every plant is political" (2007, 32).

However, guerrilla gardening's capitalization on "Che," part of a global commodification of the figure, also calls the movement's claim to subversive alternativeness into question. Indeed, Alberto Korda's iconic photograph of Guevara has been featured in Taco Bell and Smirnoff vodka ads and plastered on T-shirts, pins, and haute couture bikinis (Caspari 2013). Such commercial misappropriations displace the cultural and historical significance of Guevara. Although the application of the figure's name to contemporary revolutionaries—such as the "Guevara of Gaza," Palestinian Mohammad Al-Aswad, and even guerrilla gardeners[11]—may be more germane, it still makes troublingly misleading parallels (Selbin 2010, 38). As political scientist Eric Selbin notes, even if such appellations "are illuminatory, they just as often prove obfuscatory and limiting, encouraging us to interchange, even interpolate, people, places, events, and processes" (2010, 38). Thus, while the capitalistic commodification of Guevara through advertising is a direct contradiction of the figure's Marxist stance, the misattribution of Guevara's name to other revolutionaries untethers both from their historical and cultural specificity.

A similar untethering has occurred with the commercialization of guerrilla gardening. As Green Guerillas member Donald Loggins notes, the group was quite radical when it first began (as cited in *Vox* 2021), and, in aligning itself with Guevara's ethos, sought both to greenify the Lower East Side and to challenge the privatization and dereliction of city spaces. And, yet, just as the mass production of Korda's iconic photograph of Guevara replaces the original's Communist underpinnings with consumerism, so too has the radical agrarian reform of early guerrilla gardeners become diluted through the mass sale of seed bombs. Indeed, while there are countless do-it-yourself seed bomb recipes on blogs and on TikTok, there are just as many seed bombs for sale on Amazon, Etsy, and other shopping sites. For instance, a simple internet search reveals heart-shaped seed bombs stacked in a sleeve of cellophane; flower-shaped seed bombs in drawstring burlap pouches or jewelry boxes; and "Garden Bon Bons," which the seller describes as "gourmet seed bombs" packaged in boxes like fine chocolate (Dowell 2018). "Bombs away!" and "Throw 'N' Grow!" chirps one Etsy seller (RecycledIdeas 2022), while another claims to give buyers the "most 'bang for your buck.' We give you the most seeds per bomb than any other shop on Etsy!" (Plantables 2022). Advertised as popular party favors for every occasion from weddings to birthdays to—of course—Earth Day, the seed bombs are presented as eco-friendly, often consisting of non-GMO seeds and plant-based or recycled packaging.

And, yet, while most of the sellers tout greenifying messages, their statements are toothless, devoid of any of the radical political ideology of the actual guerrilla gardening movement. No mention is made of where buyers or their intended recipients might throw the seed bombs. While seed bomb sellers may capitalize on guerrilla gardening, then, they disregard the very ethos of the movement for many guerrilla gardeners: to upset spatialized boundaries of private and public space and to engage in collective, vegetal activism. In contrast to the Green Guerillas and other guerrilla gardeners who used seed bombs to access fenced-off properties, seed bomb sellers' artful presentation and generic messaging turn radical seed bombs into novelties. Whereas the throw 'n' go methods of the Green Guerillas early on were tactical improvisations born out of necessity, in the seed bomb ads, throw 'n' go becomes a sales pitch for a vegetal one-off. As Robin Wall Kimmerer (Potawatomi) writes, there is no "*inherent* obligation" to something one has purchased (2013, 26, emphasis in original). Contrasting settler notions of private property and commodity culture to Indigenous gift-thinking, in which gifts are made or harvested, not purchased, Kimmerer argues that "common resources were the rule" before colonization constructed a commodity culture, replacing connections and responsibilities to the land with economic transactions (2013, 31). While early guerrilla gardeners looked to Guevara for inspiration rather than to Indigenous gift-thinking, both share a belief in common resources and in the land belonging to itself. Thus, although marketed seed bombs mimic the playfulness of guerrilla gardening, the very fact that they are sold goes against the ideology of many guerrilla gardeners by reasserting a monetary-based, transactional exchange.

Battling "The Man"

While the commodification of seed bombs is one way in which the goals of guerrilla gardening can be displaced, another is through the overemphasis on the illicitness of guerrilla gardening. The thrill of seemingly unlawful behavior for a perceived greater good may obscure the systematic environmental injustices which necessitate intervention in the first place. Take, for example, a White Seattle writer's gleeful recount of her first foray into guerrilla gardening; after describing herself as a law-abiding citizen who does not even speed, Elizabeth Kwak-Hefferan playfully writes, "But, I realize now that all along, I've just been waiting for the right weapon with which to battle The Man. Wildflowers, of course" (2013). Like the Green Guerillas before her, the writer relishes the illicit allure and subversive militancy of guerrilla gardening, throwing her self-made seed bomb over a fence while muttering, "Take that!" (2013). Even as Kwak-Hefferan's narrative, and the larger guerrilla gardening movement, highlights the fact that gardening, land distribution, and its management are all political, it simultaneously obscures the specific politics, preferring to facetiously, vaguely wage war with "The Man," rather than consider land politics' connection to race and class. Of course, playfulness is a crucial tactic of the guerrilla gardening movement and Kwak-Hefferan is only leaning into this. However, the essay reveals how the "little wars" that guerrilla gardeners fight within specific geographic and cultural contexts can easily become generalized and amorphous. Referring to herself as Marlon Brando, a "modern-day Janie Appleseed," and a "true rebel" (2013), Kwak-Hefferan is able to experience the thrill of rebellion while still maintaining her position as a good, White citizen.

For the writer, and other "'fraidy cats," as Kwak-Hefferan self-deprecatingly calls herself, guerrilla gardening is a way to feel like a rebel without taking any real risks. For example, when the writer learns that the Girl Scouts made seed bombs the previous year, she jokes, "Fight the power, Brownies!" (2013). Much like the guerrilla gardening group San Francisco in Bloom (@sfinbloom), which posts TikTok videos of members skateboarding to electronic music while sprinkling native wildflower seeds from shakers or shooting them from water guns, Kawk-Hefferan glibly contrasts the rebellious tone of guerrilla gardening with the benign act of gardening. On the one hand, such performances may attract more interest in guerrilla gardening with their "cool nerd" vibe and broadly may critique the regulation of land by railing against "The Man." On the other hand, they can just as easily conceal land inequity and green space inaccessibility beneath vague, generalized battle cries and an overemphasis on tongue-in-cheek anarchy.

Just as guerrilla gardening can be commodified and decontextualized, it can also lead to the conflation of war and gardening, following Guevara's own use of expressions like the "fruits of destruction" (as cited in Reynolds 2008, 20–7). Take, for example, British guerrilla gardener and author Richard Reynolds, who turned to guerrilla gardening while living in a bleak high-rise apartment in Elephant and Castle, surrounded by traffic and shopping centers. One of the most famous guerrilla gardeners alive today, Reynolds has not only worked to beautify London but, in 2004, created a blog for guerrilla gardeners around the world to share their digs with one another. Nonetheless, he takes a combative stance in *On Guerrilla Gardening*, extending his battle with the city of London to the land itself:

> My crime was gardening on public land without permission and battling whatever was in the way...Our gardens are scenes of savage destruction. Animals uproot, frosts cripple, winds topple, rains flood. The guerrilla gardener shares this constant battle with nature with other gardeners. But we have other enemies and ambitions
>
> *(2008, 9).*

Here, Reynolds gradually returns to his primary foes—city bureaucrats who privatize and mismanage public spaces—but not before reinforcing a familiar "man versus nature" conflict. Certainly, gardening is laborious and intensive work, and guerrilla gardeners are particularly dependent on the weather to help a tossed seed bomb take root. And, yet, the "constant battle" with gardens "of savage destruction" creates an adversarial relationship with the land.

As the book goes on, Reynolds directly compares gardening to war:

> In both exploits you wrestle forces beyond your control, you shape the landscape and you get messy. There are winners and losers. Both war and gardening are creative as well as destructive. Flower and power go together; they are not opposites
>
> *(2008, 27–8).*

The association of flowers with power is not novel. The poet Allen Ginsberg coined the slogan "flower power" in 1965 to describe anti-Vietnam War protests in the US, captured in iconic photographs like *The Ultimate Confrontation* (Riboud 1967), in which a high schooler breathes in a chrysanthemum in front of a row of soldiers directing bayonets at her, and *Flower Power* (Boston 1967), in which a young man slips carnations into soldiers' rifle barrels. Both images are powerful because the protestors meet military might, capable of death and destruction, with flowers, symbols of life and peace. Flowers are powerful because they are the antithesis of manmade wars and weapons. Take, for example, the video of an elderly, Ukrainian civilian telling a Russian soldier invading her town to "Take the seeds and put them raw in your pockets. At least sunflowers will grow there where you fall on our soil" (as cited in Marder 2022). The clip went viral because of the woman's brave defiance in the face of an oppressor but, as Michael Marder notes, "the gesture was oriented toward the postwar future, the germination and growth of sunflowers" out of the corpses of the soldiers (2022). This scene is powerful because it highlights the potential for vegetal life to spring up in the wake of death and violence, as well as the endurance and autonomy of plants, which will continue to grow despite human decomposition.

But, for Reynolds, the power of vegetal life stems not from its contrast to war but rather from its similarities. For him, gardening can be a destructive zero-sum game, like war, where there are clear-cut winners and losers. Although he is critical of Mao Zedong's frequent misappropriation of vegetal language for violence (Reynolds 2008, 7–8), Reynolds himself conflates gardening and war. In her book

Mao's War Against Nature, Judith Shapiro writes, "Maoist ideology pitted the people against the natural environment in a fierce struggle" (2001, 3). This resulted, Shapiro argues, in an interconnected abuse of people and the environment. Although Reynolds' enemies are primarily city bureaucrats and privatization, by projecting human violence onto the land itself, he ultimately reasserts the very notions of land ownership that he seeks to subvert. While Reynolds effectively draws on Mao's and Guevara's communist principles of the deprivatization of land and their guerrilla tactics of staging little wars against far more powerful enemies, he also adopts their resourcism. By suggesting that there are "winners and losers," or victors and victims, in gardening, Reynolds echoes normative notions of land possession rather than alternative notions of collective land. Arguably, Reynolds intends for guerrilla gardening to subvert more traditional gardening practices in which land and wealth are linked. However, his joyfully ubiquitous employment of military jargon—"arsenal," "armament" (121), "warfare," "horticultural weapons" (2008, 122), and so on—only serves to further conflate war and gardening. While the Green Guerillas and more recent groups also play with militant language, what sets Reynolds apart is his view of gardening and war as similar rather than antithetical. For the Green Guerillas, for example, seed grenades are also "seed green-aids" ("Our History"), suggesting that their use of militant language, while Vietnam War protests were still ongoing, was about subverting militaristic warmongering with a green antidote rather than waging war with the soil. While linking the destruction of war and gardening may bolster and aggrandize Reynolds' mission, it also turns the garden into a site of violent contention rather than a site of collective performance.

And, yet, given Reynolds struggles with his south London council, his focus on contested space is understandable. Living and gardening in Elephant and Castle,[12] a major road junction in south central London, Reynolds must contend with traffic congestion, pollution, and construction. In 2012, he began a two-year protest of Transport for London, whose widening of the Elephant and Castle roundabout significantly shrank public space, leaving behind only three trees (Reynolds 2014). Over the years, he has had a number of run-ins with the Southwark Council, which destroyed a pavement garden even after giving him permission to keep it (Reynolds 2013). Such concerns have largely led the guerrilla gardener to turn to small pavement openings in sidewalks where, in a campaign begun in 2010, Reynolds encouraged people to "Pimp Your Pavement" (Reynolds 2013). While the word choice is unfortunate, suggesting control and power over the land, the gardening itself reflects laborious commitment to vegetal life. Growing bite-sized, colorful guerrilla gardens in literal gaps in the concrete, Reynolds not only contests the privatization of public spaces but also horticultural homogeneity.

At the same time, while Reynolds' vegetal interventions are heterogenous, his villains are not. As Adams and Hardman argue, in stressing guerrilla gardening's resistance to powerful city bureaucracies, Reynolds disregards the ways in which spatial meanings are altered and affected by every new performative action (2014, 1109). Thus, even as he makes spatial interventions with his improvisational gardens, he continues to emphasize what he sees as homogenized management and use of city space. Such an emphasis can overshadow the constant fluctuation of spatial meanings, particularly as they are horticulturally performed. For instance, the Liz Christy Community Garden's performance tactics, style of gardening, and spatial significance have evolved over time. However, essentializing guerrilla gardeners as resistant to corporate forces is common in guerrilla gardening practices and scholarship (Adams and Hardman 2014, 1108–9). Adams and Hardman argue that, although there is significant scholarship on guerrilla gardening as a form of subversion, far less scholarship has considered how guerrilla gardening functions as a source of social activity and community (2014, 1107). They suggest that public sites that have been ignored or neglected by city planners can be "reanimated" by guerrilla gardeners as sites of "communal gathering" (2014, 1107). Similarly, I would suggest that sites tied to violence and death can become recuperated through communal acts of guerrilla gardening. For example, George Floyd Square began as a site of racist trauma and violence, the place of Floyd's murder, and, while it is still that, it has also evolved to become a site of healing.[13] With gardens, sculptures, and murals maintained by volunteer caretakers, the square has drawn mourners from around the country. Although it was desecrated by the Minneapolis Department of Public Works in 2021, it was restored by volunteer gardeners and artists (Martin 2021). Thus, alongside the heightened performance of some guerrilla gardeners, who lean into the subversiveness and illicitness of the movement, are often gardeners with much less sensational goals of communal healing through gardening.

Nonetheless, the subversive appeal of guerrilla gardening can be a valuable recruitment tool; the rebellious veneer of guerrilla gardening is a performance technique that draws nascent gardeners, or even people who have never considered gardening before, into the movement. In the case of the early Green Guerillas, Richard Reynolds, and TikTok sensations like San Francisco Bloom, whose members scatter wildflower seeds while skateboarding, the appeal of guerrilla gardening stems from the fact that it is different from more traditional gardening: more accessible, more fun, and more radical. The many international Troop Dig stories and images on Reynold's website (GuerrillaGardening.org) frequently take delight in the spontaneous, covert aspects of guerrilla gardening. And, yet, while it is the illicitness that gets many guerrilla gardeners in the door, it is the gardening itself that is most transgressive. Whether it is in median strips, potholes, vacant lots, or art museums,[14] Reynolds and other guerrilla gardeners continue to plant, and, in doing so, bring vegetal life into all aspects of urban life. Certainly, as I have tried to demonstrate, there are numerous ways in which the more "guerrilla" aspects of gardening can become commodified, generic, and combative. And, yet, these same guerilla elements, in contrast to powerful capitalistic forces, assert a collective human and vegetal "right to the city" (Lefebvre 1968). It is important to situate "little wars" against city officials and property owners within the broader context of systemic land inequities and not to colonialistically project those wars onto the soil itself. At its best, though, guerrilla gardening lowers the barrier to entry for new gardeners and contests spatial inaccessibility and inequity through vegetal intervention.

Guerrilla Gardening and Whiteness

Different forms of guerrilla gardening contest spatial inaccessibility in a variety of ways. As I suggested earlier in the chapter, guerrilla gardeners do not have a singular identity or purpose, and the performance can evolve over time. The human involvement in some guerrilla gardening performances may be limited to tossing seed bombs or sprinkling seeds, and, at that point, the performance may be taken up by the seeds themselves with the help of some rain and air. Other guerrilla gardening projects turn into endurance performances, whereby gardeners seek to grow and protect gardens from demolition. Similarly, some gardeners focus on native wildflowers to attract pollinators, some on biodiversity, and some on fruits and vegetables. The various performances and identities guerrilla gardeners enact, though, are not always by choice. There is no separating racial, gendered, or class identities from a guerrilla gardening identity, even when the gardener takes on a code name or persona. Furthermore, even though many guerilla gardeners share the ethos that people have a right to the city and that all public spaces should be truly public, the risks of acting on this belief are much higher for guerrilla gardeners of color than they are for White gardeners. While much scholarship has focused on guerrilla gardening as a subversion of the capitalistic privatization of public space (McKay 2011; Reynolds 2008; Tracey 2007), far less attention has been paid to the ways in which, as Whiteness studies scholar George Lipsitz argues, "Race is produced by space" (2011, 5). No matter how "race neutral" a city site may seem, it contains "hidden racial assumptions and imperatives" (Lipsitz 2011, 15). As I discussed in the previous chapter, the dispossession and exclusion of people of color from environmental spaces codes such sites as White. Given that guerrilla gardening is often an illicit activity that is not officially sanctioned, a guerrilla gardener of color may be perceived as doubly illegitimate: both for guerrilla gardening and for performing in environmental activities and spaces historically intended for White people.

Take, for example, a TikTok by one of the White founding members of San Francisco in Bloom, Shalaco McGee (2021). Responding to a question about whether it is legal to scatter seeds on public property, McGee says, "Let's check in at our police department." The camera focuses on a patch of wildflowers right in front of a police cruiser, while McGee says, "Yeah, they seem pretty cool with it," explaining that he scattered the seeds six to eight months before. The camera then shifts to him sprinkling seeds between the bars of the gated police station, which bears a red sign that states: "RESTRICTED AREA. POLICE PERSONNEL ONLY." As he shakes out the seeds, McGee gives a final disclaimer: "I'm not a lawyer. This is not legal advice." With a hint of a smile at the beginning and end of the video, McGee simultaneously suggests that guerrilla gardening is both rebellious and all in good fun. But what is meant to reassure viewers that guerrilla gardening is harmless may have quite a different impact on viewers of color, particularly on Black Americans who are criminalized at five times the rate of White Americans (Nellis 2021, 5). While I do not wish to disparage the work San

Francisco in Bloom does to spread seeds for pollinators and to publicize the importance of pollinator-friendly native plants, I want to highlight the ways in which guerrilla gardening is racialized not just, as I have already discussed, in terms of the appeal of performative illicitness for many White guerrilla gardeners but also in terms of spatial mobility. On the one hand, guerrilla gardening in front of a police station asserts that even highly monitored public spaces belong to the people. On the other hand, such an act reveals the White privilege of the gardener, who can transgress spatial norms without fear of arrest. Whether it is San Francisco in Bloom members using bright pink water guns to shoot seeds or Reynolds comparing guerrilla gardening to "drug smuggling" (as cited in Adams and Hardman 2014, 1107), the performance of White guerrilla gardeners cannot be separated from their racial privilege.

Just as a guerrilla gardener's race affects their spatial mobility and performative choices while gardening, so too might their race and class influence what seeds they plant. For example, the original Liz Christy Community Garden began as a farm, but, as the neighborhood gentrified and fresh fruits and vegetables became more readily available, the garden became more oriented toward ornamental plants. Meanwhile, the contemporary Green Guerillas continue to focus on food justice in largely BIPOC neighborhoods with limited access to fresh fruits and vegetables like Harlem and the South Bronx. While there are certainly exceptions and while identity cannot be essentialized, the ability to grow ornamental plants is often a privilege; without having to worry about sustaining oneself, it becomes possible to think about sustaining pollinators and gardening aesthetics. A middle-class, White guerrilla gardener will have options in terms of where and what to plant that may be denied to many poor gardeners of color. It is important to consider this aspect of guerrilla gardening, because as Lipsitz argues, a White emphasis on Black disadvantages shifts the focus away from White privilege (2011, 2). As I, a White writer, shift to thinking about food justice and guerrilla gardening, I want to emphasize the privilege embedded in guerrilla gardening while White: the privilege to trespass without fear of serious harm; the privilege to call one's seed ball a "bomb" without fear of being labeled a terrorist; and, if middle- or upper-class, the privilege to focus on non-food-bearing plants.

Guerrilla Gardening as Food Justice

Growing food-bearing plants is typically associated with community gardening rather than guerrilla gardening because such initiatives require sustained time and attention. To benefit from a fruit and vegetable garden, one cannot throw and go. And, yet, many food-bearing gardens may begin as guerilla gardens, either because the gardeners are unaware of a space's restrictions or because, as with the early Green Guerillas, the gardeners are renters with no other access to land. As such, guerrilla gardening can play a key role in the food justice movement, itself an offshoot of the environmental justice movement.

In contrast to the larger food movement's "predominately white and middle-class character" (Alkon and Agyeman 2011, 2), wherein buying local and organic is the primary focus, food justice addresses "both food insecurity and unequal food access" (Garth and Reese 2020, 1). While it is important to consider the pesticides in one's food, the White food movement in the US tends to myopically focus on scientific discourse related to genetically modified organisms, thereby overlooking underlying food injustices. As Japanese ecocritic Masami Yuki argues, "an uncritical acceptance of science keeps us from paying attention to and questioning the deeper causes of contamination, namely, the way modern industrial societies operate" (2012, 734). Food justice in the US not only attends to the inequities in the US food system, but also "the conditions that produce such disparities" (Garth and Reese 2020, 3). As food sovereignty activist Leah Penniman argues, the racism embedded in the US food system is "built on stolen land and stolen labor, and needs a redesign" (2018, 5; Garth and Reese 2020, 2). Because guerrilla gardening contests the privatization of public spaces and the capitalistic norms of property laws, it raises questions about who owns the land and what it means to be a steward of the land. Thus, in addition to providing food-insecure people—the majority of whom are of color (Coleman-Jensen et al. 2016)—with greater access to fresh produce, guerrilla food gardening can play a crucial role in exposing the connections between racism and land practices within the US food system.

While the link between food insecurity and poverty is fairly transparent, the connections between food inequities and legacies of enslavement, dispossession, and redlining are often obscured. As I have noted elsewhere, the term "natural disaster" is often used to ascribe naturality to human messes caused by corruption, oversight, and greed (Ryan 2019). Similarly, the term "food desert," widely used to describe areas with a lack of access to fresh food, suggests a naturally occurring state rather than one created by racist government and corporate practices. The term not only erases the role local and federal government and companies play in creating food injustice, but also the ways in which food injustice is racialized. As Reese suggests, the use of the word "desert" may cause people to "imagine a barren, empty place," further deemphasizing who is most affected by food injustice (2019, 6). Although they are less utilized than the term "food desert," terms like "supermarket redlining" and "food apartheid" make visible the connection between food injustice and racism (Reese 2019, 6–7). While "supermarket redlining" draws attention to how grocery stores resist serving low-income areas, "[a]partheid brings forth visceral connections to the politically and socially imposed racial hierarchies and inequities in South Africa and forces us to grapple with how the state policies, and practices normalize inequality" (Reese 2019, 7). Terms like "supermarket redlining" and "food apartheid" highlight the fact that food insecurity is not race neutral or coincidental; rather, it is part of a larger, racist food system.

Perhaps the most famous guerrilla gardener to expose the racist underpinnings of food injustice is Ron Finley. A self-titled "gangsta gardener," Finley gained international acclaim with his 2013 TED Talk, which, as of this writing, has been viewed 1.3 million times. Two years prior to the talk, Finley and his collaborators founded LA Green Grounds, a volunteer organization that plants vegetable gardens in people's front yards and in neglected parkways, strips of land between the

sidewalk and the street. The group's first project was the stark parkway right outside Finley's rented house in South LA,[15] a predominately Black and Latinx
neighborhood.[16] Finley, tired of traveling over 45 minutes for organic produce,
planted everything from pumpkins to kale, much to the delight of his neighbors,
with whom he shared his harvest. It did not take long for the LA Bureau of Street
Services to fine Finley for planting on city property and to go so far as to issue a
warrant for his arrest. However, neighbors and fellow guerrilla gardeners joined
Finley in protesting the warrant and, with additional pressure from an *LA Times*
news story, the city council reversed course.[17] Finley and his supporters saved the
garden again in 2017, when the home Finley was renting went into foreclosure,
and, today, the parkway garden, as well as a larger garden in the nonfunctioning
in-ground pool in Finley's backyard, remain intact and are owned by Finley's
nonprofit, The Ron Finley Project (Swann 2017).

Finley begins his TED Talk by projecting photos of liquor stores, fast food
chains, and vacant lots in his neighborhood. Calling South LA "home of the drive-
through and the drive-by," Finley projects a photo of a convenience store fridge that
purports to carry "fresh produce" but is completely empty (2013). In pointing out that
the "drive-thrus are killing more people than the drive-bys" (2013), Finley highlights
what Reese calls "slow, walking, everyday deaths" caused by fast food conglomerates
and the lack of access to fresh food (2019, 3). Although he is careful not to mention
the word "racism," which in a TED Talk for a largely White audience in 2013 would
likely not be well-received, Finley's meaning is clear. Drawing viewers' attention to
the many wheelchairs and dialysis centers in his neighborhood, Finley asks them to
consider how they would feel if they were surrounded by "the ill effects that the
present food system has on your neighborhood" (2013). In asking the largely White
live audience members to put themselves in his shoes, Finley encourages them to
compare their own access to green spaces and fresh produce to his and to recognize the
inequities embedded in the US food system. As Reese argues,

> We only have to look at the uneven development of neighborhoods across the
> United States, the historic and ongoing disinvestment in cities with Black
> majorities, and the current global crisis of gentrification to see how these
> contradictions are embedded geographically, demonstrating that geography is
> not race neutral
>
> *(2019, 3).*

Finley gestures to this uneven development in a variety of ways, first through
photographs of his dilapidated neighborhood, and, subsequently, through thinly
veiled references. For example, he says, "I refuse to be a part of this manufactured
reality that was manufactured for me by some other people," and that young
people of color are "just on this track that's designed for them, that leads to
nowhere" (2013). Even though Finley does not mention systemic racism directly,
his pointed use of the words "manufactured" and "designed" highlight that the
disinvestment in Black communities is methodical and deliberate.

While Finley situates his lived experience within the larger, oppressive food system, he is not interested in focusing on what Reese calls "an all-encompassing narrative of lack" (2019, 12), preferring to see the potential for "sustainable life" through gardening (Finley 2013). Innovative food justice initiatives like Finley's are not only vital for their ability to generate fresh produce but also for their ability to create food sovereignty, enabling gardeners to plant and consume on their own terms. As Jamiah Hargins, another South LA gardener and founder of Asante Microfarm, suggests, "It's a matter of power to me. I felt powerless, so now I don't feel powerless" (Saldivar 2021). The racial disparities within the US food system are connected to other racial inequities, like incarceration[18] and poverty (Benninger et al. 2021) and historical redlining (Li and Yuan 2022). Gardeners like Finley and Hargins not only meet some of the immediate dietary needs of their communities by providing access to fresh fruits and vegetables, but they also provide opportunities for self-empowerment. As Finley says, teaching children to garden helps them learn "the joy, the pride, and the honor in growing your own food" (2013). Going beyond overly simplistic questions of food access and distribution, Finley offers the potential for self-reliance, which, as Reese argues, has always been a necessary component to Black liberation in education, food justice, and business (2019, 9–11).

However, the visibility of self-reliant, Black vegetal experiences and practices is often obscured by stories of lack (Reese 2019, 12)—particularly food desert narratives—and by a whitewashed food movement. Not only does Finley's open, parkway garden create opportunities for food access, learning, and self-empowerment, but his widely viewed TED Talk creates an alternative narrative of improvisational, innovative self-reliance. Rather than entrust their food security and well-being to systems that have repeatedly failed communities of color, gardeners like Finley and Hargins take control of their own vegetal access and narratives. Celebrating anticapitalistic sweat equity, Finley proclaims, "Growing your own food is like printing your own money!" (2013). As the public face of guerrilla food gardening in the US, Finley suggests that the popular African American saying and practice of "making a way out of no way" is not just about survival; it is about thriving and creating one's own style of food justice.

Performing Gangsta Gardener

For Finley, gardening is an art form. Formerly a successful fashion designer (Weston 2020), he sees the soil as "a piece of cloth" or a "canvas" where, much like a graffiti artist, he beautifies and embellishes it (Finley 2013). This emphasis on artistry is important because it reveals the layered possibilities of guerrilla gardening, as a source of both physical and artistic sustenance. Too often, there is a division between need-based and desire-based guerrilla gardening, in which the former results in utilitarian rather than aesthetic gardening. However, Finley takes precious time in his ten-minute TED Talk to emphasize the therapeutic aspects of guerrilla gardening. Projecting a photo zoomed in on the center of a sunflower head, containing hundreds of disk flowers, he marvels at the flower's ability to affect people. In this sense, gardening is as much about psychological well-being for Finley as it is about physical health. As he declares, "Gardening is the most therapeutic and defiant act you can do, especially in the inner city" (2013). This dual emphasis on healing and rebelling sets Finley apart from guerrilla gardeners like Reynolds, San Francisco in Bloom, and the early Green Guerillas who tend to highlight the illicitness of their performances, even as their vegetal practices are in fact therapeutic.

In the last minute of his TED Talk, though, Finley shifts from focusing on gardening as therapy to considering how to make it "sexy" (2013). Amping up the TED Talk to take on a self-described "gangsta gardener" identity, Finley, much like other guerrilla gardeners, stylizes his performance to make gardening more broadly appealing and accessible, particularly to young people. Whereas the early Green Guerillas and Reynolds, both performing during US wars,[19] draw on militarism and, in the Green Guerillas' case, flip the script on it, Finley taps into the antiauthoritarian coolness of gangsta culture and seeks to subvert its more violent characteristics. Because the word "gangsta" is laden with many contradictory cultural meanings, it is worth considering some of its previous iterations and how they inform Finley's strategic use of the term. For example, "gangsta" is most often defined via gangsta rap, which has at times been read as "resistance to marginalization" (White 2011, 69) and to "hegemonic structures of power" (Nyawalo 2013, 472). Indeed, N.W.A.'s 1988 single "Fuck tha Police", criticizing police harassment and racial profiling, continues to be a protest anthem against police brutality today (Grow 2020). However, both Black studies scholars Miles White and bell hooks ultimately see gangsta rap as part of the US's capitalistic system (White 2013, 69; hooks 2004, 25). Whereas White traces "hardcore" gangsta rap to African American blackface minstrelsy, in that both trade on "racial desire" (2013, 69), hooks argues that "[g]angsta culture is the essence of patriarchal masculinity" (2004, 26). For hooks, gangsta culture is capitalistic culture, in which mainly corporate, White men operate in "a modern Babylon with no rules;" the primary difference between a White gangsta and a Black one is that the former is rarely punished whereas Black men are excessively criminalized (2004, 25).

For hooks, the solution to the trap of gangsta culture is clear:

> Black male material survival will be ensured only as they turn away from fantasies of wealth and the notion that money will solve all problems and make everything better, and turn toward the reality of sharing resources, reconceptualizing work, and using leisure for the practice of self-actualization
> *(2004, 29–30).*

Finley's own solution aligns with hooks. In gardening as an art form, a therapeutic act, and as a way to reduce his participation in the capitalistic food system, Finley survives and thrives and provides opportunities for others to do the same. To recruit young people to his cause, he declares,

I want all of us to become ecolutionary renegades, gangstas, gangsta gardeners. We gotta change; we gotta flip the script on what a gangsta is. If you ain't a gardener, you ain't gangsta. Get gangsta with your shovel and let that be your weapon of choice

(2013).

Like many other guerrilla gardeners, Finley attempts to convert urbanites to gardening through hyperbolic, provocative, and rebellious language. Whereas Reynolds depicts guerrilla gardening as a battle that is waged for (and against) the earth, others, like Tracey, play up and take delight in the criminal risks involved in illicit gardening.[20] Finley, meanwhile, draws on popular culture's glorification of gangsta rap to make gardening attractive even as he simultaneously attempts to redefine the term by flipping "the script." Much like Reynolds' use of military terminology, Finley's use of gangsta culture seeks to masculinize gardening's perceived image of feminine domesticity, as well as its association with Whiteness and home-ownership. However, unlike Reynolds, Finley casts guerrilla gardening as "defiant" and "therapeutic," thereby highlighting its function as both a political act and a restorative one.

In contrast to the LA Council which, as Finley jokes early on in the talk, renamed South Central without making any real changes, Finley performs his gangsta gardener identity as a material practice to "change the composition of the soil" in his neighborhood (2013). On a literal level, this can speak to the need for soil remediation when soil has become contaminated by industrialization, common in poor neighborhoods of color (Jones et al. 2022). Metaphorically, changing the composition of the soil may mean grappling with sedimented injustice; as eco-theater scholar Angenette Spalink suggests, "To unearth dirt is to bring history to the surface" (2017, 86). In deploying the term "gangsta," historically associated with violence and contextually meaningful in South LA, where gangs like the Bloods and Crips began, Finley strives to make being gangsta synonymous with gardening. In encouraging people to trade in a weapon for a shovel, he speaks directly to the gun violence often embedded in gangsta culture. However, in calling for "ecolutionary renegades," Finley calls for a rebellion against a far more insidious violence: the capitalistic structure that creates racist conditions in the first place.

Leaning into the coolness of gangsta culture while subverting its capitalistic violence, Finley seeks to redefine what it means to be gangsta. As his website states, gangsta is "projecting strength on one's own terms, hip, cool, innovative, revolutionary, resolute, vital, the cutting edge" (Ron Finley Project 2022). Emphasizing self-reliance and originality, Finley's definition of "gangsta" offers self-empowerment without self-commodification. This is evident in the final moments of the TED Talk when Finley tells the audience not to bother calling him to sit in some "cushy chairs" and talk about doing something (2013). Instead, he says, "If you want to meet with me, come to the garden with your shovel, so we can plant some shit" (2013). Rejecting idle do-gooder discussions for the material practice of gardening, Reynolds puts the final emphasis on the self-actualizing act of growing vegetal life. Deploying a gangsta gardener identity as a tactic to change misconceptions about the act of gardening and the identity of gardeners, Finley not only subverts the stereotype of a gangsta but also the stereotype of a White, bourgeois gardener. Like the Green Guerillas, Reynolds, and other guerrilla gardeners, Finley exposes the environmentally unjust underpinnings of land distribution and accessibility by pushing the boundaries of private and public space, but he also begins to transform his neighborhood from a state of food insecurity to a food collective. Creating a degree of food justice in South LA, Finley invites neighbors to freely take from the garden, but, more than that, to join in the gardening. Most importantly, while Finley's illicit gardens begin as creative improvisations, they continue as durational performances, maintained and protected but never fenced off.

Through guerrilla and community gardening, activists like Finley reconnect people to the soil and to their food. If globalization, as scholars from Marx to Lefebvre to Harvey have argued, truncates "spaces of production and consumption," then food justice initiatives work to "resist economic globalization," making small dents in agribusiness by materially reconnecting people and plants (Carruth 2013, 7). On one hand, these small, localized interventions are minor compared to global food systems. For example, Monsanto, an international chemical and agricultural biotechnology megacorporation, merged with Bayer in 2016 and makes up ten percent of the commercial seed market and roughly 90 percent of the genetically modified organism (GMO) industry (Carruth 2013, 14–15). The company's monopolizing reach has made it nearly impossible to avoid Monsanto products, despite micro-scalar seed saving banks and practices. Meanwhile, guerilla vegetable gardens, community gardens, and farmer's markets can only make up a minor percentage of all vegetal needs (McClintock 2011, 113). Thus, as urban geographer Nathan McClintock suggests, "The passion and vigor with which food justice activists break new ground…must extend also to rethinking and rebuilding the entirety of the metropolitan and regional food system—production, processing, distribution, retail, and waste recovery—in both urban and peri-urban areas" (2011, 113). However, by exposing the food apartheid embedded in the US food system and by offering an alternative, albeit it on a micro-scale, Finley urges people to rethink the entire food system. Even as he advocates for self-reliance by growing one's own food, Finley simultaneously critiques a food system that has failed him and the 17.1 million people who have inadequate access to grocery stores[21] (USDA 2021). Like the early Green Guerillas and Reynolds, Finley resists capitalistic land ownership, but he also challenges food systems through his revolutionary gangsta gardening performance.

Performing Guerrilla Gardening

In this chapter, I focused on three distinct guerrilla gardeners, all of whom demonstrate that the performance of guerrilla gardening identities and practices are dependent on a gardener's own identity, situational needs, and geographic context.

As Adams and Hardman insist, there is no singular guerrilla gardening identity (2014, 1109), and I would add no fixed urban space. Rather, gardeners like Christy, Reynolds, and Finley deploy highly specific, situational, and improvisational performances based on local, socio-spatial gaps and cracks. In a country in which property laws legitimized land dispossession and enslavement, US guerrilla gardeners especially must deploy creative tactics to challenge the privatization of public space. As de Certeau argues, "The space of a tactic is the space of the other," and, thus, a tactic must "poach" heavily surveilled spaces (1984, 36). The tactic "creates surprises in them. It can be where it is least expected. It is a guileful ruse" (1984, 36). Whether through seed bombs or gangsta gardening, guerrilla gardeners dig out pockets of vegetal space, turning nominally "public" spaces into actual public spaces through vegetal and tactical performances. Together, the Green Guerillas, Reynolds, and Finley suggest that guerrilla gardening can not only denaturalize land ownership but also create and, where possible, maintain collective gardens.

In contrast to more legitimized forms of gardening, guerrilla gardening has "metaphoric appeal" for subversives who appreciate "the sheer interstitiality of it all," the gaps and margins that guerrilla gardening fills (McKay 2011, 187). While the heightened performance tactics of many guerrilla gardeners can serve to attract more people to gardening, they can also create a generic guerilla gardening identity and abstract ecological and racialized particularities of place. I would argue that the best guerrilla gardening simultaneously exposes sedimented environmental injustices and enacts ecological practices that adapt and improvise based on geographical and environmental necessity. As a political and vegetal performance, guerrilla gardening has the potential to highlight the unequal privatization of land, the mismanagement of city grounds, and the regulation of seemingly "public" spaces by making tactical, material interventions. Ultimately, though, I would suggest that if guerrilla gardening is to be an egalitarian practice that benefits diverse people and plants, rather than a privileged game for some humans, a balance must be maintained between improvisational, guerrilla tactics and long-term gardening performance.

Notes

1 As of June 2022, #PlantTok had 2.2 million views.
2 Guerrilla gardeners did not invent seed balls; they have been used in farming for centuries and were reinvented and improved upon by "do-nothing" Japanese farmer Masanobu Fukuoka in the early twentieth century (Setboonsarng and Gilman 1999). However, guerrilla gardeners popularized and politicized seed balls by renaming them seed bombs or seed grenades and throwing them on private or public property.
3 Although this book primarily focuses on case studies in the US, Reynolds is a very influential figure in the guerrilla gardening movement and thus warrants consideration.
4 For instance, over 1,000 years ago, the Romani people traveled from northwestern India to the Balkans and, eventually, to Europe. As they traveled, they dropped potato seeds on private and public land, knowing that they would return to harvest the crop later (Tracey 2007, 20).

5 The Green Guerillas spell "guerrilla" with one "r."

6 The garden was closed from 2005 to 2007 while AvalonBay erected a second apartment complex. When the garden was reopened, the unique, rose-covered trellis fence that was original to the garden had been replaced by "a standard-issue Parks Department fence" (Edwards 2007). As then Liz Christy Garden member Brandon Krall said, "It is part of the homogenization that is taking place all over the city…They took our unique fence and replaced it with a generic one" (as cited in Edwards 2007).

7 After building one luxury apartment complex across the street from the LCCG, the AvalonBay real estate company erected another right next to the garden, digging three feet into it, despite volunteers' protests. NYC Parks negotiated between the garden and AvalonBay and, as a result, the real estate company was forced to fill in the area where they dug into the garden and pay $50,000 in damages (Jones 2022).

8 In my interview with Jones, she stressed that the Picturesque style of the garden was specifically implemented to create the illusion of expansive space (2022).

9 Particularly influential was the occupation of the People's Park in Berkley in 1969, when students and police clashed over the University of California's ownership of the park.

10 In 1975, Adam Purple began creating his garden on five vacant lots on Eldridge Street in Manhattan. The garden, more of a large earthwork, became an international tourist attraction before being demolished in 1986 (Ferguson 1999, 87–8).

11 The title of a *VICE* news article, featuring British guerrilla gardener Chris Tomlinson, is "The Che Guevara of Gardening" (Goodey 2009).

12 According to Reynold's Twitter bio (@Richard_001), he is now located mostly in Castle Street.

13 Another example of guerrilla gardening coming out of acts of violence and death is the Grenfell Garden of Peace, begun by Tayshan Hayden-Smith following the Grenfell Tower fire in West London that killed 72 people (Hayden-Smith 2022).

14 In 2015, Reynolds and his collaborator Vanessa Harden seedbombed the Tate Modern, interpreting the artist Cruzvillegas' installation of London soil as an open invitation to garden (Reynolds 2015).

15 In his TED Talk, Finley refers to his neighborhood as South Central. Although city council members voted in 2003 to change the name to South LA in order to destigmatize its violent representation in the media (Myrow 2003), Finley suggests that they only changed the name without addressing any of the underlying injustices.

16 South LA is a historic Black neighborhood that has become increasingly Latinx; according to the LA Department of Planning, as of 2017, the area was 61% Latino and 27.9% Black (City 2017).

17 As a direct result of Finley's public protest, the LA City Council changed its gardening guidelines in 2013. Urban LA gardeners may plant in parkways if they observe existing street safety requirements, but they are liable if anyone trips and falls or is otherwise injured by the garden (Fox 2013).

18 Finley himself has made overt connections between food apartheid and incarceration by calling his neighborhood a "food prison" (as cited in Weston 2020).

19 The Green Guerillas began in 1973, the same year the US withdrew its troops from Vietnam after eight years of direct intervention. In 2008, when Reynolds wrote *On Guerrilla Gardening*, both the US and the UK were five years into the Iraq War.

20 Tracey writes that readers can go to jail for guerrilla gardening before explaining that "the warning was just a ruse to get the naysayers out of the room" (2007, 3). Nonetheless, he provides new guerrilla gardeners with a list of "10 Lines to Try if You Get Stopped in the Middle of a Planting Project" (2007, 32).

21 According to the US Department of Agriculture, 17.1 million people live in low-income areas that are anywhere from one to 20 miles away from a supermarket (2021).

References

Adams, David and Michael Hardman. 2014. "Observing Guerrillas in the Wild: Reinterpreting Practices of Urban Guerrilla Gardening." *Urban Studies* 51 (6): 1103–1119.

Adams, David, Michael Hardman, and Peter Larkham. 2015. "Exploring guerrilla gardening: gauging public views on the grassroots activity." *Local Environment* 20 (10): 1231–1246.

Alkon, Alison Hope and Julian Agyeman. 2011. "Introduction: The Food Justice Movement as Polyculture." In *Cultivating Food Justice: Race, Class, and Sustainability*, edited by Alison Hope Alkon and Julian Agyeman. Cambridge: MIT Press: 1–20.

Benninger, Elizabeth, Gwendolyn Donley, Megan Schmidt-Sane, Jill K. Clark, David W. Lounsbury, Dominque Rose, and Darcy Freedman. 2021. "Fixes That Fail: A System Archetype for Examining Racialized Structures Within the Food System." *American Journal of Community Psychology* 68 (3–4): 455–470.

Boston, Bernie. 1967. Flower Power. First featured in *The Washington Evening Star*, October 21.

Brooks, Steve and Gerry Marten. 2005. "Green Guerillas: Revitalizing Urban Neighborhoods with Community Gardens (New York City, USA)." *The EcoTipping Points Project*, June. https://tinyurl.com/2p89t32t.

Carruth, Allison. 2013. *Global Appetites: American Power and the Literature of Food*. Cambridge: Cambridge University Press.

Caspari, Sarah. 2013. "Global Perception of Che Guevara." *Pulitzer Center*, February 22. https://tinyurl.com/3fc96mwz.

City of Los Angeles Department of City Planning. 2017. "South Los Angeles Demographic Profile." https://tinyurl.com/2p8b6pft.

Coleman-Jensen, Alisha, Matthew P. Rabbitt, Christian A. Gregory, and Anita Singh. 2016. Household Food Security in the United States in 2015, ERR 215, U.S. Department of Agriculture, Economic Research Service, September. https://tinyurl.com/5uzujj42.

Coyle, Patrick. 2020, "Planting the Future: Guerrilla Gardening in Ireland." *Trinity News*, May 12.

Crane, Annie, Leela Viswanathan, and Graham Whitelaw. 2013. "Sustainability through intervention: a case study of guerrilla gardening in Kingston, Ontario." *Local Environment* 18 (1): 71–90.

de Certeau, Michel. 1984. *The Practice of Everyday Life*. Trans. Steven Rendall. Berkeley: University of California Press.

Dowell, Anne. 2018. Gardenbonbons. *Etsy*. Last updated March 6. https://www.etsy.com/shop/Gardenbonbons.

Doyle, Michael William. 2002. "Staging the Revolution: Guerrilla Theater as a Countercultural Practice: 1965–1968." In *Imagine Nation: The American Counterculture of the 1960s and '70s*, edited by Peter Braunstein and William Michael Doyle, 71–98. New York: Routledge.

Edwards, Brooke. 2007. "Liz Christy Garden reopens but with some changes." *The Villager*, January 18. https://tinyurl.com/35d8ac5n.

Ferguson, Sarah. 1999. "A Brief History of Grassroots Greening on the Lower East Side." In *Avant Gardening: Ecological Struggle in the City and the World*, edited by Peter Lamborn and Bill Weinberg, 80–90. Brooklyn, NY: Autonomedia.

Finley, Ron. 2013. "A guerrilla gardener in South Central LA." TED, *YouTube*, March 6. https://tinyurl.com/4smy23ku.

Fox, Hayley. 2013. "LA residents may soon plant gardens in green space between sidewalk and curb (updated)." 89.3 *KPCC*, October 23. https://tinyurl.com/3d2jfymk.

Garth, Hannah and Ashanté M. Reese. 2020. "Black Food Matters: An Introduction." In *Black Food Matters: Racial Justice in the Wake of Food Justice*, edited by Hannah Garth and Ashanté M. Reese, 1–28. Minneapolis: University of Minnesota Press.

Goodey, Jan. 2009. "The Che Guevara of Guerrilla Gardening." *VICE*, November 12. https://tinyurl.com/43f6prvc.

"Green Guerillas Fact Sheet". 1973. *Green Guerillas*. https://tinyurl.com/4uu2werb.

Grow, Kory. 2020. "How N.W.A.'s 'Fuck the Police' Became the Perfect Protest Song." *Rolling Stone*, June 9. https://tinyurl.com/3xufc9sx.

Hardman, Michael et al. 2018. "Guerrilla Gardening and Green Activism: Rethinking the Informal Urban Growing Movement." *Landscape and Urban Planning* 170: 6–14.

Hayden-Smith, Tayshan. 2022. "Guerrilla gardening took me back to my roots—and to the Chelsea flower show." *The Guardian*, May 25. https://tinyurl.com/3cyufp6t.

hooks, bell. 2004. *We Real Cool: Black Men and Masculinity*. New York: Routledge.

Jenks, Chris. 2003. *Transgression*. London: Routledge.

Jones, Daleniece Higgins, Xinhua Yu, Qian Guo, Xiaoli Duan, and Chunrong Jia. 2022. "Racial Disparities in the Heavy Metal Contamination of Urban Soil in the Southeastern United States." *International Journal of Environmental Research and Public Health* 19 (3): 1105.

Jones, Penny (Member, Liz Christy Community Garden). 2022. Interviewed by Courtney Ryan. May 29.

Kimmerer, Robin Wall. 2013. *Braiding Sweetgrass: Indigenous Wisdom, Scientific Knowledge, and the Teachings of Plants*. Minneapolis: Milkweed Editions.

Kwak-Hefferan, Elisabeth. 2013. "Flower Power: Fighting the Man with Guerrilla Gardens." *Grist*, May 3. https://tinyurl.com/yckuxm5j.

Lefebvre, Henri. 1968. *Le droit à la ville*. Paris: Anthopos.

Li, Min and Faxi Yuan. 2022. "Historical Redlining and Food Environments: A Study of 102 Urban Areas in the United States." *Health & Place* 75: 102775.

Lipsitz, George. 2011. *How Racism Takes Place*. Philadelphia: Temple University Press.

Loggins, Donald. 2007. "Houston between Bowery & Second Avenue: Garden History." http://lizchristygarden.us.

Magelssen, Scott. 2020. *Performing Flight: From the Barnstormers to Space Tourism*. United States: University of Michigan Press.

Mahany, Barbara and Brian Cox. 2008. "Guerrilla Gardeners Attack!" *Chicago Tribune*, September 29.

Marder, Michael. 2022. "Vegetable Redemption: A Ukrainian Woman and Russian Soldiers." The Philosophical Salon, A *Los Angeles Review of Books* Channel, February 26. https://tinyurl.com/3sttvdst.

Martin, Frank Edgerton. 2021. "In Minneapolis, as George Floyd Square is cleared, so too is the historic landscape." *The Architect's Newspaper*, June 10. https://tinyurl.com/2wxn8bf2.

McClintock, Nathan. 2011. "From Industrial Garden to Food Desert: Demarcated Devaluation in the Flatlands of Oakland, California." In *Cultivating Food Justice*, edited by Alison Hope Alkon and Julian Agyeman, 89–120. Cambridge: MIT Press.

McGee, Shalaco (@sfinbloom). 2021. "Is it legal to scatter local seeds in your neighborhood?" *TikTok*, May 2. https://tinyurl.com/59aud4ks.

McKay, George. 2011. *Radical Gardening: Politics, Idealism, and Rebellion in the Garden*. London: Francis Lincoln Limited.

Millie, Andrew. 2022. "Guerrilla gardening as normalised law-breaking: Challenges to land Ownership and aesthetic order." *Crime Media Culture* 1–18. doi:10.1177/17416590221088792.

Myrow, Rachael. 2003. "L.A. Council Votes to Name South Central." *All Things Considered*. *NPR*, April 9. https://tinyurl.com/2dxnk28r.

Nellis, Ashley. 2021. *"The Color of Justice: Racial and Ethnic Disparity in State Prisons."* The Sentencing Project (Washington D.C.), 1–25. https://tinyurl.com/2p89c7s6.

Nyawalo, Mich. 2013. "From 'Badman' to 'Gangsta': Double Consciousness and Authenticity, from African-American Folklore to Hip Hop." *Popular Music and Society* 36 (4): 460–475.

"Our History." Green Guerillas. https://www.greenguerillas.org/history (accessed May 24, 2022).

"Our Programs." Green Guerillas. https://www.greenguerillas.org/programsummary (accessed June 7, 2022).

Penniman, Leah. 2018. *Farming While Black: Soul Fire's Farm Practical Guide to Liberation on the Land*. White River Junction, Vermont: Chelsea Green Publishing.

PlantablesAndPaper. 2022. "NEW—50 Herb Seed Bombs." *Etsy*. Listed May 2. https://tinyurl.com/bdesjkw4.

RecycledIdeas. 2022. "Flower Seed Bombs Rainbow Gardening Gift Pack." *Etsy*. Listed May 20. https://tinyurl.com/2v35c45f.

Reese, Ashanté M. 2019. *Black Food Geographies: Race, Self-Reliance, and Food Access in Washington D.C.* Chapel Hill, North Carolina: UNC Press.

Reynolds, Richard. 2008. *On Guerrilla Gardening: A Handbook for Gardening without Boundaries*. New York: Bloomsbury.

Reynolds, Richard. 2013. "Guerrilla gardening in Elephant and Castle: Richard Reynolds at TEDxNewham." TEDx, *YouTube*, June 5. https://tinyurl.com/2p8z73wj.

Reynolds, Richard. 2014. "Twists & Tricks." GuerrillaGardening.org.

Reynolds, Richard. 2015. "*Seed Bombing the Tate*." GuerrillaGardening.org, October 20.

Riboud, Marc. 1967. *The Ultimate Confrontation: The Flower and the Bayonet*. First featured in *Look Magazine*, December 30, 1969.

Ron Finley Project. 2022. https://ronfinley.com.

Ryan, Courtney B. 2019. "BPCares: Sinking Oil, Spreadable Détournement." *ISLE: Interdisciplinary Studies in Literature and Environment* 26 (4): 882–900.

Saldivar, Steve. 2021. "South L.A. doesn't have easy access to fresh food. One man wants to change that by turning lawns into microfarms." *Los Angeles Times*, May 7. https://tinyurl.com/tnh2x8jj.

Schleiden, Cydney, Kristy Soloski, Kaitlyn Milstead, and Abby Rhynehart. 2020. "Racial Disparities in Arrests: A Race Specific Model Explaining Arrest Rates Across Black and White Young Adults." *Child & Adolescent Social Work Journal* 37 (1): 1–14.

Scott, Alister J., et al. 2013. "Disintegrated development at the rural urban fringe: Re-connecting spatial planning theory and practice." *Progress in Planning* 83: 1–52.

Selbin, Eric. 2010. *Revolution, Rebellion, Resistance: The Power of Story*. New York: Zed Books.

Shapiro, Judith. 2001. *Mao's War Against Nature: Politics and the Environment in Revolutionary China*. Cambridge: Cambridge University Press.

Spalink, Angenette. 2017. "Taphonomic Historiography: Excavating and Exhuming the Past in Suzan-Lori Parks's The America Play." *Modern Drama* 60 (1): 69–88.

Swann, Jennifer. 2017. "Ron Finley, Gangster Gardener, Emerges Victorious from Eviction." *LA Weekly*, May 3. https://tinyurl.com/2k3xnp9w.

Taylor, Diana. 2003. *The Archive and the Repertoire: Performing Cultural Memory in the Americas*. Durham: Duke University Press.

Tracey, David. 2007. *Guerrilla Gardening: A Manualfesto*. Gabriola Island, BC: New Society Publishers.

USDA Economic Research Service. 2021. "Food Access Research Atlas: Definitions." Last updated May 24. https://tinyurl.com/38p4uxre.

Vox. 2021. "How Radical Gardeners Took Back New York City." *Missing Chapter*. https://tinyurl.com/2p8r46v7.

Weston, Phoebe. 2020. "'This is no damn hobby': the 'gangsta gardener' transforming Los Angeles." *The Guardian*, April 28. https://tinyurl.com/bdhh66fn.

White, Miles. 2011. *From Jim Crow to Jay-Z: Race, Rap, and the Performance of Masculinity.* Chicago: University of Illinois Press.

Young, Greg. 2021. "Liz Christy and the Community Gardens of the East Village." *The Bowery Boys*, April 22. https://tinyurl.com/3tyyyff8.

Yuki, Massami. 2012. "Why Eat Toxic Food? Mercury Poisoning, Minamata, and Literary Resistance to Risks of Food." *Interdisciplinary Studies in Literature and the Environment* 19 (4): 732–750.

4

"TOUCH THE WATER"

Performing the Los Angeles River

I am racing down Woodley Avenue in the Los Angeles (LA) San Fernando Valley, rushing to make it to my LA River Expeditions kayak tour. I see wide streets, brush, and dust but no river. Following the directions in my information packet, I park and walk to Burbank Boulevard and a bridge, from where I can see the Sepulveda Dam and the LA River. The kayak launch site below is marked by concrete, graffitied barriers, bags of trash, and a fleet of grocery carts. The tour itself is no less disorienting. Ecologist Ellen Mackey leads a group of ten kayakers through the Sepulveda Basin, one of two recreational zones within the 51-mile long, mostly concrete LA River. Fifteen feet above us, cars zoom past, but, in the river, all is quiet except for our oars in the water. I spot a pelican in the lush foliage and forget for a moment that I am right off a major freeway, the 405. But then an overturned armchair in shrubs, grasses, and forbs and the "Los Angeles moss" (Fletcher 2008, 42)—plastic bags dangling from trees—remind me that I am in an unfamiliar and dizzying place (see Figure 4.1)

Like the ash trees that loom above me, crowding out the native black willow and cottonweed trees, the river is a hodgepodge of urban discards—clothing, grocery carts, and furniture—and unruly nonhuman nature. Mackey explains that, since summers in LA are dry, the water we are rowing in is actually discharge from the Tillman Water Reclamation Plant. Curious, I lower my head to smell it, and Mackey shouts, "Don't touch it!" Although the river was deemed "navigable" by the Environmental Protection Agency (EPA) in 2010, it is still too polluted to swim in or drink from.[1] As I paddle along, my disorientation increases: there is corn growing at the edge of the sun-dappled water not far from an unhoused encampment; there are tree canopies above half-submerged grocery carts; and tree branches tangled with T-shirts. We are almost back to the launch site when I spot a mossy stiletto heel resting on what appears to be an algae-encrusted oil drum (see Figure 4.2). The water ripples and the heel slips off the drum and sinks. This is the LA River.

DOI: 10.4324/9781003203766-5

FIGURE 4.1 An overturned chair in the LA river. Photograph by the author.

Civil engineer David Fletcher calls the river "flood control freakology" for its unique mix of nonhuman nature and urban infrastructure (2008). Meanwhile, poet Standard Schaefer describes it as "Smog typhoid celery like a ghost splashing out of a beaker" (2005, 59). Both writers allude to the state and federal technocratic management that has made the LA River what it is today. Encased in concrete by the US Army Corps of Engineers (USACE) after a series of devastating floods, the river, from an aerial view, could easily be mistaken for yet another freeway. Indeed, until recently, most Angelenos[2] were unaware of the river's existence, even though it flows 51 miles from the San Gabriel and Santa Monica Mountains, through the San Fernando Valley, past downtown LA, and out to the Pacific Ocean (Fletcher 2008, 36). And yet many people have seen the river without knowing it, because it has been featured in movies, television shows, commercials, video games, and music videos. The riverbed has been used for car chase scenes, for example in *The Dark Knight Rises* (2012) and *Ambulance!* (2022) and for drag races, most famously in *Grease* (1978). A site for mutant creatures, body dumps, and covert meetings, the LA River has sundry iterations, most of which are rarely traced back to the river itself. Like many sites in and around Tinseltown, the river gives visitors a sense of déjà vu, provoked by both its ubiquity in media and its displacement as a free-flowing river.

It is this very paradox that has made the LA River an object of fascination for scholars, journalists, and artists since its 20-year conversion into a concrete flood

FIGURE 4.2 A mossy high heel rests on a barrel in the LA river. Photograph by the author.

channel was completed in 1959. As nature writer Jenny Price writes, "What makes the L.A. River so peerlessly amazing is that its city actively 'disappeared' it: We stopped calling the river a river. And it all but vanished from our collective memory" (2001). Along similar lines, ecocritic T.S. McMillin asks, "Can a river really cease to be a river if it still flows, albeit in a concrete channel? What makes a river a river, and what can render it a river no longer?" (2018, 156). When it was useful to the city—as a source of drinking water and irrigation—the LA River was deemed a river, but, when rapid urbanization made its floods increasingly deadlier, it had to be contained, controlled, concreted.

In 1986, when poet and founder of Friends of the LA River (FoLAR) Lewis MacAdams cut a hole through the chain-link fence that surrounded the river, there was little cultural awareness of the river's existence or past, but, since then, there has been mounting interest in revitalizing the river (LA River 2020, 48). LA County and LA County Public Works' 2020 LA River Master Plan, an update and expansion of the 1996 plan, offers a 25-year vision for a "reimagined river" that is at the center of city life (8). The 2020 planning committee, unlike its predecessor, took social equity into consideration, meeting with East LA residents concerned about rising housing costs due to the river's gentrification; in response, the county created a land bank to build low-income housing along the river (Schexnayder 2022). However, the master plan emphatically stated that it would not be possible to remove the concrete in the river due to urbanization. This decision, combined with a controversial park design by architect Frank Gehry that envisioned concrete park platforms over the river, and the exclusion of Gabrielino-Tongva[3] tribal members from the committee, led many environmental groups like FoLAR and East Yard Communities for Environmental Justice to withdraw their support for the plan (Schexnayder 2022; City News 2022).[4]

As this latest disagreement suggests, the LA River, which passes through 17 cities, is a complicated and contested site multilayered with political, ecological, and performative significance. A palimpsest of Hollywood settings, environmental histories, and ongoing environmental injustices, the LA River is paradoxically both a highly site-specific place and a non-place; it is both here, local and contextual, and not here, a stand-in for whatever site Hollywood needs it to be. How it is viewed—as a film set, a sewer, a channel, a dump, a fishing spot, a river, or a nonentity—is often dependent on the viewer. While the river's contested meanings have made it a popular source of discussion among scholars, the river has rarely been examined from a performance perspective. What does it mean to perform with a river—particularly one that has been culturally de-rivered and re-rivered? How might a spatialized eco-performance center a river that has been technocratically contained, backdropped in media, and endlessly spoken for? Can spatialized eco-performances focused on the river highlight sedimented environmental injustices and riparian spatial mobility?

The LA River's fluctuating spatial significance makes it an ideal site from which to explore urban, riparian spatiality in performance, and, although I focus specifically on the LA River, the practices and performances in this chapter may be relevant to the examination of other rivers that have been diverted, tamed, or forced underground. Adapting Henri Lefebvre's and Edward Soja's spatial theories, I posit that the LA River is a highly spatialized site with a multiplicity of shifting spatial meanings, and that eco-performance can play a key role in articulating these various meanings and in actualizing the river. Analyzing the spatial significance of water in the film *Chinatown* (1974) and Cornerstone Theater Company's site-specific

Touch the Water: A River Play (2009), I argue that, in unique and divergent ways, each one shifts the cultural narrative about the LA River from abstraction, by way of concrete channelization, to concrete materiality. In the following paragraphs, I introduce Lefebvre's and Soja's spatial triad before delving into the history of the river and its representation in eco-performance.

Toward a Spatio-Environmental Justice

The relationship between abstraction and concreteness is crucial to the LA River, which has been disappeared by technocratic management, and to Lefebvre, who posits that space is often represented as universal, fixed, and abstract, when it is actually an unfixed variable constantly being produced and reproduced. To combat what he sees as a constructed gap between abstract and concrete space, Lefebvre proposes an interconnected spatial triad made up of spatial practice (perceived, mental space), representations of space (conceived, social space), and representational spaces (lived, physical space) ([1974] 1991, 38–9). The constant tension among perceived-conceived-lived spaces can serve to undermine the domination of generalized, absolute space and, with it, the abstracted, capitalistic production of space (1991, 57). In other words, if space is seen as universal and fixed, its capitalistic production and uneven exploitation go unexamined. As Lefebvre warns, if the production of space is not denaturalized, "(physical) natural space" will increasingly be "lost to *thought*," abstracted even as it is extracted (1991, 30–1, emphasis in original). Considering how space is perceived, conceived, and lived in by different stakeholders reveals contested and multifaceted aspects of spatial production.

The spatial triad is taken up by Soja who, paraphrasing Lefebvre, refers to it as "the center-periphery relation [...] between the 'conceived' (*concu*) and the 'lived' (*vecu*)" (1996, 30). Lefebvre "saw these two dialectical pairings (center-periphery, conceived-lived) as homologous, arising from the same sources, and often mapped them directly on one another" (Soja 1996, 30). Lefebvre's notion of perpetual mapping is applicable to the LA River, which simultaneously occupies the physical center of the city—running right through it—and the periphery of urban perceptions and experiences. For the spatial triad to effectively reveal the production of space, though, it cannot be reduced to a dualism (such as space/place or abstract/concrete), or it becomes locked in a hermetic system of oppositions (Lefebvre 1991, 39). Likewise, if the triad is only deployed in abstract terms, space yet again becomes lost to thought (Lefebvre 1991, 40).

As sociologists Brian M. Napoletano, John Bellamy Foster, and Brett Clark argue, Lefebvre is invaluable to environmental sociology today—and to my understanding of spatialized eco-performance—for his insights "regarding the growing rupture between natural processes and spatial dynamics" (2021). Furthering Lefebvre's work, Soja argues for a "spatial justice," a "consequential geography" directly connected to social and political action (2010, 1–2). Taking a spatial perspective of social justice, Soja considers how justices and injustices alike become spatially embedded in local and regional geographies. To analyze the spatialization of social justice and build on existing environmental justice practices, which advocate for equal access to clean air, water, fresh food, and parks, I use what I call spatio-environmental justice. With this term, I combine the environmental justice movement's emphasis on humans and their shared environments with Lefebvre's and Soja's focus on the spatializing practices that forge and alter such environments. I consider how eco-performance, with its emphasis on material and ecological meaning, can articulate the spatial tensions and injustices around conceived, perceived, and lived experiences of the LA River.

While there are other, more recent performances of the LA River, like River LA's ambitious *Rio Records* (2020), a digital "choose your own adventure" style performance with over 700 minutes of potential content from more than 70 different artists, I focus on *Chinatown* (1974) and *Touch the Water: A River Play* (2009) because of their shared emphasis on the spatial histories and ongoing spatio-environmental injustices of the river. And yet, each offers disparate interpretations of the river's spatialized production and highlights different historical and ecological aspects of its spatialization. For example, *Chinatown* (1974) focuses on water corruption and places the properties of the LA River center stage, while *Touch the Water* (2009) exposes uneven spatio-environmental injustices but also posits a multi-perspectival approach to the river and its revitalization. Displacing some representations and foregrounding others, the two works perform multivalent narratives of the river and take multiscalar approaches to it. Together, they suggest a variety of ongoing perceived, conceived, and lived spatial representations and understandings of the LA River.

Both performances also obliquely or directly refer to two of the biggest water controversies in LA's short history: the Owens Valley water acquisition and the LA River's concrete channelization. The former is so infamous that a common expression in US water politics is, "We don't want another Owens Valley" (Libecap 2007, 2). Meanwhile, the concrete beds that line the LA River have been so successful in suppressing the water's flow that, up until recently, even Angelenos forgot the river existed. Geographers, historians, and economists have written at length about both controversies, but there has been little focus on the role performance has played in shaping Owens Valley and LA River narratives and activism.[5] I will discuss the Owens Valley controversy as it relates to, and differs from, *Chinatown*, but, since the spatial histories at work in the two performances are, at best, partial and fragmented, I first begin with a brief background of the river and the rapid changes it underwent throughout the twentieth century.

The River Then and Now

The Los Angeles Basin was home to the Tongva people, who lived in villages along the LA River for 7,000 years until their enslavement by Spanish colonizers and missionaries beginning in 1769 ("Tribal History" 2022).[6] The US acquired California from Mexico in 1848, and Anglo-Americans descended upon the land in search of gold, decimating Indigenous populations, like the Tongva and Chumash peoples, and beginning to destroy the LA River. As librarian Michael McLaughlin (Winnebago) points out, "It should be no mystery that the Californian Indian population dropped 95% between 1850 and 1900" (as cited in Meares 2016). Although California has the highest number of Indigenous peoples in the US today, with 700,000 residents (Davis-Young 2016), there is a lack of awareness of Indigenous histories in California and, as gender studies scholar Mishuana Goeman (Tonawanda Band of Seneca) notes, a persistent "stereotype that Indian people are dead" (as cited in Davis-Young 2016). The attempts by Spain and the US to disappear Indigenous peoples in many ways anticipated and were connected to the exploitation and eventual de-rivering of the LA River.

Until the completion of the LA Aqueduct in 1913, which will be discussed in relation to *Chinatown*, the river was LA's primary source of drinking water and was used to irrigate the city's first orange groves and vineyards. However, despite its immense importance to the development of the city, the river was never a selling point for easterners heading west. As geographer Blake Gumprecht argues, the river was always more significant to the city economically than it was aesthetically, which explains why it was so utterly exploited by industrialists and residents alike (2005, 123). Eastern settlers unaccustomed to LA's semi-arid climate were unimpressed by a river that looked more like a stream nine months out of the year; it was only during the three winter months that the river surged and often flooded, destroying the houses foolishly built on its banks (Gumprecht 2005, 118–19). The LA River significantly flooded in 1815, 1825, 1884, 1914, and 1938, and 177 people died from the 1914 flood alone. Although floods were always common to the LA River, they were not always as devastating. The railroad, built in 1869 only a half mile west of the river, destroyed the agricultural land near the river and prompted urban development in the area; factories, warehouses, and small houses soon sprung up alongside the train depot (Gumprecht 2005, 131). Historically, flash flooding could change the entire course of the river; in fact, one 1825 flood was so powerful that it "shifted its mouth twenty miles down the coast" (Gumprecht 2005, 130). Since LA was still relatively undeveloped at that point, this shift was not too destructive; however, by the late nineteenth century, it proved catastrophic. Floods, exacerbated by the city's rapid deforestation, now wreaked havoc where they otherwise would have been relatively harmless.

Although the city considered flood control measures after the particularly severe flood in 1914, there was simply not enough funding to initiate them (Gottlieb 2007, 140). After another devastating flood hit in 1938, its damage worsened by deforestation, river mismanagement, and development along the river, the USACE began covering the 51 miles of river with a concrete bed and walls. Three and a half million barrels of cement, 147 million pounds of steel, and 460,000 tons of stone later, the already damaged river had become a flood control channel for storm drain runoff (Elrick 2007, 73). While there is no question that the USACE acted drastically in its construction of the concrete channel, the severity of the latest flood required prompt action. Certainly, the USACE's intervention was forceful and hasty, and its single-minded goal to quickly direct water from the San Gabriel

Mountains to the sea left no room for environmental or aesthetic considerations. However, as Gumprecht makes clear, the USACE, so often blamed for the LA River becoming a concrete channel, only put the final coating on a river that had already been destroyed by exploitation and contamination—its topsoil stripped for farmland, its water drained by underground pumps, its sand and gravel hauled out for construction, and its bed turned into a common dumping ground (1999, 5). Thus, while the USACE's flood control strategies were extreme, it was Angelenos' disregard for the river in the first place that necessitated such strategies. As geographers Jason Michael Post and Perry Carter succinctly put it, "The city's evolution has been a mirrored image of the river's devolution" (2022, 210; Marsh 2012).

The effects of rapid industrialization and deindustrialization have left their mark on the river and its neighborhoods, especially those east of the river. Indeed, most industrial waste sites are in East LA where, according to the US Census Bureau, 95.9% of the population is Latinx (2021). This environmental injustice can be traced back to the 1920s when suburbanization allowed working-class White people to move out of the city center; people of color moved inward, and "near suburbs became the inner city" (Pulido 2000, 27). Zoning laws pushed industry and Latinx communities east of the river, a lucrative location for developers at the time, because the railroad already ran along the river and labor unions—like those forming downtown—did not exist in East LA (Pulido 2000, 26–7). Today, East LA continues to suffer from environmental racism, with worse air quality and less access to trees and grocery stores than LA County as a whole (Neighborhood Data for Social Change 2021). The river, meanwhile, remains on the outskirts of the bustling, sprawling city despite running right through it; as aerial views of the river reveal, the railway and I-5 freeway run alongside it, often separating it from street level and infrastructure more central to the city. As we will see, much of the environmentalism surrounding the LA River emphasizes restoration and revitalization, a return to an idyllic time when the river was central to Angeleno life. However, as Gumprecht insists, since colonization, such a time did not exist (1995); thus, while LA River narratives often pinpoint the USACE's concretization of the river as a moment of sudden loss, its devastation was far more gradual, just as its ecological improvements will likely be.

Welcome to *Chinatown*

If the USACE's channelization of the LA River has become a tale of paradise lost, the buy up of Owens Valley to create the LA Aqueduct is often deemed a tale of treachery, a narrative cemented in the 1974 neo-noir film *Chinatown*, directed by Roman Polanski[7] and starring Jack Nicholson and Faye Dunaway. Although it is one of many films that have been shot in and around the LA River, it is unique in that it is not only set in and near the river but also stars it and the water politics surrounding it. While the film is set in LA in 1937, its story is actually based on the California Water Wars, which took place throughout the first quarter of the century. Highlighting the convoluted corruption surrounding water politics in

California, *Chinatown* speaks to the subterfuge embedded in the California Water Wars. While much of the chicanery depicted in the film is fictionalized, *Chinatown* nonetheless underscores the inescapable fact that "metropolitan interests appropriated the Owens Valley for their own expansionary purposes through the use of blunt political power" (Walton 1992, 232). Drawing attention to past and ongoing spatio-environmental injustices in Owens Valley, *Chinatown* sparked renewed protests in the 1970s and captured the uneven power relations at play in California's water acquisition and distribution.

Much has been written about *Chinatown* already. Film scholars have focused at length on the main character, J.J. "Jake" Gittes (Jack Nicholson), a jaded private eye: Glenn Man emphasizes the fallibility of Gittes's subjective point of view (1994b, 144), while Phillip Novak argues that, despite suggestions to the contrary, the film critiques Gittes's cynicism rather than endorses it (2007, 257). Other film scholars focus on the unknowability of the femme fatale (Maxfield 1996, 127) and her connection to the equally indecipherable Chinatown (Belton 1991, 945–6; Shetley 1999, 1102). However, while *Chinatown*'s characters, including Chinatown, have been closely analyzed, the environmental history in the film and the role of water as a character in its own right have received less attention. Thus, after describing the film, I consider its interpretation of the Owens Valley controversy before turning to the film's spatialization of water and marginalized characters of color.

The neo-noir film follows Gittes, who is seemingly hired by Evelyn Mulwray to find proof that her husband Hollis Mulwray, chief engineer for the Los Angeles Department of Water and Power (LADWP), is having an affair. Gittes spies on Mulwray, first observing him in a town hall meeting where the engineer opposes the construction of a new dam and later taking photos of him with a young woman. He gives the pictorial evidence to "Mrs. Mulwray" only to see it on the newspaper's front page the next day. The *real* Evelyn Mulwray (Faye Dunaway) comes to see Gittes, demanding to know why he claims that she hired him. The investigator quickly realizes that he was tricked by someone who wanted him to smear Mulwray's reputation. Before Gittes can alert the engineer, Mulwray is found dead in the Oak Pass Reservoir. The detective begins to realize that nothing is quite as it seems, but the more he discovers about the murky machinations of water moguls, the less he can actually do about it.

After visiting the supposedly dry LA River, only to discover that water gushes into it at night, Gittes realizes that the city is not actually experiencing a drought, despite the LADWP's claims to the contrary. In a subsequent visit to the San Fernando Valley, the detective is run off the road by angry farmers convinced that he is from the LADWP and is there to poison their wells and blow up their water tanks, as other businessmen have already done. While both incidents hint at a misappropriation of water, it is the phone call that Gittes receives from Ida Sessions (Diane Ladd), the woman who posed as Evelyn Mulwray, which offers the greatest clue. Distraught over the engineer's death, Sessions suggests that Gittes check the paper's obituary section for insight into Mulwray's murder, but when the detective visits her home to follow up, he finds her dead body. Based on Sessions's tip, though, he gradually discovers that nearly all the land in the San Fernando Valley has recently been purchased in the names of residents of the Mar Vista Inn retirement home. However, the residents themselves know nothing of the transactions, and one of the supposed "buyers" has purchased land postmortem. With Evelyn Mulwray's assistance, Gittes connects the misuse of the elderly people's names to Noah Cross, Evelyn's father and Hollis Mulwray's former business partner. As occurred historically as well, the land in the valley is being cheaply purchased by rich tycoons who know that its value will rapidly multiply once the valley has unlimited access to water.

Gittes suspects Noah Cross of Mulwray's murder, but his suspicions shift when, after following Evelyn, he witnesses her appearing to confine and quiet the young woman from the photographs with Mulwray. Considering the possibility that Evelyn killed her husband in a bout of jealously, Gittes thinks his suspicions are confirmed when he finds what he believes are the engineer's glasses in the Mulwrays' pond. The detective reports Evelyn to his former police partner, Lieutenant Lou Escobar, before violently confronting her himself. Evelyn finally admits that the young girl, Katherine Cross, is both her sister *and* her daughter, the product of incest. As Gittes reels from this revelation, Evelyn mentions that the bifocals the detective found do not belong to her husband. Deducing that the glasses belong to Noah Cross, the investigator tries to help Evelyn and Katherine flee him, as well as the police. In the denouement, which leads all the central characters to Chinatown, Evelyn shoots her father in the arm and drives away with Katherine, only to be killed by a police officer for fleeing the scene. As Evelyn's body slumps forward, Katherine's screams are muffled by her illicit father, who will now gain control of the daughter and the water (Shetley 1999, 1092). Thus, in true noir fashion, Noah Cross's murky crimes of water corruption and incest will not only go unpunished but will likely be repeated.

Chinatown and the Owens Valley Purchase

What makes *Chinatown* so compelling is that much of its narrative of corruption and greed is inspired by real events. In actuality—but unrepresented in the film—Paiute peoples native to the Payahuunadü region (the Californian Owens Valley) were displaced by US settlers in the mid-nineteenth century, especially following the Homestead Act of 1862 (Wei 2016). In the early twentieth century, the settlers themselves were displaced by water imperialists intent on diverting Owens Valley water to LA. Although the film is fictional, its focus on the politics and topography of water distribution highlights how "the spatiality of (in)justice…affects society and social life just as much as social processes shape the spatiality or specific geography of (in)justice" (Soja 2010, 5). By recalling the acts of LA water imperialists in the early twentieth century, the film accounts for the spatialized conditions of its own time, the 1970s. Indeed, a second aqueduct south of Owens Valley was completed in 1970, just four years before *Chinatown* was released, suggesting that the spatio-environmental injustices begun a century prior were still very much in effect in 1970. Thus, *Chinatown* is both a critique of historical corruption and of ongoing water politics.

Early in the film, Gittes observes Hollis Mulwray at a public hearing on the proposed Alto Vallejo Dam, a fictional stand-in for the LA Aqueduct, which in actuality was constructed from 1908 to 1913, and, at 233 miles, was the longest dam to date, stretching from the northeastern Owens Valley to Los Angeles (Prud'homme 2011, 152–3). Gaining permission to undertake such a project took money, power, and position. It was the combined clout of Frederick Eaton, then mayor of LA, and William Mulholland, self-made engineer and mayor-appointed superintendent of the LADWP, that made the aqueduct possible. Beginning in 1900, the two men envisioned that, with unlimited water, LA, then a small city with a population of around 100,000, could be developed into a thriving metropolis to rival Chicago and New York in size and influence (Prud'homme 2011, 151). Owens Valley, with the Inyo Mountains to its east and the Sierra Nevada to its west, had immense potential as a water source, and, at 200 miles northeast of LA, was the closest option. However, the Bureau of Reclamation, "the federal agency responsible for water management in the West," had already agreed to assist Owens Valley farmers by creating an irrigation system (Prud'homme 2011, 152). If Eaton and Mulholland were to be successful, they would need to stop the irrigation project before it began. With the support of investors like the publisher of the *Los Angeles Times* Harrison Gray Otis and his son-in-law Harry Chandler, Eaton and Mulholland got Theodore Roosevelt's administration to suppress the irrigation initiative. Eaton, concerned that speculators would soon descend, began covertly and cheaply purchasing land and water rights in Owens Valley (Prud'homme 2011, 152).

Eaton and Mulholland managed to keep their activities quiet until 1905, by which point it was too late for Owens Valley residents to stop the Bureau of Reclamation's abandonment of the irrigation project. However, this did not prevent residents from running Eaton and his son out of town when the story broke, an event which only marked the beginning of the farmers' wrath (Nadeau 1950, 21). This tension between LA moguls and valley farmers is twice depicted in *Chinatown*. The first time is at the public hearing that Gittes observes, which is disrupted by a farmer and his baying sheep; the former calls out, "You steal the water from the valley, ruin the grazing, starve my livestock—who's paying you to do that, Mr. Mulwray, that's what I want to know!" (Towne 1997, 12). Although the farmer is dressed in a blazer, his overalls, flat cap, shepherd's staff, and woolly companions make him a stark contrast to the dark-suited bureaucrats. Like the rest of the courtroom, Gittes laughs at the unexpected appearance of the farmer and the sheep, and the scene, viewed through the investigator's eyes, ends on a dismissive, comical note. However, as with many other revelations in the film, the significance of the farmer's protest does not become evident until much later.

The film's second depiction of Owens Valley farmers occurs after Yelburton of the LADWP claims that the water Gittes saw gushing from the reservoir was to help irrigate Owens Valley farms, and the detective decides to investigate for himself. Passing numerous "SOLD" signs in the valley, he pulls into a grove marked "PRIVATE PROPERTY," only to be shot at by suspicious farmers. Gittes's car crashes into a tree, and, echoing an earlier shot in the film, his radiator ruptures. A farmer beats the investigator with his crutch, prompting Gittes to call the men "dumb Oakies." This further inflames the farmers, and the leader asks whether Gittes is with the "Water Department or the real-estate office" (Towne 1997, 89). When the detective explains that he is there to see if the land has been getting irrigated by the Water Department, the farmer exclaims, "Irrigating my land? The Water Department's been sending people to blow up my water tanks!" (Towne 1997, 90). While in actuality it was the desperate farmers who dynamited parts of the aqueduct from 1924 to 1927 (Prud'homme 2011, 153), the scene nonetheless speaks to other real-life injustices that incited the farmers' anger. For example, Fred Eaton and city officials posed as "cattle buyers" in Owens Valley to buy up the land without alerting farmers or speculators to their true intent (Nadeau 1950, 17). Similarly, Eaton and Mulholland told Angelenos in 1905 that the aqueduct would only be used in the city of LA domestically; they failed to mention that it would also supply the arid San Fernando Valley, which had already been cheaply bought up by investors like Chandler and Otis (Prud'homme 2011, 152). LA annexed the San Fernando Valley in 1915, and it prospered while Owens Valley gradually became desertified (Prud'homme 2011, 153). Despite vigilante resistance from the farmers, LA had gained control of 90% of the valley's water rights by 1928, and agriculture in Owens Valley soon became a thing of the past (Prud'homme 2011, 153).

Hence, *Chinatown*, released in 1974, offers retrospection not only colored by the spatio-environmental injustices of the California Water Wars but also by more recent injustices, like the LADWP's second aqueduct from Owens Valley, built in 1970. The film's temporal layers—the time in which it is set (1937), the time of the events it recreates (1905–1928), the time in which it is made (1974), and its "prophetic modernism" (Scott 2007, 5)—reveal how spatial injustices are compounded, reproduced, and magnified over time. And yet, while the film highlights injustices experienced by the poor, White farmers, it erases racial injustices, like the initial displacement of Indigenous peoples in the mid-nineteenth century and the incarceration of Japanese Americans in Owen Valley's Manzanar during World War II.[8] Once the lake ran dry, Owens Valley became "the largest source of dust in North America," affecting the respiratory health of Indigenous peoples and former ranchers turned environmentalists (Colgan 2020). Thus, as Soja posits, "Justice and injustice are infused into the multiscalar geographies in which we live," and they create "lasting structures of unevenly distributed advantage and disadvantage" (2010, 20). While *Chinatown* only gives voice to one group in Owens Valley affected by enduring structures of spatial injustice, it nonetheless captures the insidious corruption embedded in water extractivism. Contrasting the spatial realities of the farmers with the misperceptions of urbanites like Gittes and the technocratic conceptions of water moguls, the film surfaces the "selfish, profit-driven presentism" sedimented in Los Angeles's foundation (Davis 1998, 65).

"Water on the Brain"

Although the central characters in the film are J.J. Gittes and Evelyn Mulwray, water acts as an omnipresent entity, enigma, and motivator. Indeed, the plot's neo-noir mystery hinges on a distinction between freshwater and saltwater: Mulwray's body is found at the Oak Pass Reservoir and is full of saltwater, leading Gittes to assume that it was dumped in the ocean. It is only when Evelyn's gardener reveals that the Mulwrays' pond contains saltwater, not freshwater, that the detective realizes where the murder actually occurred. In another scene, the investigator is puzzled by the coroner's insistence that a drunk man drowned in the LA River, protesting, "Well, he ain't exactly gonna drown in a damp riverbed...I don't care how soused he was" (Towne 1997, 48). The incongruity of a man drowning during a drought leads Gittes to examine the river more closely and discover that, though it is "bone-dry" by day, it has gallons of water dumped into it by night (Towne 1997, 48). Thus, unraveling the film's complex plot depends on particularities like the salinity and quantity of water.

In the rare scenes of *Chinatown* where water is not discussed, it is still aurally or visually prominent. The film, like its character Hollis Mulwray—a loose stand-in for the real-life William Mulholland—has "water on the brain" (Towne 1997, 16). From dripping faucets to streaming showers, from radiator ruptures to car washes, water features in nearly every scene, never letting Gittes and, through him, the audience forget its significance. Ironically, water is never more present than when it is only an offscreen sound effect. Take, for example, the scene in which Gittes discovers Ida Sessions's body: ominous, dissonant music sets the tone, as the investigator slowly creeps toward the kitchen, where Ida and her groceries are sprawled out on the floor. Gradually layered over the music is a steady, dripping sound eventually revealed to be the kitchen faucet. The leak not only heightens the scene's dramatic tension, but it also acts as a literal reminder of why Ida was killed. Water corruption and misappropriation are at the film's center, and aural cues like this one ensure that, even when water is out of sight, it is never out of mind.

Water corruption is visually highlighted in another scene, in which the detective is getting his hair cut and reads the newspaper headline "Department of Water and Power Blows Fuse," just as a passing car's radiator overheats (Towne 1997, 19). This moment is echoed when the detective's own radiator bursts in the drought-ridden valley. The spurting coolant in both scenes visually imitates the gushing water secretly being released from the reservoir at night, discovered by Gittes when he stands in the reservoir and is swept off his feet by a torrent of water that knocks him into the chain-link fence. The repetitive images of water bursting free of its mechanized containment are instances of what political ecologist Maria Kaika calls the "urban uncanny" (2005, 51), moments when unexpected leaks and ruptures cross erected boundaries between inside and outside, culture and nature (2005, 54). The coolant that shoots from the two vehicles in *Chinatown* interrupts the human drama in order to emphasize the ordinarily hidden production and properties of water. Similarly, Gittes's fall into the reservoir, an isolated site fenced off from the public and below street level, demonstrates both the water's powerful flow and its (mis)management. As the drenched detective scrambles out of the reservoir, his one remaining water-logged, leather shoe squeaks, offering yet another instance of the urban uncanny. Taken together, the three scenes highlight the pressure, flow, and production of water, qualities that are typically concealed within or beneath the city. The water's surge from its contained spaces, in this case a sleek automobile and a remote reservoir, is an unexpected reminder of the socio-spatial management, necessity, and presence of water in the city.

Art historian Homay King links the film's emphasis on dirty water seepage to its fear of immigrants when he writes, "The water in *Chinatown* is already contaminated: stolen and rerouted, but also accented…and infused with the salt of the Pacific Ocean that separates the Asian continent from the American one" (2010, 87). Just as water in the film bursts through pipes, so too might immigrants flood the city, breaking tenuously constructed boundaries between water and its containment, LA and Chinatown. On the one hand, the latter is marginalized, despite being the movie's title (Man 1994a). Only the last scene occurs there, and the film's use of foreboding music and broken neon lights to signify Chinatown not only foreshadows Evelyn's imminent demise but also reinforces Hollywood representations of Asia as inscrutable and enigmatic. For Gittes, Chinatown is convoluted and unlucky; he vaguely tells Evelyn that he once failed to save a woman there, and, by the narrative's end, he has failed yet again. The screenwriter, Robert Towne, saw Chinatown not as a place but as "Jake Gittes's fucked-up state of mind" (as cited in Evans 1997, 257). Thus, on the other hand, Chinatown permeates the film, albeit abstractly, represented as an overdetermined hyper-performance of Asian stereotypes and an empty signifier. Film scholar John Belton argues that since Chinatown is not seen until the last scene, "its meaning—i.e., what it designates—floats. The object or place to which the word refers remains unseen, enhancing its status as place of mystery and enabling it to function abstractly" (1991, 946).

While this abstraction is at odds with the film's grounded, textured representation of water, there are two moments in particular where otherwise marginalized bodies and water properties converge. In the first, the Mulwrays' gardener (Jerry Fujikawa) mumbles the phrase "bad for glass," meaning "grass," while probing at the overflowing pond (Towne 1997, 33). The first time Gittes overhears the gardener, he misunderstands and dismisses him outright: "Yeah sure. Bad for the glass," sarcastically emphasizing the latter two words. As King points out, the scene reaffirms some Hollywood clichés, disregarding ethnic difference by casting the Japanese American Fujikawa as a Chinese gardener and emphasizing the character's pronunciation for comic relief (2010, 80). At the same time, it suggests that, from the very beginning, the gardener knows something that the protagonist does not. Quick to dismiss the Chinese laborer, Gittes fails to understand him until much later in the film when the gardener elaborates, "Salt water velly bad for glass" (Towne 1997, 123). This off-camera revelation, delivered to Gittes's back, stops the detective in his tracks; slowly turning back toward the gardener, he finally realizes that, if the pond is in fact saltwater, then Mulwray's body may just as easily have been drowned there. In King's estimation, "Some encoded form of knowledge resides with the Chinese gardener. As a result, the gardener's off-hand, accented remark takes on an unexpected authority, and the film's enunciation gets an accent" (2010, 80–1). Although Gittes mocks the gardener's seeming linguistic mistake, it is he who ultimately fails to understand correctly.

Not only does the gardener possess the crucial information that the detective needs to solve the case, but he is also the one to fish the evidence—Noah Cross's bifocals—from the pond. During their first encounter, the gardener probes the overflowing pond with a pole, pulling out a clump of dead grass, and, during the second encounter, it is he who steps into the knee-deep water, rolls up his sleeve, and searches for the glasses, wound around yet another clump of grass. Meanwhile, the dry detective stands above him waiting. Thus, the gardener's seeming mispronunciation is validated as grass and glass become entwined, together offering literal and figurative clues. "In *Chinatown*," King posits, "the film's enunciation seems to side with the gardener, not with Jake, in this exchange" (2010, 83). Creating an affinity between the saltwater and the gardener, the film suggests that it is Gittes who fails to see[9] and hear clearly.

Similarly, it is Gittes who fails to understand in an earlier exchange with a Mexican boy on horseback (Claudio Martínez). Gittes stumbles down an LA River embankment in search of clues, and his leather-clad shoe sinks into the muddy, shallow water. In his pin-striped suit and soaked shoe, the detective is clearly out of his element, in contrast to an approaching boy on horseback who, in a loose, cotton tunic and sombrero, seems far more at ease. On the horse, the boy is at eye level with Gittes, but is not only physically elevated but also more knowledgeable about the river than the clueless detective. Gittes spied the boy telling Mulwray something before the latter was killed, and now he wants to know what it was. However, the boy hesitates to answer, leading the detective to ask rudely, "Speak English? Habla Inglés?" (Towne 1997, 49). Just as in his encounters with the gardener, Gittes assumes that it is the other character who lacks language when, in fact, it is he who misunderstands and fails to see clearly. The boy finally chooses to reveal that the water "comes in different parts of the river—every night a different path" (Towne 1997, 50). The detective watches the boy's slow retreat before confusedly turning to face the camera; as he takes in the rubble under the nearly dry Hollenbeck Bridge, Gittes struggles to comprehend how the boy's words fit with the urban blight before him.

Like the gardener, the boy possesses knowledge of the water that the citified detective fails to grasp, and, thus, the film grants him a superior position to Gittes. On the one hand, the film privileges the Chinese gardener's and the Mexican boy's embodied knowledge, undercutting the authority of the traditional noir protagonist with that of marginalized characters. Likewise, as journalist Victor Valle suggests, the presence of the Mexican boy, in addition to Detective Escobar, offers "rooted specificities" that journalists who interpret the film as a universal metaphor miss (2009, 1). The spatial specificity of the marginalized characters, and of water in the film, resists abstraction. On the other hand, *Chinatown*'s conflation of the

Chinese and Mexican characters with nonhuman nature, particularly water, essentializes both as marginalized others, "innately" one with their environments.

Ultimately, the film's deployment of materialized water in a variety of contexts suggests that water is ubiquitous in urban life. At the same time, it questions how long the water can last, in light of deeply embedded water exploitation, mismanagement, and overconsumption. Inequitable access to water is also highlighted, as in the scene in which Gittes pointedly takes in the Mulwrays' verdant grass, streaming fountain, and gushing gardening hose. Through the detective's eyes, the camera exposes the disparity between the city's water restrictions, enforced during the supposed drought, and the Mulwrays' own excessive water consumption. Through such instances of aural and visual repetition, the film attempts to put water on the brains of everyone, including viewers. Not only is such a detailed focus on the actual properties of water unique in film, but it is also unique in academia. In geographer Bruce Braun's estimation, "A great deal is written about water, but nary a word is said about the *properties* of water, and how these might influence the sociospatial development of cities. Water flows" (2005, 645, emphasis in original). While subfields like the blue humanities and critical oceanic studies[10] have exploded since Braun's writing, rivers continue to be difficult to articulate, because they are complex, often visible enmeshments of nonhuman nature and culture, ecological adaptation and modern alteration. As historian Jason Kelly argues, rivers are "a useful locus for analyzing flows, intersections, and cycles that are central to understanding the human-environment nexus" (2018, xx). By centering the LA River and emphasizing the properties of water—the flow, changeability, and salinity—*Chinatown* suggests the major role that water has played and might continue to play in the uneven spatio-environmental development of LA. Furthermore, by highlighting the Chinese gardener's and Mexican boy's experiential knowledge, the film alludes to the embodied labor that built the city and was marginalized by it.

Imagining the LA River: Cornerstone Theater's *Touch the Water*

Whereas water is the undercurrent and throughline of *Chinatown*, it is the setting and focus of the 2009 production *Touch the Water: A River Play*. Informed by interviews with East LA residents, the play, which ran from May 28 until June 21, was written by Julie Hébert and directed by Juliette Carrillo for the LA-based Cornerstone Theater Company. As with most Cornerstone productions, the performance developed out of the local community, featuring both professional and amateur actors, as well as activists, who play a wide range of characters with varied, conflicting intentions toward the LA River. The characters include the comically pretentious eco-activist who goes by the code name Roger Vadim!, the well-meaning but sometimes misguided experts Joe Swift (an Army Corps biologist) and Jade Kenton-Denton (a green architect and activist), the ticket-toting Parks and Recreation's officer, and wide-eyed, curious students. In addition to the human characters, there is a chorus of flora and fauna led by Maniisar, a ghost of a Tongva girl. Two of the other featured characters are animals: the poisoned turtle, Ridley (named after the olive ridley sea turtle), and an imposing crow, Corvus (named for the crow's genus name, *Corvus*). While *Touch the Water* is undoubtedly a biodiverse ensemble piece, its story centers on the river and two characters who live along it: Luis Otcho-o, who witnessed a murder and refused to testify, and Isa Pino, the woman whose little brother was murdered. At the play's start, Luis has just been released from prison and has returned to his mother's condemned house, reigniting Isa's anger and guilt. He arrives in time to witness Roger Vadim!'s attempt to "free the river" by taking a jackhammer to its concrete bed (Hébert 2009, 2). The activist unwittingly calls the ghost Maniisar, who floats up through the hole in the concrete and helps Luis and Isa begin to find peace with each other, themselves, and their environment. Thus, *Touch the Water* promotes a reciprocal relationship between humans and the environment, but it also asks who represents, and who should represent, the river and its interests. The play warrants closer analysis, because it considers spatio-environmental justice in the LA River and stages site-specific, multi-vocal debates about the river's past, present, and future.

Whereas *Chinatown* emphasizes the properties of water over the properties of place, *Touch the Water* is firmly connected to the LA River and the people who live along it. The play's site-specificity is very much in keeping with the practices of the community-oriented Cornerstone Theater Company, which has been tackling issues of social relevance to the Angeleno community for over 30 years. Frequently casting residents from the towns in which productions are staged and collaborating with local organizations in the area, the company emphasizes collective activism. For *Touch the Water* in particular, Cornerstone collaborated with Friends of the Los Angeles River (FoLAR), Metabolic Studio/Farmlab, and South Asian Network (SAN). FoLAR led free pre-show river walks for those interested and, at the end of every performance, circulated a petition to protect the river. Thus, the production, part of a four-year Justice Cycle, was very much a community effort that included local artists, actors, environmentalists, scholars, and residents.

By situating the narrative and the characters on the banks of the LA River, the play literally and figuratively places the river center stage. However, the production itself complicates this specificity by not taking place in the play's exact setting. *Touch the Water* is set in Elysian Valley or, as it is locally known, Frogtown and draws on the area's history of industrialization and its recent gentrification. The production, meanwhile, takes place in Taylor Yard along the northeast side of the LA River across from Frogtown. Furthermore, while the production is indeed performed on the bank of the LA River, its set includes a shallow, rectangular box of water that runs the length of downstage and serves as a stand-in for the nearby river. Placed at a 90-degree angle to the actual LA River, the box, made of reclaimed wood, contains two inches of collected rainwater; on the floor of the model river are alternating black and silver squiggly lines that hint at the river's flow and its toxicity. Characters frequently walk, dance, fish, wash, drink, and kayak in the miniature river, suggesting the many hopeful uses for the actual river.[11] Their embodied experiences in the water encourage new perceptions and conceptions of the river as a potential site of communal interaction.

Although it may seem rather absurd to place a model of a river on the very bank of that river, this spatializing choice highlights the long-term inaccessibility of the LA River, and it is almost fitting that a model stand in for a river that has historically been disregarded by Angelenos, closed off by the USACE, and recast as countless other places by Hollywood. The river set piece reveals the disjuncture between the play's hopes for the river and the reality of the river, which is still largely inaccessible. Indeed, the production team that chose the location immediately ruled out the river, because it would have been unsafe, particularly for cast and audience members in wheelchairs (Woolery 2012). The use of a model, abutting the material river, makes clear that the play's vision of the river is just that: an imagined future rather than an idyllic past or a fully realized present. By setting the production in the "wrong" site, Cornerstone highlights the need for improvements to the "right" site. *Touch the Water* quite literally asks its characters— and audience—to imagine touching the waters of the LA River to reconnect with themselves and their environment.

Multivalent Performances of Spatio-Environmental Justice

The strength of Hébert's writing lies in its ability to consider the multivalent perspectives that the characters—people and animals alike—have toward the river without dismissing anyone's viewpoint. Take, for instance, the play's portrayal of the debate between those who advocate for removing all the concrete from the river and those who favor more cautious measures. At one end of the spectrum is Roger Vadim!, so desperate for a "real" river that he is willing to take matters into his own hands: "Let the people see Nature, man, let them touch it, it will heal them. Free the river from her concrete corset!" (Hébert 2009, 2). Here, Hébert mocks Vadim!'s gendered personification of the river, as well as his appropriation of the code name Roger Vadim!, a real-life French film director. Emulating the director's sartorial style and French dialect, the activist attempts to imbue his cause with European, artistic sophistication. However, in taking on Vadim's name and mannerisms, the activist also imitates his misogyny. Arguably most famous for directing actresses in highly sexualized roles and subsequently marrying them, the real Vadim goes so far as to recount his intimate experience of the women in *Bardot, Deneuve, Fonda: My Life with the Three Most Beautiful Women in the World* (1986), a self-serving account of how he educated and rescued the actresses before liberating them. Similarly, *Touch the Water*'s Vadim! wants to rescue the feminine river, freeing her from her "concrete corset." Just as the real-life director hypersexualizes women in his films, the eco-activist imagines the river as an unbridled, untamed woman simply in need of a male liberator. Thus, Hébert mocks activists like Vadim! who gender nature, simultaneously casting it as helplessly passive and wildly uncontrollable. Performing what ecocritic Nicole Seymour (2018) calls "bad environmentalism," Hébert uses absurdity and irreverence to critique Roger's— and by extension the environmental movement's—sanctimony and disconnection from people's actual experiences of the environment.

However, despite the playwright's comedic critique of Vadim!, and many of the other characters, she never outright dismisses the eco-activist or his ideas, no matter how flawed they are. For example, just after Roger has been derided by the other characters for ludicrously telling them to call him "River Boy," he breaks out of his affected French persona (Hébert 2009, 53). Sans accent and hyperbole, he confesses that he is really from the San Fernando Valley where his part of the river is dry: "The river is more than water, it's a way of sustaining our spirits. I've lived in L.A. all my life and I will die here—I can't wait fifty years, or twenty years—I need my water now" (Hébert 2009, 55). Thus, Hébert establishes Vadim! as a misogynistic, excessive eco-activist only to later complicate this image. Roger suggests that he took on the role of Vadim! simply to draw attention to the river's condition, but in dropping the act, he realizes that his own experience as an Angeleno is far more influential. Like everyone else in the play, Roger needs to reconnect with the actual river, as opposed to projecting his gendered assumptions on to it.

At the other end of the spectrum is the biologist Joe Swift, who works for the USACE. Compared to Roger Vadim! and sustainability architect Jade Kenton-Denton, Joe is hyper-rational, occasionally telling the other two to calm down and mistaking their metaphorization of the river for scientific error. Advocating small, gradual changes to the river, the biologist is viewed with distrust by many of the other characters, largely because of the way in which the USACE turned the river into a concrete channel without considering less drastic measures. For example, Jade says, "Our defining geologic feature is the Los Angeles River, which—before it was so rudely interrupted by men short on vision and long on concrete—flowed in a natural cycle for nine thousand years" (Hébert 2009, 14). Indeed, the fact that the USACE still regulates the river is a further source of discontentment for those Angelenos who feel that flood control officials are a part of "a concrete cult" unsupportive of greening initiatives (Gumprecht 2005, 116). However, as Gumprecht convincingly argues, there was never a point in the city's short history that the river was viewed as the center of life, even when LA was primarily agricultural. While the river was indeed central to the Tongva people who lived along it prior to Spanish colonization in the eighteenth century, it was not central to Angelenos (Gumprecht 2005, 118). The fact that the railroad and, later, the I-5 freeway follow the river suggests not that it is the center of the city, but that it is the outskirts. Thus, Joe must contend with both Angelenos' legitimate complaints about the USACE's river management and their nostalgia for a river that their own ancestors helped destroy.

Just as Hébert adds shades of complexity to Roger's character, she depicts Joe as someone who is genuinely intent on improving the river. Rather than reinforce the familiar vilification of the Army Corps, she complicates this image through Joe, who claims that the USACE is becoming more environmentally conscious:

> We're changing, we have to. We want to adapt the system so it works *with* Nature instead of trying to control it. As always, our main objective is to protect the city from flooding, but we can do that and add greenspace
>
> *(Hébert 2009, 20, emphasis in original).*

The character's statement is reflective of a current trend within the USACE, LA District, which has united with the city and with nonprofit organizations to generate strategies to improve the river's environment without increasing flood risks. However, although Joe (and, through him, the USACE) seems to understand that human and environmental needs are intertwined, he, like Roger and Jade, nonetheless privileges the river over its inhabitants. This is evidenced by the fact that, within the play, the greenspace USACE wants to add will require tearing down a condemned house, the home where Luis grew up and has returned to following his imprisonment. Hence, the greenifying vision of both Joe and Jade is in tension with the needs of the actual residents. While both Joe and Jade express interest in the community's wishes, they fail to recognize how their visions for the river might conflict with the community's day-to-day needs.

Never is this learning gap more apparent than when the biologist and the architect are preparing to take apart Luis's home. The house now belongs to the city, which has given permission for a pocket park to be built on the grounds. Unable to save his childhood home from demolition and desperately in need of work, Luis asks if he can help tear down the structure. Although Joe readily agrees, the irony of the situation is not lost on the inquisitive teenager Cachoo, who is doing a video documentary of the river for school. When she asks Joe and Jade why they would tear down someone's house, Jade replies, "There have to be a few sacrifices" (Hébert 2009, 50). Tellingly, though, the sacrifices are not made by those outside the community but those within it. Unable to find work after his imprisonment, Luis cannot risk losing a potential job and merely tells Cachoo not to ruin this opportunity for him. The contrast between Luis's economic straits and Jade's and Joe's ecological vision is jarring: when Luis asks, "So, how's this supposed to work?," the biologist and architect provide a lengthy explanation of the greening process only to have Luis respond with, "I meant how're we supposed to take my house down. You got a sledgehammer?" (Hébert 2009, 48). Through this juxtaposition, Hébert exposes the fact that environmental injustice can not only be found in projects that pollute an area but also in those that purport to improve it.

While historically environmental justice scholarship tends to focus on how people of color are unequally and unfairly exposed to toxins and pollutants, gentrification is also an environmental injustice, because it provides both economic and environmental benefits to White gentrifiers by actively displacing people of color (Vázquez 2019, 204–05). *Touch the Water* suggests that sometimes the solution can be worse than the problem, especially if the solution only addresses the environment and ignores the people within that environment. Not only can greening projects destroy existing habitats, like Luis's home, but, as Isa fears, they can also gentrify a place to the point that it becomes unaffordable for its own residents. This is one reason why art historian Miwon Kwon, drawing on Iris Marion Young and Jean-Luc Nancy, argues "against the common notion of the community as a coherent and unified social formation—equally valorized by neoconservatives and the liberal left—which often serves exclusionary and authoritarian purposes in the very name of the opposite" (2004, 7). By juxtaposing Jade's and Joe's privileged aspirations with Luis's lived experience, Hébert challenges the environmental assumption that green spaces are always beneficial to a community and demonstrates the dangers of treating social and environmental injustices as separate issues.

Furthermore, she shows, through Isa's and Luis's experiences, how environmental injustice is spatially and historically compounded. As Isa tells Joe, "My mother's family has lived here for four generations—Chavez Ravine before Elysian Valley, Sonora Town before that. When I-5 got built—we lost our doctor's office, the grocery story, the bakery" (Hébert 2021, 21). The construction of Interstate 5 through Elysian Valley was just one instance of the displacement of residents of color for the sake of "development." As Black studies scholar Gaye Theresa Johnson writes, in the mid- to late-twentieth century, "Los Angeles emerged as one of the most visible examples of spatial hegemony: several Black and Brown neighborhoods were eviscerated, even from maps themselves, as if no one had ever lived there" (2014, 320). For example, Mexican Americans in Chavez Ravine, a mile and a half northwest of downtown LA, were forcefully evicted in the 1950s. The city promised to build affordable housing on the razed land but instead sold it to the LA Dodgers in 1958 (Llamoca 2017). Meanwhile, East LA bore the brunt of highway construction for 20 years, culminating in the East LA Interchange in 1961, where four major highways (I-5, I-10, Rt. 101, and Rt. 60) cut right through Boyle Heights (Estrada 2005, 290). As urban historian Gilbert Estrada succinctly puts it, "Ravine residents were displaced to accommodate the Dodgers; East Los Angeles residents were expelled to build freeways" (2005, 289). While freeways decimated East LA, plans to build freeways in White suburbia were scrapped (Estrada 2005, 290). The Interchange, called a "spaghetti bowl" by contractors, is "one of the most concentrated pockets of air pollution in America" (Estrada 2005, 301).

The effects of these environmental injustices are ongoing. As Pulido demonstrates, there is ample evidence showing that environmental racism—in the form of environmental hazards like air toxins, toxic waste, and waste management—disproportionately affects Latinx communities, especially in East LA (2000, 20–1). To show people the extent of this environmental racism, East Yard Communities for Environmental Justice organizes what it calls the "LA River Toxic Tour," during which cyclists travel 17 miles along the river from East LA to Long Beach, experiencing firsthand the effects of ultra-fine particles (mostly caused by transportation energy) and urban heat islands (Guzman 2016). In *Touch the Water*, Hébert connects past displacements and injustices, like those in Chavez Ravine and East LA, to the action in the play, in which Luis's house is to be razed for a pocket park. In doing so, she suggests that environmental improvement is no different from industrial development if it lacks a holistic approach. Similarly, the set of *Touch the Water*—littered with tires, shopping carts, and trash collected from the surrounding area—is a material reminder of the ongoing effects of freeways, industrialization, and deindustrialization in East LA. Making visible often deliberately ignored acts of environmental racism, *Touch the Water* highlights what sociologists Melvin Oliver and Thomas Shapiro call the "sedimentation of racial inequality" (1995, 5). Revealing the ongoing legacies of spatio-environmental injustices through the set design and the characters' lived experiences, the production suggests that even when harmful effects are invisible, like ultrafine particles from emissions, they are no less impactful.

A question of prime importance in revitalization projects, then, is who is improving the quality of life for whom and for what purpose. Hébert considers this question in her focus on contested perceptions, conceptions, and lived experiences of the river. While, for Joe—and the developers who bulldozed through Chavez Ravine and East LA in the mid-twentieth century—the area is perceived as a slum, to residents it is home. In *Touch the Water*, Luis is just one example of the many people who will be displaced if Jade's and Joe's project, which entails greening 700 streets, is completed. While Joe claims that USACE representatives went to every house explaining the greening project, tellingly, none of the residents seem to have been informed. This hints at the city's long history of imposing economic and environmental "development" on East LA without consulting the actual inhabitants, a problem that exists in largely White, US environmental organizations as well.[12] The failure to consult residents is not only unjust but also a missed opportunity; as Latinx scholars argue, "Latinx cultures hold the potential to make visible key aspects of the exploitation of the earth" because of their diverse cultural values and their own historical and ongoing lived experiences of exploitation (Wald et al. 2019, 3). Although the USACE initiative in the play will most likely improve the river quality for flora and fauna, it may adversely affect neighborhood residents already suffering the impacts of spatio-environmental injustice. Not only will Luis lose his home, but—as Isa points out—locals will now have to contend with an influx of curious visitors eager to enjoy the beautified river—or to gawk at residents like the character Ruth Betsy, who lives in an abandoned car in the river and will undoubtedly be displaced at some point during the revitalization project.[13] Ruth and Luis are examples of what environmental studies scholar Sarah Jaquette Ray calls "ecological others," bodies that are treated with "environmental disgust" and seen as "bad" for nature (2013, 2). For environmentalists like Joe and Jade, cleaning up the river means removing unsightly bodies and homes—Luis's condemned house and Betsy's car. In critiquing the ecological othering of marginalized characters, Hébert speaks not only to the history of gentrification and environmental disregard for people in LA but also to that in US cities and environmental organizations more broadly.

Although Hébert is critical of Jade's and Joe's project for its failure to consider the people of Frogtown, she nonetheless emphasizes the need for environmental improvement. For instance, the failing health of Ridley the sea turtle serves as a warning of the danger of leaving the river in its current condition. Poisoned by urban runoff like oil and antifreeze and choked by a plastic bag around his neck, Ridley gradually dies. The turtle's fate illustrates the need for greening projects like Joe's and Jade's, which involves filtering street runoff into a gravel catchment basin underground (Hébert 2009, 48). Such a project might not only improve the quality of life for the water, flora and fauna, but also for East LA residents, many of whom fish in the river. Materializing the interdependency of "spatiality-historicality-sociality" (Soja 1996, 3), Hébert highlights the need for environmental improvements, even as she suggests that equitable change is only possible if residents who have been excluded and displaced by environmentalists, engineers, and developers are brought into the decision-making process.

At the same time, the complex ecology of the urban LA River means that, in addition to considering multivalent human perspectives and needs, any environmental project must also consider the many native and non-native species that have amalgamated in the river over the years. Fletcher uses the word "freakology" to describe the river's seamless blend of organic and artificial elements caused by urban runoff (2008, 42). Although pollution cannot be said to benefit the ecosystem, it has nonetheless become integrated into the environment. As Fletcher points out,

> recent studies suggest that, although trash obviously has its own hazards for ecology, it has become a vital component to the riparian ecosystems; loose debris gets incorporated into the vegetative community, binding and forming a structural substrate that holds organic nutrients and silts
>
> *(2008, 42).*

Examples of this are visible in the production's set, where plants grow out of tires, through paper cups, and around an abandoned car. Of course, Fletcher is not suggesting that the debris should remain perfectly intact, but rather that environmentalists should consider the needs of the actual environment rather than attempt to return to a river paradise that never was. For instance, several non-native plants have sprung up or been planted along the river over the last two centuries. To uproot all these plants simply because they are not native is to traumatize the complex river ecosystem rather than to recognize how it has adapted and evolved (Fletcher 2008, 46). Thus, in addition to considering the needs of human and animal residents, river environmentalism must strive to work within rather than overhaul the existing ecosystem. In spatializing sometimes contradictory perspectives and needs, Hébert demonstrates, as tourism scholar Abhik Chakraborty argues, that while it is easy to recognize that the human control of rivers is anti-ecological, it is much harder to propose viable alternatives (2018, 2).

Non-Indigenous Representations of Tongva Spatiality

In staging the multi-perspectival perceptions, conceptions, and lived experiences of the river, Hébert stresses the importance of taking diverse animal, riparian, and human needs into consideration. While the human characters have a vested interest in the river, so too do the animals, all of whom demonstrate their unique dependency on the river. For example, Ridley the sea turtle, poisoned by antifreeze and wounded by a fishing hook, is dying when he calls out, "Touch the water, I need to touch the water" (Hébert 2009, 57). All the characters rely on the river in various ways, and the polyphony of voices and needs within the play demonstrate a mutual dependence on the river for physical and spiritual sustenance. At the same time, the non-Indigenous writing of Tongva characters presents representational challenges and questions worth considering further, given that non-Indigenous playwrights like Hébert are still grappling with what it means to stage Indigenous characters ethically and generatively.

For example, Maniisar, a "ghost of a Tong-va girl killed in the river long ago," is summoned from the river's concrete bed only to vanish once she has helped Luis and Isa forgive each other by appealing to their shared love of the river (Hébert 2009). A combination of healer and spiritualist, Maniisar uses lyrical music to lead the characters to "channel the river" (Hébert 2009, 39). Thus, the seemingly omniscient spirit, who knows the characters' needs and desires better than they do, acts as the play's spiritual and environmental guide. It is not surprising that Maniisar, as a spectral figure from the afterlife, would be represented as more in tune with the river than the living characters. Depicted as a three-foot puppet in a long shroud and an inanimate mask for a face, Maniisar is operated by two women who also give her voice.[14] In her puppet form, she is more abstracted than the human and animal characters, all played by people, and is more ethereal than material. The puppeteers hold her by stick arms and bob her about in the air, floating her toward and away from the other characters. Some of Maniisar's statements are cryptic and the operators' eerie delivery only makes them seem more mysterious. The spirit is already marked by her otherworldly demeanor, but her Tongva heritage, which she mentions early on, also separates her from the other characters. When she sees the water, Maniisar asks, "What have they done to my river?" (Hébert 2009, 7). Calling herself a "river-ghost-girl," the spirit's attunement with the river is contrasted with Luis's and Isa's disconnection with the water, themselves, and each other (Hébert 2009, 7).

On the one hand, the decision to include Tongva characters, Maniisar from the past and Luis from the present,[15] is an important one that materializes the lived experiences of Tongva people whom the US has tried to erase both then and now. On the other hand, as eco-theater scholar Lisa Woynarski argues, inserting an Indigenous savior into a Western, linear narrative can be problematic given that most Indigenous storytelling is nonlinear (2015, 187, building on Stanlake 2009). Likewise, the dualistic alignment of Maniisar with a pristine, pre-contact paradise essentializes the ghost and, by proxy, pre-colonial Tongva people. As anthropologist Shepard Krech argues, the stereotype of the "Ecological Indian" as "ecologist and conservationist" has been a staple of American and European literature and art since the beginning of North American colonization (1999, 16). It has been used to obscure the imperialistic displacement and genocide of Indigenous peoples by focusing on a romantic oneness with nature rather than on how White colonizers forcefully removed people from their land. It persists today, forcing Indigenous peoples into stereotypically environmental roles or what Seymour calls "unfair performative binds" (2018, 152). Anthropologist Kimberly TallBear (Sisseton Wahpeton Oyate) posits that the trope "helps perpetuate divisive identity politics underway in Indian Country, and de-legitimizes the efforts of tribes to govern ourselves if we are not perceived as *traditional* according to a narrow, generic, and romanticized view of what is traditional" (2000, 2, emphasis in original). For example, the Makah tribe of

Washington is a whaling community that has experienced legal barriers and protests from animal activists who deem their whaling practices anti-ecological (Murphy 2022). Indigenous peoples face pressure to perform ecologically within the narrow, Western binds of the Ecological Indian stereotype, while, at the same time, because they live in what decolonial theorist Macarena Gómez-Barris calls "extractive zones" (2017, xvii–xx), they are also forced to defend their land and water from the onslaught of extractive capitalism.

In *Touch the Water*, many of the characters like Luis, Isa, and Roger identify with the river, but, until the end of the play, it is only Maniisar who is represented as attuned with the river. For example, early in the play, Isa, working on her scraggly community garden in the river, sows a white sage/Kasili seed, a venerated blessing or prayer plant in Tongva culture. Twenty-four hours later, "Maniisar flies down to the hole in the concrete and causes the sage to emerge," which unites all the characters; her work done, Maniisar proclaims, "Speak, my river, speak" before disappearing back into the concrete (Hébert 2009, 69–71). As a "river-ghost-[Tongva]-girl," Maniisar is not only signified by her heritage and ghostliness but also by her gender (Hébert 2009, 7). In ecofeminist Noël Sturgeon's words, the generalized category of "indigenous woman" is often seen as the "ultimate ecofeminist," since, historically, both women and Indigenous peoples have been linked to nature (1997, 115). Maniisar's ability to grow the sage plant and to speak to the river read as essentialized tropes of the female Ecological Indian.

Importantly, the character of Luis serves as a contrast to Maniisar: whereas Maniisar grew up in pre-colonial times, the "daughter of the Chief," Luis introduces himself as the "son of nobody" (Hébert 2009, 5). His name, Luis Otcho-o Authemont, connects him to the river, because Otcho'o is one of the names the Tongva people have for the river (Linton 2005). And, yet, like his childhood friend Isa, he connects to the river's trauma rather than its vitality. As he sings early on: "I am this river, muck and all/Wounded, scarred, choked with crap/Still not still" (Hébert 2009, 13). Having suffered generational traumas like being beaten by his father, Luis sees the river's mistreatment and confinement as an extension of his own upbringing and imprisonment. Living in the same space of the LA River at very different times, Maniisar and Luis embody the contrast between pre-colonial and neocolonial, urban experiences of the river. Revealing the spatio-historical layers of the river, the characters demonstrate what Soja calls "the consequential geographies of justice," meaning "how social and spatial processes intertwine to produce oppressive as well as enabling geographies" (2010, 2, 193). Weaving together the social and environmental injustices suffered by Luis, Isa (whose family was displaced by freeways and development), the poisoned Ridley, and other characters, Hébert stages consequential geographies. At the same time, since Maniisar and Luis are the only explicitly Indigenous characters in a play by a non-Indigenous writer, their characterization takes on increased symbolic weight, signaling the need for more representation. As Goeman writes, "I also encourage us to move toward spatialities of belonging that do not bind, contain, or fix our relationship to land and each other in ways that limit our definitions of self and community" (2013, 11). While Maniisar and

Luis share a connection to the LA River, they are bound to it, incapable of forming other spatial communities or moving on from it.

"We Are the River": Riparian Projection, Identification, and Longing

In addition to its non-Indigenous representation of Indigenous characters, *Touch the Water*, like many eco-performances, must consider how best to represent the environment, in this case the central figure and setting of the LA River. Unlike the animal characters, Corvus and Ridley, the river never speaks but is instead spoken for. In addition to Luis, who sees his own trauma mapped on the river, there is Isa who, grieving the murder of her younger brother, sees an angry river. Until the end of the play, each human character projects their own desires and emotional state onto the river. For example, Maniisar encourages Isa to "channel the river" rather than her own anger and guilt (Hébert 2009, 39). However, Isa's attempt to do so only leads her to project her own anger onto it: "The river wants to flood, wants to kill. The river wants vengeance" (Hébert 2009, 40). Unable to imagine the river beyond her own grief, Isa learns nothing from it—the way it moves, the way it survives, the way it adapts. When Maniisar tells Isa that *she* is the one who wants vengeance, not the river, the woman defiantly responds, "I am the river," only to finally admit that, in her current emotional state, she cannot channel anything but her own anger and grief (Hébert 2009, 40). Isa's confession illustrates the central problem of speaking for an environmental other; it is difficult to do without one's own feelings and beliefs shaping the perception of space.

Through the characters' projections onto the river, Hébert highlights the limits of representation and suggests that human identification with nonhuman nature can be untrustworthy. Slyly sending up many of the characters' tendencies to gender or personify the river, Hébert exposes the ways in which people cast the river in their own image, or in the image that is most helpful for their own purposes. For instance, to Roger Vadim! the river is feminine and mystical, fighting through her manmade entrapments, while, to Luis, the river is masculine in its brute strength and power. The latter imagines the river as himself whereas the former imagines the river in a helpless, weakened state that will make people more sympathetic to it. Luis needs the river to fight back where he himself failed to do so, while Vadim!, as his chosen code name suggests, needs the river to play damsel in distress to his heroics. Just as Hébert suggests that some environmental action is misguided, she implies that some environmental representation is misrepresentative.

At the same time, the playwright insinuates that while humans should not pass their own emotions off as the environment's sentiments, they can nonetheless experience healing through environmental connection. For example, after confessing that she cannot channel or call the river beyond her own anger, Isa picks up a stone to throw at Luis's house. Maniisar urges her to place the stone in the river, singing: "Pour out your rage and fury, drain all your righteous wrath/The water's never judge or jury, it's just seeking out the easiest, the simplest path" (Hébert 2009, 41).[16] Importantly, rather than personify the river, Maniisar emphasizes its physical properties, the way in which it flows. While Isa has previously attempted to improve her environment, starting a languishing community garden on the river's embankments, her anger and grief leave her disconnected from the river, the garden, and her neighbors. Consumed by guilt and resentment over her brother's death, Isa cannot grow a healthy garden—or unite a community around it—until she forgives herself and Luis. Catharsis only comes for Isa when she lies down in the river: Maniisar asks her to "Look beneath the surface. Take in the water, what do you see?" (Hébert 2009, 65). Isa lays down and replies, "I see...Nothing" (Hébert 2009, 65). Rather than claim to know what the river feels without actually experiencing it, Isa admits that she cannot even see it. In considering how one can speak of a traumatic event without betraying it, comparative literature scholar Cathy Caruth suggests that witnessing begins from a place of incomprehension, a place of not knowing and not seeing from the site of trauma (1996, 56). Prior to this moment, Isa vehemently insists that her brother Rana's death was Luis's fault, just as she insists that the river is furious over its channelization. It is only when she physically connects with the water, laying down in it, that she can relinquish her preconceptions and resentments.

Hébert thus suggests that a reciprocal relationship with the environment cannot be forged without a physical connection to place that continuously extends beyond oneself and one's private patch of land. It is not enough to act upon or for the environment, as Jade, Joe, and Isa believe they do. Without recognizing their interdependence with the river, plants, animals, and other humans, Isa and the other characters fail to establish mutually beneficial relationships. After the sage plant grows with Maniisar's help, the play ends with all the human and animal characters drinking or touching the water and, as an ensemble, declaring, "We are the river" (Hébert 2009, 71). Shifting from an individually centered identification with the river, in which they project themselves onto the water, they now speak as a collective:

We are each other's homes
Longing for shelter but destined to roam
Connecting us one and all
Streaming with life, pulled to answer the call

Drop by drop by drop
We are the river

(Hébert 2009, 72).

On the one hand, the finality and certainty of this declaration is a bit troubling. The statement "We are the river" seems to swallow the river whole, assimilating it with the human characters. On the other hand, through touching and experiencing the water directly, the characters' spatial perceptions of it evolve. Recognizing the river as "streaming with life" despite being displaced, like many of the characters, the ensemble collectively begins to channel the river, rather than their individualistic desires, "drop by drop by drop" (Hébert 2009, 72). Staging shifting spatialities, *Touch the Water* embraces collectivism while highlighting uneven spatio-environmental injustices, creating an expansive and multilayered sense of place.

Performing Spatiality in the LA River

Kwon argues that the uneven conditions between one place and another, one person's spatial experience and another person's, is what current site-specific art must address or else sites really do become "one place after another" (2004, 166). Focusing on contested perceived, conceived, and lived productions of space in the LA River, this chapter not only highlights spatial particularities unique to the LA River, but also exposes disproportionate scales of spatio-environmental injustice embedded within the river's ecology. Both performances analyzed here represent the river in radically different ways: *Chinatown* highlights water corruption and the properties of water and *Touch the Water* offers multi-perspectival, material interpretations of the river. Despite their differences, both works deploy socio-spatial practices that foreground the historically displaced, abstracted LA River and highlight its ongoing spatial production. By emphasizing the river's particularities of place, these performances turn the typically invisible site of the LA River into one of heightened visibility.

To varying degrees, they both interact with and in the river, casting it as a pivotal character in the action rather than a mere backdrop. For instance, in *Chinatown*, the urban Gittes must go down to the river and observe it closely to unravel the city's water corruption; stumbling down the river's steep slope until his loafer-clad foot plops into the water, the detective is taken out of his element—the concrete city above the river—and forced into contact with the river's elements—its changeable water levels, salinity, and scattered rocks. Meanwhile, *Touch the Water*, staged on the banks of the LA River, is a meditation on the necessity and joys of establishing a life-long relationship with the river. Fostering multivalent understandings of the river, the play imagines a future in which all people may engage with it more fully—swimming, fishing, and navigating its waters. Together, both performances stage highly spatialized relationships with the LA River, in which divergent perceived, conceived, and lived spatial understandings of the river tussle and tangle. Materializing the interplay of Lefebvre's spatial triad, the performances highlight diverse spatial realities, misconceptions, and potentialities. In *Chinatown*, water gushes, gurgles, drips, and flows. In *Touch the Water*, a miniature river stands in for the actual river just behind it, rippling and gleaming in the moonlight, waiting. This is the LA River.

Notes

1 The lake is more polluted in the winter's wet season, when urban runoff like trash and bacteria pours into the more than 2,000 storm drains along the river (Guerin 2018).
2 Like many distorted Spanish names in the Southwest, "Angeleno" is a misspelling of "Angelino" or, even more accurately, "Angeleño."

3 The Tongva people lived in California for 7,000 years and were renamed "Gabrielinos" following Spanish colonization in the eighteenth century. The Gabrielino-Tongva Indian Tribe was officially recognized by California in 1994 but, as of 2022, has not been federally recognized ("Tribal History" 2022).

4 To hear from the environmental group representatives directly, listen to their interview on Eco Justice Radio (Eidt 2021: https://tinyurl.com/mvkmavzt).

5 While most Owens Valley scholars at least touch on the impact that the film *Chinatown* (1974) had on public opinion, few go into much depth. Sociologist John Walton (1992) is unique in that he not only highlights the influence of the film but also of early twentieth century literature that dramatizes the Owens Valley events.

6 Ten thousand years ago, Hokan-speaking peoples lived near the river before being "absorbed into or displaced by the Tongva" peoples (McMillin 2018, 153).

7 It is important to acknowledge that Polanski plead guilty to the charge of unlawful sexual intercourse with a minor in the US in 1977 and has since been accused of rape by multiple women. While I condemn his actions and do not think that an artist can be fully separate from his art, I agree with philosopher Mary Beth Willard that art is not "fungible" (2021, 13–14). *Chinatown*'s treatment of water politics and materiality is unique and worth examining further.

8 For a better understanding of how the injustices toward imprisoned Japanese Americans, Indigenous peoples, and Owens Valley ranchers are interconnected, see the documentary *Manzanar, Diverted: When Water Becomes Dust* (Kaneko 2022).

9 Much has been written about vision and doubled vision in *Chinatown*; for instance, Man argues that Gittes has "limited vision" which is "clarified" too late (1994b, 144–5).

10 For more on the blue humanities, see DeLoughrey (2019), Dobrin (2021), Ingersoll (2016), and Sharpe (2016).

11 In 2009, when the play was produced, fishing with a license was the only activity permitted in the river.

12 Green 2.0, an environmental watchdog organization that has tracked diversity among environmental NGOs for the last five years, found upward trends in POC representation in 2021. However, it notes that environmental organizations "will need to greatly increase their rate of change (from 30% POC to 50% POC) to keep up with the country's changing demographics" (Green 2.0 and Puritty 2021, 15).

13 In April 2022, LA Councilmember Nithya Raman received $1.7 million from the state to create permanent housing for the more than 60 people who live along the river (Herández 2022).

14 The overall effect is similar to a Bunraku puppet.

15 Luis never explicitly identifies himself as Tongva, saying he is "a little bit of everything" when asked (Hébert 2009, 33), but Ruth Betsy, who claims to have known his grandfather, suggests he is.

16 Music by Shishir Kurup and lyrics by Kurup and Hébert.

References

Belton, John. 1991. "Language, Oedipus, and Chinatown." *MLN* 106 (5): 933–950.

Braun, Bruce. 2005. "Environmental Issues: Writing a More-Than-Human Urban Geography." *Progress in Human Geography* 29 (5): 635–650.

Caruth, Cathy. 1996. *Unclaimed Experience: Trauma, Narrative, and History*. Baltimore: Johns Hopkins University Press.

Chakraborty, Abhik. 2018. "Introduction: The Rivers and Society Debate Revisited." In *Rivers and Society: Landscapes, Governance, and Livelihoods*, edited by Malcolm Cooper, Abhik Chakraborty, and Shamik Chakraborty, 1–8. London: Routledge.

Chinatown. 1974. Dir. Roman Polanski. Perf. Jack Nicholson and Faye Dunaway. Paramount Pictures.

City News Service. 2022. "County OKs LA River master plan, despite opposition from environmental groups." *Spectrum News* 1, June 14. https://tinyurl.com/2b67de78.

Colgan, David. 2020. "Effort to Limit Dust Pollution in Owens Valley Is Advancing, but Still Room to Improve." *UCLA Newsroom*, March 3. https://tinyurl.com/yf26adhm.

Davis, Mike. 1998. *Ecology of Fear: Los Angeles and the Imagination of Disaster*. New York: Metropolitan Books.

Davis-Young, Katherine. 2016. "UCLA project maps LA's indigenous communities," *Take Two. KPCC*. https://tinyurl.com/58ds9dss.

DeLoughrey, Elizabeth M. 2019. *Allegories of the Anthropocene*. Durham, NC: Duke University Press.

Dobrin, Sidney I. 2021. *Blue Ecocriticism and the Oceanic Imperative*. New York: Routledge.

Eidt, Jack. 2021. "Los Angeles River Revitalization: A Master Plan Gone Awry." *Eco Justice Radio*, April 2. https://tinyurl.com/mvkmavzt.

Elrick, Ted and the Friends of the Los Angeles River. 2007. *Images of America: Los Angeles River*. Charleston, SC: Arcadia Publishing.

Estrada, Gilbert. 2005. "If You Build It, They Will Move: The Los Angeles Freeway System and the Displacement of Mexican East Los Angeles, 1944–1972." *Southern California Quarterly* 87 (3): 287–315.

Evans, Robert. 1994. *The Kid Stays in the Picture*. London: Aurum Press.

Fletcher, David. 2008. "Flood Control Freakology: Los Angeles River Watershed." In *The Infrastructural City: Networked Ecologies in Los Angeles*, edited by Kazys Varnelis, 36–51. Barcelona: Actar Distribution.

Goeman, Mishuana. 2013. *Mark My Words: Native Women Mapping Our Nations*. Minneapolis: University of Minnesota Press.

Gottlieb, Robert. 2007. *Reinventing Los Angeles: Nature and Community in the Global City*. Cambridge, MA: MIT Press.

Green 2.0 and Chandler Puritty. 2021. "2021 NGO & Foundation Transparency Report Card." https://tinyurl.com/3ujd48h4.

Guerin, Emily. 2018. "LA Explained: The Los Angeles River." *LAist*, June 22. https://tinyurl.com/474fhxrv.

Gumprecht, Blake. 1999, *The Los Angeles River: Its Life, Death, and Possible Rebirth*. Baltimore: Johns Hopkins University Press.

Gumprecht, Blake. 2005. "Who Killed the Los Angeles River?" In *Land of Sunshine: An Environmental History of Metropolitan Los Angeles*, edited by William Deverell and Greg Hise, 115–134. Pittsburgh, PA: University of Pittsburgh Press.

Guzman, Christian L. 2016. "Exposing Injustice at the LA River: A Bike's-Eye View from Maywood to Long Beach." *Random Lengths News*, September 2. https://tinyurl.com/3a5w6k65.

Hébert, Julie. 2009. *Touch the Water: A River Play*. Dir. Juliette Carrillo. Cornerstone Theater Company. Los Angeles, May 28–June 21. https://tinyurl.com/5yz65uyy.

Hernández, Caitlin. 2022. "Permanent Homes Coming for Unhoused People Living by LA River." *LAist*, April 1. https://tinyurl.com/bdcyb72d.

Ingersoll, Karin Amimoto. 2016. *Waves of Knowing: A Seascape Epistemology*. Durham, NC: Duke University Press.

Johnson, Gaye Theresa. 2014. "Spatial Entitlement: Race, Displacement, and Sonic Reclamation in Postwar Los Angeles." In *Black and Brown in Los Angeles: Beyond Conflict and Coalition*, edited by Josh Kun and Laura Pulido, 316–340. Berkeley: University of California Press.

Kaika, Mara. 2005. *Cities of Flows: Modernity, Nature, and the City*. New York: Routledge.

Kaneko, Ann. 2022. *Manzanar, Diverted: When Water Becomes Dust*. KPBS TV. Aired July 18.

Kelly, Jason M. 2018. "Preface." In *Rivers of the Anthropocene*, edited by Jason M. Kelly, Philip V. Scarpino, Helen Berry, James Syvitski, and Michel Meybeck, xv–xxvi. Oakland, CA: University of California Press.

King, Homay. 2010. *Lost in Translation: Orientalism, Cinema, and the Enigmatic Signifier*. Durham, NC: Duke University Press.

Krech, Shephard, III. 1999. *The Ecological Indian: Myth and History*. New York: W.W. Norton & Company.

Kwon, Miwon. *One Place After Another: Site-Specific Art and Locational Identity*. Cambridge, MA: MIT Press, 2004.

LA River Master Plan. 2020. Prepared by Geosyntec, Olin, and Gehry Partners, LLP for Los Angeles County and Los Angeles County Public Works. https://tinyurl.com/4se8btwv.

Lefebvre, Henri. 1991. *The Production of Space*. Trans. Donald Nicholson-Smith. Malden, MA: Blackwell Publishing.

Libecap, Gary D. 2007. *Owens Valley Revisited: A Reassessment of the West's First Great Water Transfer*. Stanford: Stanford University Press.

Linton, Joe. 2005. *Down by the Los Angeles River: Friends of the Los Angeles River's Official Guide*. Berkeley, CA: Wilderness Press.

Llamoca, Janice. 2017. "Remembering the Lost Communities Buried under Center Field." *Code Sw!tch*, October 31. https://tinyurl.com/48yvrawf.

Man, Glenn. 1994a. "Marginality and Centrality: The Myth of Asia in 1970s Hollywood." *East-West Film Journal* 8 (1): 52–67.

Man, Glenn. 1994b. *Radical Visions: American Film Renaissance, 1967–1976*. Westport, CT: Greenwood Press.

Marsh, E.M. 2012. *A Concrete Reality: Spatial Injustice and the Los Angeles River*. London, UK: London School of Economics and Political Science.

Maxfield, James. 1996. *Fatal Woman: Sources of Male Anxiety in American Film Noir, 1941–1991*. Cranbury, NJ: Farleigh Dickinson University Press.

McMillin, T.S. 2018. "The End of the Los Angeles River: A paradox." In *Rivers and Society: Landscapes, Governance, and Livelihoods*, edited by Malcolm Cooper, Abhik Chakraborty, and Shamik Chakraborty, 150–168. London: Routledge.

Meares, Hadley. 2016. "Genocide, Slavery, and L.A.'s Role in the Decimation of Native Californians." *KCET*, June 29. https://tinyurl.com/2p8h2uct.

Murphy, Andi. 2022. "The Revival of Indigenous Subsistence Whaling Hangs in the Balance." *Civil Eats*, February 8. https://tinyurl.com/mtj5fvww.

Nadeau, Remi. 1950. *The Water Seekers*. Santa Barbara: Crest Publishers.

Napoletano, Brian M., John Bellamy Foster, and Brett Clark. 2021. "Antinomies of space and nature or an open totality? Neil Smith and Henri Lefebvre on nature and society." *Human Geography*, November. https://doi.org/10.1177/19427786211051384.

Neighborhood Data for Social Change. 2021. "The Most Pressing Environmental Health Conditions for Latinx Communities in Southeast L.A." *KCET*, September 9. https://tinyurl.com/y3mpyfce.

Novak, Phillip. 2007. "The Chinatown Syndrome." *Criticism* 49 (3): 255–283.

Oliver, Melvin L. and Shapiro, M. Thomas. 1995. *Black Wealth, White Wealth*. New York: Routledge.

Post, Jason Michael and Perry Carter. 2022. "Unnatural Nature: Anglers Reimaginings of the Los Angeles River as Parkland." *Geographical Review* 112 (2): 207–227.

Price, Jennifer. 2001. "In the Beginning." *LA Weekly*, August 8. https://tinyurl.com/52vd3mw7.

Prud'homme, Alex. 2011. *The Ripple Effect: The Fate of Freshwater in the Twenty-First Century*. New York: Scribner.

Pulido, Laura. 2000. "Rethinking Environmental Racism: White Privilege and Urban Development in Southern California." *Annals of the Association of American Geographers* 90: 12–40.

Ray, Sarah Jaquette. 2013. *The Ecological Other: Environmental Exclusion in American Culture*. Tucson: University of Arizona Press.

Schaefer, Standard. 2005. "The L.A. River." In *Water & Power*, 59. New York: Agincourt Press.

Schexnayder, C.J. 2022. "The Reimagining of the LA River." *ENR California*, July 15. https://tinyurl.com/6622zbsy.

Scott, Ian S. 2007. "'Either You Bring the Water to L.A. or You Bring L.A. to the Water': Politics, Perceptions and the Pursuit of History in Roman Polanski's *Chinatown*." *European Journal of American Studies* 2 (2): 1–12.

Seymour, Nicole. 2018. *Bad Environmentalism: Irony and Irreverence in the Ecological Age*. Minneapolis, MN: University of Minnesota Press.

Sharpe, Christina. 2016. *In the Wake: On Blackness and Being*. Durham, NC: Duke University Press.

Shetley, Vernon. 1999. "Incest and Capital in *Chinatown*." *MLN* 114 (5): 1092–1109.

Soja, Edward W. 1996. *Thirdspace: Journeys to Los Angeles and Other Real-and-Imagined Places*. Malden, MA: Blackwell Publishers.

Soja, Edward W. 2010. *Seeking Spatial Justice*. Minneapolis: University of Minnesota Press.

Stanlake, Christy. 2009. *Native American Drama: A Critical Perspective*. Cambridge: Cambridge University Press.

Sturgeon, Noël. 1997. *Ecofeminist Natures: Race, Gender, Feminist Theory and Political Action*. New York: Routledge.

TallBear, Kimberly. 2000. "Shepard Krech's *The Ecological Indian*: One Indian's Perspective." *International Institute for Indigenous Resource Management Publications*, September, 1–5. https://tinyurl.com/mrxm3hf5.

Towne, Robert. 1997. *Chinatown*. New York: Grove Press.

"Tribal History." 2022. Gabrielino-Tongva India Tribe. https://tinyurl.com/9wt978hf.

United States Census Bureau. 2021. "Quick Facts: East Los Angeles, CDP, California." https://tinyurl.com/h234eb5v.

Vadim, Roger. 1986. *Bardot, Deneuve, Fonda: My Life with the Three Most Beautiful Women in the World*. New York: Simon and Schuster.

Valle, Victor. 2009. *City of Industry: Genealogies of Power in Southern California*. New Brunswick, NJ: Rutgers University Press.

Wald, Sarah D., David J. Vázquez, Priscilla Solis Ybarra, and Sarah Jaquette Ray. 2019. "Introduction: Why Latinx Environmentalisms?" In *Latinx Environmentalisms: Place, Justice, and the Decolonial*, edited by Wald et al., 1–34. Philadelphia: Temple University Press.

Walton, John. 1992. *Western Times and Water Wars: State, Culture, and Rebellion in California*. Berkeley: University of California Press.

Wei, Clarissa. 2016. "How the Owens Valley Paiute Made the Desert Bloom." *KCET*, December 15. https://tinyurl.com/2p9fsb2a.

Willard, Mary Beth. 2021. *Why It's OK to Enjoy the Work of Immortal Artists*. New York: Routledge.

Woolery, Laurie. 2012. *Telephone interview with author*, September 10.

Woynarski, Lisa. 2015. "Ecological Sentinels: Indigenous Heroes or Colonial Cliché?" *RiDE: The Journal of Applied Theatre and Performance* 20 (2): 186–190.

5

PERFORMING ECOLOGICAL IRRESOLUTION IN THE 2010 BP OIL SPILL

In a 2014 episode of HBO's *VICE*, Shane Smith interviews Louisianans still suffering the effects of the 2010 BP oil spill in the Gulf of Mexico. Smith appears surprised to learn that negative environmental impacts, ranging from respiratory and skin issues to mutated, oily seafood, are still emerging four years after the spill was supposedly cleaned up. But, as Plaquemines Parish's Coastal Zone Director, P.J. Hahn explains, once BP and the Coast Guard sunk the oil, it was "out of sight, out of mind. There's no story if you don't see the oil" (2014, 00:12:50–00:12:55). This refrain of invisibility is echoed throughout the episode by victims who understand all too well the direct link between visibility and media viability, between invisibility and limited liability. The episode's title, "Crude Awakening," signals itself as a wakeup call, a material refutation of the corporate and federal narrative that the disaster was cleaned up and resolved when its oily seepage was no longer visible on the water's surface.

As other oil spills like the 1989 *Exxon Valdez* spill in Alaska suggest, the long-term effects of fossil fuels stretch far into the past and future. According to human ecologist Andreas Malm, today's weather may be a "product of past emissions" while today's car emissions "are so many invisible missiles aimed at the future" (2016). The emissions of the Industrial Revolution have now disproportionately begun to affect people, particularly islanders, just as today's emissions will have dire consequences for future generations. Where Malm considers the fossil economy's emergence from a historical standpoint, tracing its origins to steam-powered coal in Britain, cultural theorist Imre Szeman takes a literary approach, analyzing "existing 'end of oil' narratives" and what they might teach a left with the unenviable job of thinking beyond oil (2007, 808). While these narratives diverge in their focus—be it geopolitics, technology, or the environment—Szeman finds them equally "unable to mobilize or produce any response to a disaster we know is a direct result of capitalism—limitless accumulation" (2007, 821). I would posit that state, corporate, and individual inaction in the face

DOI: 10.4324/9781003203766-6

of catastrophic, fossil-fueled climate change is only partly due to global entrenchment in a fossil economy. Another major factor is the disaster narrative, which, because of its calamitous quality, lends itself to monolithic crises and solutions perceived only in the short-term. The very word "disaster," notes ecocritic Stephanie LeMenager, is often a misnomer, because it comes "[f]rom the Greek *astron*, or star" and "suggests an unforeseen calamity arising from the unfavorable position of a planet" (2011, 26). Given the excesses and deregulations within the US fossil economy, the consequences of petrocapital are anything but unforeseen and, yet, when predictable outcomes like the 2010 BP oil spill erupt, they are met with shock and disbelief. Disasters are cataclysms that wash away past and future causations in their focus on the immediate crisis.

In a mediascape where recency is the primary consideration, to speak in the language of disaster is to speak in the present tense. As ecocritic Rob Nixon argues, visceral, sudden disasters, those with "burning towers" and "exploding heads," are easier to narrate than stories of long-term disasters with invisible, gradual consequences (2011, 3). The latter are what Nixon calls instances of slow violence, "a violence that occurs gradually and out of sight, a violence of delayed destruction that is dispersed across time and space, an attritional violence that is typically not viewed as violence at all" (2011, 2). Slow violence may seem like a contradiction of terms given that violence is typically associated with forceful outbursts, and yet the damage it causes is even more powerful because of its gradualness, relative invisibility, and breadth. For Nixon, the primary question is how, "in an age when media venerate the spectacle," we can create compelling stories about gradual emergencies like climate change (2011, 3). For me, the question is how, even in the throes of an explosive, mesmerizing disaster, we can tell multivalent stories that speak to both the immediate violence and the slow violence that precedes and follows, trickling out so diffusely that it is often made invisible and truncated from the hypervisual disaster narrative. One prime example of the combined effects of spectacular and slow violence is the 2010 BP oil spill, which began with the explosion of the *Deepwater Horizon* oil rig that killed 11 rig workers before turning into an ongoing saga of gushing oil. Represented by the media, artists, and BP itself, the spill produced rivaling narratives of hypervisibility and invisibility, explosivity and protraction. Thus, I am less interested in the 2010 spill itself than in how its subsequent narratives represented, misrepresented, or subverted the event's paradoxical tropes of immediacy and futurity, visibility and invisibility.

Because it was an unfolding drama, the 2010 spill initially remained highly visible in the news. However, its coverage came to a sudden halt when, after 87 long days of mishaps, BP succeeded in partially capping the well on the Gulf of Mexico's ocean floor. While the near complete drop-off in media coverage implied an end to the disaster, the intensive ad campaign by BP during and after the spill sought to manage the catastrophe's optics, suggesting a narratival resolution and, with it, an ecologically impossible return to the status quo. In other words, because the scope of BP's and the news' narratives were limited to the present—the explosion and the oil leak—it became possible to represent the disaster as fixed, solved, complete when the leak was plugged, even though its far-reaching consequences were just beginning. Similarly, while the gripping disaster film *Deepwater Horizon* (2016) gives the rig's explosion the big budget treatment, it fails to consider the systemic oil deregulation that preceded and followed the blaze and the long-term ecological effects of the spill. Although the *Deepwater Horizon*'s spectacular explosion and surging oil captured public attention, the spill's slow violence—the dispersed, long-term effects of the sunken oil and the dispersant agent Corexit—has not. Indeed, since the 2010 BP disaster, there have been 85 international oil spills ("List of Oil Spills" 2022), many of which have received little attention, highlighting the need for extensive, relational representations of the slow petroviolence that precedes and follows spectacular bursts like the 2010 disaster.

To better explore the contrasts between representations of spectacular violence and slow violence, hypervisibility and invisibility, and narrative resolution and irresolution, I turn to five media representations of the spill, each with its own distinct narrative. I argue that the first representation, TV news—particularly 24-hour news shows—framed the disaster as a spectacle in the Debordian sense of the word. Collapsing the past and future of petrocapital into the mesmerizing "now" of the explosion and gushing oil, much of the news coverage obfuscated the role that the relentless fossil economy played in the spill and the disproportionate, durational effects on the Gulf's ecologies. Meanwhile, BP commercials visually overlaid the spill with what I call spectacular resolution, by which I mean a false sense of narrative closure made possible through the visual obfuscation of the spill's slow violence. In contrast, satirical tweets from the Twitter handle @BPGlobalPR disrupted the oil company's false sense of closure by parodying BP's own public relations department. From spectacular resolution to disruption, I turn to performances of "trans-corporeality" (Alaimo 2010) and "tentacular thinking" (Haraway 2016, 30–57). Analyzing Look Left Look Right's *NOLA: A Documentary Play about the BP Oil Spill* (2012) and Caridad Svich's play *The Way of Water* (2013), I argue that, together, the two plays perform an ecological irresolution that resists spectacular resolution and embodies invisible forms of slow violence. Ultimately, I suggest that, in contrast to the news' spectacle and BP's narrative of disaster resolution, @BPGlobalPR's tweets, *NOLA*, and *The Way of Water* reveal the spill's invisible, slow violence and challenge the narratival drive toward crisis resolution.

Spectacular Murkiness

On April 20, 2010, the *Deepwater Horizon*'s drilling rig exploded, killing 11 people; several days later, a large oil leak was discovered. In the ensuing months, the media tracked the story as one attempt after another to plug the well failed. By the time the leak appeared to be sealed five months later,[1] 4.9 million barrels of oil had been spilled. The unfolding story was primarily a televisual one, taking up 22% of all news for 100 days following the explosion ("100 Days" 2014); thus, it is worth considering the primary TV narratives that emerged from the disaster and their long-term effects. On the one hand, TV news reportage of the spill, prompted by the public's insatiable interest, was unusually attentive, following the event for 14 weeks when most stories receive screen time for only one or two weeks ("100 Days" 2014). On the other hand, the near-total drop in media attention after such extensive coverage inadvertently suggested that the crisis had been cleaned up, resolved on or shortly after the 87th day, when in fact the story had just shifted from the visually captivating oil leak to the largely invisible effects of crude oil and Corexit. But for a few largely local exceptions, news coverage of the spill rapidly declined following the well's partial sealing on July 15, 2010.[2] Meanwhile, from Louisiana to Florida, entire ecosystems—animals, plants, water, and people—continue to suffer from their exposure to crude oil and Corexit.[3]

Ironically, whereas the drop-off in media coverage belied the slow violence still occurring in the Gulf, the initial monolith of coverage on the disaster's immediacy obscured the petrocapital histories and dependencies driving the spill. Marxist theorist Guy Debord speaks to the erasure of history in representations when he writes, "The history that is present in all the depths of society tends to become invisible at the surface" ([1967] 2014, 78). For Debord, this invisibility means that, if we cannot see our economic history, we cannot change the existing *"time of things"* (78, emphasis in original). In the case of the 2010 spill, while there was a deluge of hypervisual news coverage that featured the immediate *Deepwater Horizon* explosion and oil plumes, oil as a commodity was not historicized and, thus, never questioned. LeMenager, however, would disagree with my Debordian assertion. As she sees it, "[t]his 'disaster' did not work as spectacle, in Guy Debord's sense of the mystification of modern means of production through screen imagery," because "a plethora of visible data" on the blowout prevented the abstraction of oil as a commodity (2011, 26). I would contend, though, that this very plethora of data, along with the live stream from BP's so-called "spill cam" on the ocean floor, proved dazzling in its overwhelming hypervisibility.

As feminist scholar Anne McClintock suggests of the spill cam, "This spectral, nightly close-up became a form of blindness" (2012). The monopolizing visual spectacle of the surging oil, paired with a running tally of days and gallons lost since the spill occurred, supplanted the material and ecological significance of the disaster. It obscured the spill's relationality to prior spills worldwide, its (entirely human) causation, and its ongoing consequences for diverse bio-organisms and environments. The murkiness of the spill cam became a metaphor for the repetitive, spectacular coverage of the spill, which visually emphasized the newfound "enemy"—oil—over the people and animals affected by deregulation and extractivism. Closely capturing the oil's slightest shift in flow and volume, the spill cam, and its TV transmission, visually privileged the non-living commodity over the living ecologies in which it spread. While viewer fascination with the spill cam stemmed in part from its close-up, live-action footage of an uncorked, ongoing disaster, it also stemmed from the cultural worship of fossil fuels as commodities. The latter was evidenced by TV news shows' tendency to interweave commentary about the latest number of barrels spilled and the latest drop in BP's stock price with the muddy visual of free-flowing oil. In a story of numbered crises—lives lost, days lost, oil lost—it became clear that loss is best understood through capital.

Since the spurting oil became a monopolizing, visual crisis—an unfolding drama—in need of instantaneous resolution, it took center stage in news coverage, to the point that, when it was mostly contained, the story of the spill seemed to be concluded. Indeed, media scholar Tamar Liebes suggests that, when catastrophes occur, news outlets turn into "disaster marathons…broadcasting from the moment when the disaster strikes (or immediately after) until the redressive ceremonial closure" (1998, 72, 74). In the case of the BP oil spill, this sense of ceremonial closure came when the well was partially capped on the 87th day of the disaster. This false sense of closure was reinforced by the seeming disappearance of oil; since most of it proved impossible to skim or burn off, the oil was instead emulsified and sunk by Corexit, which not only buried the oil beneath the ocean's surface but also made it 52 times more toxic to humans and animals (Rico-Martínez, Snell, and Shearer 2013). In contrast to the hypervisible oil caught on the spill cam, the "treated" oil was broken up into tiny beads and submerged by Corexit. Just as the oil was resolved—broken down and dispersed—so too was coverage of the spill, waning when the spectacular visual of gushing oil became an invisible and uncertain form of slow violence. Indeed, the dispersant's very name—Corexit—implies finality and resolution, suggesting that, when it is combined with oil, both will disappear.[4] The hypervisual representation of oil in the TV news and the emphasis on the immediate spectacle not only castigated oil rather than crude explorers and consumers but also made less visible aspects of the disaster that much more undetectable.

Spectacular Resolution

Whereas the TV news obscured less perceptible, and hence less spectacular, narratives of slow violence, BP promoted a spectacular resolution, a false sense of economic and environmental recovery that further concealed the toxic effects of the sunken oil and Corexit. Unable to control the oil, BP sought to manage public perception of the disaster instead. Between April and July 2010, the company, according to its own admission, spent over $93 million on advertising, triple its usual amount (Durando 2013). Once BP partially plugged the leak on July 15, the company continued its media blitz, but moved from apologizing to extolling its own efforts and the "rise" in tourism around the Gulf of Mexico. BP's deluge of ameliorating advertisements exemplified the core message of Debord's spectacle: "'What appears is good. What is good appears.' The passive acceptance it demands is already effectively imposed by its monopoly of appearances, its manner of appearing without allowing any reply" (2014, 4). BP's media blitz showed an isolated spill already contained before quickly shifting to a dazzling Gulf already recovered. Playing on visuality's cultural preeminence, the company made invisible the spill's slow violence by sinking the oil beneath the water's surface and by conducting a hypervisual media campaign that offered disaster narrative resolution. Of course, it is not at all surprising that BP would deploy advertising to control the spill's disaster narrative. However, what makes the corporation's commercials from

2010 and 2011 unique is their attempt to counteract and minimize a colossal environmental disaster as it still was unfolding. Thus, while the TV news, aided by the omnipresent spill cam, told a story of uncontainable, gushing oil, BP countered with a tale of contained oil managed by military might and corporate technocracy. While the news coverage of the disaster collapsed past and future oil dependency and the slow violence it causes into the perpetual present, BP went so far as to negate the present altogether. Then, less than a year after the partial sealing of the well, the BP narrative shifted to represent the Gulf as not only fully recovered but better than ever. From advertising a sense of containment to a sense of resolution, BP's disaster-related ad campaign strove to supplant the TV news' narrative of an unmitigated disaster, as well as to conceal the presence and consequences of the sunken oil and Corexit.

For example, a July 2010 commercial, released before the well was fully capped, features a coastline already on the mend. The ad begins with an aerial view of the Gulf, from which small splotches of seemingly stagnant oil are surrounded by a vast sea of blue, suggesting that the spilled oil is but a drop in the Gulf's endless bucket. Although dark blobs of oil are visible in the water, the camera's focus is on the containment boom[5] already in place. The distance between the lighter, apparently uninfected, sections of the water and the boom gives a sense of containment, at odds with the fact that, at the time of the commercial's release, the smallest wave could drive the oil over the boom. Featured in tranquil waters, the boom projects a technological management that obscures the fact that, in the commercial, all that stands between oil containment and exposure is a thin sheet of plastic. Of course, in actuality, the oil had already spread, and throughout July, BP worked closely with the Coast Guard, spraying Corexit in secret in the wee hours of the morning (McClintock 2012).

In the commercial, meanwhile, BP's crisis management is further emphasized by a series of action photos in quick succession: from a boat crew placing a boom in the ocean to a beach clean-up crew dragging heavy trash bags; from call center volunteers speaking with aggrieved victims to US soldiers working on the beach. Together, the scenes emphasize collective action on the part of BP, the affected communities, and the US army, and they suggest that containment and clean-up are completely under control, which, given the fact that the Macondo well continued to leak, could not have been further from the truth. Replacing harsh figures of people killed, barrels spilled, and days passed with more flattering figures, in the commercial, then BP chief executive Tony Hayward claims, "More than two million feet of boom, thirty planes, and over thirteen hundred boats are working to protect the shoreline" (climatebrad 2010). Interwoven shots of booms firmly in place and workers laying more booms visually reinforce a false sense of containment. Meanwhile, the commercial's verbal emphasis on the number of volunteers and resources dedicated to cleaning up the spill attempts to supplant other numbers, like the death toll and the spilled barrels of oil, a constantly rising figure. Turning a numbered crisis that was still being tallied into a numbered solution, BP suggests that the latter can adequately fix the former.

The commercial offers spectacular resolution, its camera lingering on images of seagulls on high rocks; the clean, tranquil birds, far above any toxic threat, stand in sharp contrast to the oil-drenched seagulls that featured so heavily in most news coverage. Similarly, still shots of the seashore in summer, where colorful umbrellas dot the beach, families lounge on the pristine sand, and young children play in the waves, visually suggest that the crisis is over and that life has resumed its usual course. Taken together, the images of communal action and rapid recovery, combined with the soothing sounds of waves and birds, suggest a false sense of corporate responsibility and environmental restoration. The commercial's visual depiction of a unified, organized clean-up seeks to overwrite BP's initial refusal to act for fear of claiming liability, as well as the corporation's chaotic disorganization and ineptitude when it finally did take action. Likewise, the wide shots of seagulls elevated above the distant, contained oil and humans at play in unblemished sand project a spectacular resolution at odds with the uncontainable oil surge less than a month earlier. If the TV news media dwelled on the murky, gushing oil to the point that all else became blurry, BP deployed commercials that suggested it was in complete control, containing and managing the oil *before* it could cause damage.

Where the 2010 commercial attempts to conceal the extent of the disaster and visually depict disaster resolution, a 2012 ad, "Come Back to the Gulf," heralds an even more explicit spectacular resolution. The commercial features tourism bureau representatives and prominent business owners from Florida, Alabama, Mississippi, and Louisiana extolling the Gulf as an ideal getaway spot. It begins with the sunny proclamation, "Last season was the Gulf's best tourism season in years!" (Bellingrath Gardens and Home 2012).[6] The tone of the commercial is optimistic and bright, as people from different Gulf States playfully compete with one another to lure tourists to their hometowns. The overall message is that the Gulf has not only recovered but is better than ever with "More suntans!," "More fun on the water!," "More people, more good times!," and more "deep sea fishing" (Bellingrath Gardens and Home 2012). Featuring several shots of seemingly pristine beaches and water, the commercial belies the fact that, according to the National Oceanic and Atmospheric Administration, the "deep sea ecosystem may take decades to recover" from the spill (Montagna et al. 2013). Advertising a return in tourism, the commercial implies an ecologically impossible resolution to the disaster, even as millions of pounds of oily materials were beginning to resurface in the Gulf ("Crude Awakening" 2014, 00:08:47–00:09:02).

Careful to avoid explicitly addressing environmental concerns, BP's tourism commercials go beyond promoting a return to the status quo, instead repeating words like "more" and "better" to emphasize improvement through consumption over conservation. In the last few seconds of the ad, the camera hovers on the BP logo while an off-camera voice enthuses, "Brought to you by BP and all of us who call the Gulf home" (Bellingrath Gardens and Home 2012). Linked, BP and Gulf residents are seen as working together to save their shared home, while viewers are urged to do their part by visiting the Gulf. Putting the burden on the consumer not to conserve resources but to consume more of them for the greater good, BP, without a hint of irony, suggests that the cure for an environmental disaster caused by overconsumption is, in fact, more consumption.

And, of course, it is this very consumption that allows oil companies like BP to manage the environmental disasters that they themselves cause. Indeed, in dissecting the apparent paradox of BP proclaiming to "go green" following the 2010 catastrophe, Peter Hitchcock argues that disrupting BP's dual narrative of exploitation and sustainability would require us to reduce our oil dependence drastically (2012). Refusal to do so means that even disasters as massive as the 2010 spill do "not necessarily negate BP's environmental credentials; on the contrary, BP has used its robust response to the accident [...] to massage its profile by claiming that its diligence in emergency response proves its commitment to ecological sustainability" (Hitchcock 2012). For example, were it not for a half-hearted apology from Hayward in the 2010 commercial, the advertisement could be mistaken for that of a nonprofit organization rushing in to provide humanitarian and environmental relief for an unanticipated natural disaster. Submerging the slow violence of the spill, like the oil itself, beneath pervasive ad campaigns, BP succeeded in projecting a narrative of environmental and economic containment and spectacular resolution.

Spreadable Détournement

In contrast to BP's narrative-driven ads, satirical tweets from the Twitter handle @BPGlobalPR, begun by an initially anonymous comedian and activist later revealed to be Josh Simpson, subverted the company's desired sense of closure and created opportunities for the general public to weigh in on the disaster in real time. As media scholars Henry Jenkins, Sam Ford, and Joshua Green note, the media "shift from distribution to circulation signals a movement toward a more participatory model of culture, one which sees the public not as simply consumers of preconstructed messages but as people who are shaping, sharing, reframing, and remixing media content" (2013, 2). On the one hand, issues like Twitter bullying and the circulation of fake news have shown that social media suffers from uneven circulation and disproportionate participation. On the other hand, because of its emphasis on circulation rather than distribution, Twitter proved an ideal platform for Simpson, and anyone who wished to participate, to disrupt BP's spectacular resolution in the very moment it was distributed. In contrast to BP's pre-packaged, finished commercials, created and distributed by the company itself, @BPGlobalPR offered a more participatory and unedited forum in which a large number of Twitter followers could contribute to the Twitter handle's content and visibility.

This relative ease of circulation is one reason why I describe the @BPGlobalPR tweets as spreadable, following Jenkins, Ford, and Green's definition of participatory media (2013, 2). The other is because Simpson's parodic tweets not only undercut BP's spectacular resolution but also make visible the spreadable slow violence surrounding the spill by highlighting an otherwise unspoken dependence on oil, an inattention to spills in the Global South, and *Deepwater Horizon*'s connection to past and future environmental disasters. Taking every opportunity to show the expansive reach of the spill, @BPGlobalPR performs a spreadable détournement that exposes BP's narrative of containment and resolution. The French word *détournement*, as defined by Debord translator Ken Knabb, "means deflection, diversion, rerouting, distortion, misuse, misappropriation, hijacking, or otherwise turning something aside from its normal course or purpose" (in Debord 2006). In the case of the BP oil spill, the @BPGlobalPR tweets disrupt and reroute BP's teleological drive for resolution. Imitating BP's own public relations tactics, @BPGlobalPR tweets in the bureaucratic tones of a BP employee and ends many tweets with the hashtag #bpcares. Often ironic and sarcastic, the tweets act as sharp barbs undercutting BP's overdetermined narrative of resolution. For instance, tweets like, "We'd like to be remembered as the company that saved the Gulf. What we saved it from is not important. #bpcares"[7] act as miniature, digital pin-pricks; released at strategic moments throughout the crisis, they serve to interrupt and deflate BP's spectacular narrative of resolution.

Such subversive tactics are not exclusive to @BPGlobalPR but are common to many social media deployed to disrupt monolithic narratives and corporate agendas. These acts are what media studies scholar Rita Raley calls "tactical media," which, though they may often vary in digital form and content, are intended to create "disturbance" (2009, 6). As Raley posits, "In its most expansive articulation, tactical media signifies the intervention and disruption of a dominant semiotic regime, the temporary creation of a situation in which signs, messages, and narratives are set into play and critical thinking becomes possible" (2009, 6). By being "set into play," dominant corporate messages and narratives are no longer hermetically fixed but are set in a digital topography in which they can be teased, altered, disrupted, negated, or subverted.

The tweets from @BPGlobalPR create not only disturbance to the dominant narrative of resolution but also spreadability in the form of retweets, likes, and links to more accurate information countering BP's own claims. Take, for example, the following tweet: "Reports of 79% of the oil remaining in the Gulf are false according to the pie chart we made ourselves" (@BPGlobalPR), which ends with a link directing followers to said reports, thereby simultaneously mocking BP's attempts at misinformation and providing more unbiased stories. Such disruptive tweets directly counter BP's own narrative; often tweeted in response to the latest BP claim or gaffe, they create an immediate and ongoing alternative to BP's visual version of events. Similarly, because @BPGlobalPR tweets in the bureaucratic tone of BP executives, it tactically subverts the company's own corporate voice, thereby exposing and mocking BP's attempt to obfuscate the scope of the disaster. For instance, the very first @BPGlobalPR tweet sent on May 19, 2010, over a month into the spill, is, "We regretfully admit that something has happened off of the Gulf Coast. More to come." The ambiguity and nonchalance of the tweet comically reflects BP's initial reluctance to take any action to stop the spill for fear of appearing responsible for it. Hyper-performing BP's obfuscation of the scale of the disaster and its role in creating it, @BPGlobalPR exposes the absurdity of the company's vague response to the spill, both in the media and in the Gulf.

And, yet, @BPGlobalPR's performance is not that ludicrous when compared to that of actual BP executives. *Newsweek* highlights the similarity between the two in an article in which readers are asked to guess whether uncredited statements were made by @BPGlobalPR or BP itself (Mascarenhas 2010). For instance, on May 14, 2010, Hayward claimed, "The Gulf of Mexico is a very big ocean. The amount of oil and dispersant we are putting into it is tiny in relation to the total water volume" (as cited in Webb 2010). Imitating Hayward's tone, @BPGlobalPR tweeted on June 4, "We've modestly made modest changes to this modest gulf. This modest incident will blow over and you'll forget how modest we were. #MODEST." Where the TV news media spectacularized Hayward's and BP's gaffes through repetitive sound bites and emphatic outrage, @BPGlobalPR mimicked Hayward's vague, assuaging tone to expose the absurdity of BP's response given the magnitude of the disaster. Not only does the tweet, weeks after Hayward's statement, remind followers of BP's disingenuous stance before its "apologetic" commercial was released, it also predicts that, once the spill is out of the public eye, people will forget their outrage.

Whereas the bulk of news coverage centered on oil containment and BP ("100 Days" 2014), the @BPGlobalPR tweets extend their criticism to the underlying issue of American dependence on a fossil economy. Despite the magnitude of the disaster, the news never questioned the US's oil dependence while, in its commercials, BP went so far as to celebrate it. As Malm suggests, "the ruling classes are constitutionally incapable of responding to the catastrophe [of fossil-driven climate change] in any other way than expediting it" (2021, 8). While @BPGlobalPR offers no alternative to a fossil economy, it nonetheless insists on making visible a factor of the disaster that was pointedly avoided elsewhere: consumers' own complicity in the spill. Tweets like "Feeling down? Why not take a long drive and blow off some steam? #bpcares" and "If you want to help clean up, drive your cars fast and often. Let's melt those glaciers and dilute this mess! #bpcares" remind followers that, even as Americans condemn BP's actions, car owners refuse to acknowledge our own complicity in the spill. This lack of reflexivity causes what eco-theater scholar Baz Kershaw calls a "double bind," wherein Americans' urge to stop environmental destruction is at odds with our dependence on oil (2007, 13). @BPGlobalPR's reflexive tweets refuse to allow American consumers to forget our own role in the 2010 spill, thus not only disrupting BP's driven narrative of spectacular resolution but also calling out American complicity in the fossil economy.

@BPGlobalPR also calls out Americans' short-term memories with tweets that celebrate the inevitability of people losing interest in the spill. For instance, one tweet bluntly predicts the expected end of the story: "SPOILER ALERT: The leak stops eventually, everyone forgets about it and we all buy another vacation home. #cantwait." Using reverse psychology to challenge followers to hold on to their ire, a tweet later the same day similarly doubts Americans' ability to hold BP accountable in the long term: "We respect your outrage, we just don't believe it's sustainable. #exxonvaldez #bpcares." Playing on the word "sustainable," a now pervasive buzz word that, like the word "conservation" in the early twentieth century, sanitizes capitalism (Alaimo 2012, 558–9), @BPGlobalPR provokes followers to maintain their anger. The reference to the *Exxon Valdez* spill also reminds followers of the biggest US oil spill prior to *Deepwater Horizon* and urges them to remember how that turned out. Although the long-term effects of the Valdez spill continue to this day, Exxon Mobil, after several court appeals, was only held accountable for a fraction of its initial damages.[8] By linking the two events, @BPGlobalPR urges followers to resist the immediate, visible resolution of the capped well and to extend their attention to the invisible slow violence to come.

Perhaps even more important than the historical links that the Twitter handle makes are the transnational links. In addition to critiquing Twitter followers' short-term memory, @BPGlobalPR highlights the fact that, had the BP oil spill occurred somewhere other than the US, it would likely have received little to no attention from Americans. Tweets like, "We feel terrible about spilling oil in American waters, we'll make sure the next spill happens where the terrorists live. #bpcares," not only expose the unequal value that the Global North places on its lives, livelihoods, and environments but also remind followers that oil spills occur on a regular basis in the Middle East and Africa. Another tweet goes further in highlighting the invisibility of spills in the Global South: "We honestly didn't think this was going to be a huge deal. No one cares when this happens in Nigeria." The tweet provides a link to a news article that claims that more oil is spilled in the Niger Delta "every year than has been lost in the Gulf of Mexico," yet there have been no legal repercussions in Nigeria (Jardin 2010). Tweets like these reveal that what really shocked Americans about the 2010 spill was less that it had occurred at all but that it had occurred *here*, in the US. Thus, the tweets are a sharp reminder that, when it comes to environmental exploitation, there can be no separation between here and there. Just as the slow petroviolence in Nigeria has been largely invisible to American audiences, the sunken oil and Corexit have been equally invisible, quietly reemerging in Louisiana marshes, inhabitants' respiratory systems, and in marine life. In connecting the 2010 oil spill to international spills like those in the Niger Delta, @BPGlobalPR suggests that the BP spill is not an isolated or exclusively American disaster but a spreadable, transnational concern that extends beyond any one particular spill.

However, although the ecological effects of the 2010 spill are still being felt in the Gulf, @BPGlobalPR has stopped tweeting.[9] A lone tweet on April 20, 2011 commemorates the anniversary of the spill: "One year ago, we thought that this terrible PR disaster would never go away. We were wrong. #StayStrongTEPCO." The tweet not only critiques the total media shift from the spectacular disaster of 2010—the BP oil spill—to the spectacular disaster of 2011—the Tokyo Electric Power Company Fukushima nuclear disaster—but also connects the two, both caused by a lack of oversight and both likely to be forgotten in the wake of the next large-scale disaster. In the bureaucratic voice of BP, the tweet speaks to the relief the company must have felt when another environmental disaster took center stage, pushing the oil spill to the recesses of people's memories. While @BPGlobalPR's coverage of the spill was far more disruptive and provocative than most news coverage, it too dramatically declined after the well was capped. Nonetheless, although

@BPGlobalPR may have gone the way of most news outlets, at least it had the audacity to predict and critique followers' disinterest, even if it too eventually conceded to it. By making visible the slow violence obfuscated in the TV news coverage and in BP's advertisements and by emphasizing ongoing irresolution and spreadable détournement, interventions like the @BPGlobalPR tweets act as mini-protests to disaster narrative resolution. Extending the conversation beyond the immediate disaster, they privilege multivalent, invisible narratives of slow violence over hypervisual numbered crises with clear-cut resolutions.

From Spectacular Resolution to Tentacular Irresolution

Whereas @BPGlobalPR performs spreadable détournement through sharp digital barbs, the verbatim *NOLA: A Documentary Play about the BP Oil Spill* (2012) does so through the juxtaposition of multivalent perspectives on the spill. The polyvocality and irresolution in *NOLA* are examples of what feminist Donna Haraway calls "tentacular thinking:" "webbed, braided" stories that resist closure and singularity (2016, 49). Like Leigh Fondakowski's verbatim play *Spill* (2017), *NOLA* considers the vying interests and perspectives surrounding the 2010 spill and its aftermath. Premiering at the Edinburgh Festival Fringe in 2012, the production featured a barebones set consisting of oil barrels and a screen on which images of the 2010 BP oil spill were projected. Four actors[10] from the English company Look Left Look Right (LLLR) portrayed the 20 different characters, whose dialogue all came from the wide-ranging interviews the company conducted throughout Louisiana six months following the 2010 spill.[11] Scuttling and scurrying between different interviewees and ideas, *NOLA* is tentacular in its stringy, sticky extensions that refuse narrative closure.

The tentacularity of *NOLA* begins with LLLR's decision to interview people six months after the spill occurred and to stage its production two years after the disaster, when most people had already stopped paying attention. This artistic choice is reflective of the company's eponymous goal to look both left and right to present as many views as possible. In contrast to the singular narrative of disaster resolution seen in much of the news media on the spill, *NOLA* extends outward, offering a multitude of perspectives from those who worked on the *Deepwater Horizon* rig, families whose loved ones were killed in the explosion, journalists, Louisiana fishers, lawyers, activists, conservationists, and even an anonymous BP executive. LLLR's polyphonic approach in *NOLA* serves as both a critique of media that focused too narrowly on the disaster, ceasing their news coverage once the well was plugged, and a multi-perspectival examination of the ongoing slow violence from the spill throughout Louisiana and beyond.

At first glance, the 2010 spill would seem to be the quintessential definition of spectacular violence, given Nixon's definition of typical violence "as an event or action that is immediate in time, explosive and spectacular in space, and as erupting into instant sensational visibility" (2011, 2). After all, it began with an explosion that killed 11 people, whereas most oil spills silently go undetected or unrepaired for years.[12] However, as I have already argued, the spectacular hypervisibility of the unfolding drama in the media and BP's overdetermined narrative of disaster resolution obscured underlying slow violences that have caused long-term, ongoing consequences for aquatic life and people,[13] especially Cajun and Indigenous communities that were disproportionately affected by the spill (Farber 2012). One major way in which grassroots theater, and eco-performance in particular, can expose slow violence is through reflective, slow art that does not share the news media's focus on recency and narrative closure. In conducting its interviews after the oil leak was capped, LLLR not only highlights the slow violence that continues in the spill's wake but also critiques the media's grand performance of disaster resolution.

For example, early in the piece, an actor playing BBC correspondent David Shukman wheels a TV onstage and recounts Shukman's experience reporting on the spill:

> By late May Louisiana was a ridiculous scene! Just sort of taken over by TV!... There were local fishermen lining up to be interviewed. I mean, they were so used to what the media wanted. It kinda became, it was almost routine...The story had been granted the sort of fully fledged status of a major national crisis, erm you know sort of like a hostage situation, this was now a numbered crisis with days....[T]heir language was just it was sort of "full strength catastrophe."[14]
>
> (NOLA 2012).

Shukman's recollection reveals how the spill's status as a "full strength catastrophe" led to a singular, grand performance intensified by the "numbered crisis" and reinforced through repetition. Full-strength catastrophes are certainly compelling, yet their very urgency can result in sweeping language and heightened drama, incompatible with details, multiplicities, and irresolution. As ecocritic Greg Garrard points out, the news media often casts environmental disasters in an apocalyptic light, "because news more easily reports events than processes," but, in so doing, it reduces "long-term issues" to "monocausal crises" with short-term solutions and temporary villains (2004, 105). In the case of the BP spill, the drama centered on capping the well: will the latest method work or will it too be an abysmal failure? Once this plotline was resolved, the story seemed to be over.

Certainly, capping the well was of utmost importance, given that it was leaking 62,000 gallons of oil every day. However, because it was a "numbered crisis with days," the crisis seemed to be resolved when the well was sealed. As Shukman recalls, once BP capped the well, it "stopped the appalling sight on the nightly news in the States, so that was a huge triumph" (NOLA 2012). After saying these words, the actor playing Shukman exits and takes the TV with him. In a play with a set consisting only of barrels of oil and a projector, the appearance and disappearance of a TV is notable. It mirrors the way in which the majority of media swept in during the full catastrophe and swept back out after the immediate crisis was resolved, thereby implying that the disaster itself was resolved. LLLR highlights this monocausal, event-drive representation of the spill to contrast it with its own nonlinear, multivalent presentation, which offers a tentacular, deliberately irresolute alternative.

In taking a step back and considering not only the immediate crisis but how that crisis came to be and its unresolved ramifications, *NOLA* serves as an example of how eco-performance can stage complex problems with long-term causations and effects. For instance, although the play begins chronologically, focusing first on the explosion and the immediate reaction to it, when it shifts to the aftermath, the linearity ends as different viewpoints and agendas butt up against one another. Rather than give one issue priority over the others, the company gives equal weight to all of them. Except for a slide to introduce each new character, the voices flow from one to the other without interruption, each perspective demanding the audience's attention. For instance, the Director of the Bird Conservation National Audubon Society in Baton Rouge emphasizes the effects of the spill on the Gulf Coast's pelican population, while the Field Monitor of the Gulf Restoration Network focuses on the widespread damage to the coastline, and an ear, nose, and threat doctor foregrounds the infected humans whom he believes were ignored by a news media fixated on affected birds and sea life. By intercutting various interviewees' voices and giving them a similar amount of time and attention, the company refuses to rank the crises.

Whereas the media's focus on the numbered crisis—the days it took for the oil well to be sealed—created a univocal, resolution-driven performance, LLLR's attention to the messy, chaotic aftermath reveals how slow violence multiplies and spreads. By ultimately refusing to privilege one voice over another, or to offer a final conclusion, *NOLA* denies the audience a sense of resolution and forces it to grapple with the multivalent acts of ongoing slow violence. Because theater and performance are not beholden to immediacy and recency in the way that news and social media are, they have potential to eschew neat, contained narratives for more complex representations that extend beyond a singular time or place. As theater scholars Una Chaudhuri and Shonni Enelow note with regard to climate change theater, if eco-theater is to collaborate with the sciences and social sciences, it must find a way to represent different "*time scales*" that challenge humanist modes of representation (2014, 25, emphasis in original). This consideration of time scales can be seen in *NOLA*'s refusal to merge, unify, or synchronize the distinct voices heard in the play. Instead, it creates a polyphonic palimpsest of perspectives that highlight differing priorities and timeframes. Take, for instance, a series of voices heard in quick succession: Alan Smith, the Chief Executive of Capital Asset Management Pension Fund in London; a lawyer; and Melanie Driscoll, Director of the Bird Conservation National Audubon Society in Baton Rouge. Together, the voices reveal three vastly different value systems surrounding the spill: economic, litigious, and ecological. By combining, juxtaposing, and interlacing distinct perspectives, LLLR offers a multilayered, irresolute portrayal that puts the onus on the audience to grapple with the spill and its ongoing effects.

This deliberate irresolution was, unsurprisingly, not well-received by critics of the 2012 Edinburgh Festival production. One faults *NOLA*'s "lack of narrative drive" and a "central story" (Bell 2012), while another complains that the production's "story of the disaster lacks any resolution" (Strachan n.d.). These reviewers mirror Western audience's desire for grand narratives that offer dramatic resolution and, in the case of the BP disaster, ecological resolution as well. If the story is resolved, it frees up mental bandwidth and attention can be turned to the next numbered crisis. By refusing a dramatic resolution or even a potential solution to the many problems it raises, NOLA frustrates audience expectations and forces us to sift through the proliferating flotsam and jetsam ourselves. Even the play's ending, which verbally seems to offer a resolution of sorts, visually denies closure. Diane Wilson, a Texan fisherwoman and activist recalls that, after not seeing a single pelican for months, she saw five, suggesting a gradual environmental recovery. Her words, however, are undercut by a projection of a pelican flying away, one last reminder in NOLA that the effects of the BP spill are anything but resolved.

Beyond irresolution, a key aspect of tentacularity for Haraway is that, at times, lines will intersect but never neatly or permanently. As she writes, "The tentacular ones make attachments and detachments; they [m]ake cuts and knots; they make a difference; they weave paths and consequences but not determinisms; they are both open and knotted in some ways and not others" (2016, 31). Such tentacular intersections and disconnections are made in NOLA, which sprawls outward to include interviews from people connected to the Texas City BP oil refinery explosion of 2005. What might at first glance appear to be a detour in NOLA's inquiry is in fact evidence that the 2010 spill is not nearly as unanticipated as it may seem. Rather, like the refinery explosion, it is the direct result of environmental exploitation and deregulation. While the Texas City explosion, an instance of spectacular violence that killed 15 workers and injured 180 more, garnered attention in the immediate aftermath, it did not lead to significant changes in worker safety or facility maintenance, even though both were key factors in the explosion (Malewitz, Collette, and Olsen 2015). In loosely connecting the 2005 disaster to the 2010 spill, NOLA urges people to look to the past to prevent future spectacular disasters spawned by attritional slow violence.

The play's tentacularity also extends to other disasters, revealing the ways in which, as Nixon argues, the poor are disproportionately affected by slow violence. As Diane Wilson explains, her small community in Tegan, Texas, was just starting to recover from Hurricane Katrina when Hurricane Gustav hit and, then, two years later, came the oil spill. Her experience highlights the extreme vulnerability of impoverished people for whom environmental injustices tend to be compounded. Nonetheless, Wilson says that the one thing that stayed the same was the

> spirit of the people that were born and raised here the people who have webbed toes because they live on the water, they live here, they earn all their money here, they teach the old ways here and uh they are stubborn enough not to be put off

> (NOLA 2012).

Wilson, a fourth-generation shrimper, sees herself as a naturally quiet and solitary fisherwoman driven to activism by corrupt chemical corporations. She and others like her are what Nixon would call "impoverished resource rebels," thrust into the unexpected role of environmentalist by "intensified assaults on resources" in their own communities (2011, 4). Their environmentalism, then, is charged with economic, cultural, and personal significance. Wilson has risked her own health by sucking discharge pipes and has been jailed for covering herself in Karo syrup resembling oil during a Senate hearing on the spill. Taking advantage of the spill's short-term hypervisibility to expose its long-term effects, Wilson stressed the ongoing ecological damage unresolved by the hearing. In ending the play with Wilson, *NOLA* privileges the environmentalism of those directly affected by spectacular and slow violence and suggests that the battle against Gulf exploitation is ongoing. By highlighting the continued activism of Wilson and others directly affected by the spill and by presenting multivalent, divergent viewpoints on the disaster, *NOLA* defies the sweeping, singular dramatic arc so often embedded in "full strength catastrophe" performances and suggests that the slow violence preceding and following the spill remains unresolved.

Sedimented Slow Violence

Both *NOLA* and Caridad Svich's 2012 play, *The Way of Water*, resist dramatic resolution by emphasizing the ongoing environmental injustices that spill victims face and by making connections between the 2010 spill and other environmental disasters. However, while *NOLA* primarily highlights the spill's irresolution by juxtaposing multiple perspectives, *The Way of Water* mainly does so by materializing the spill's underlying slow violence and its toxic infection of humans and oceanic life. Although Svich focuses on the spill's disastrous effects on one town— Plaquemines Parish, Louisiana—she also makes connections to environmental injustices around the world. Some of the injustices, like the *Exxon Valdez* spill, are forgotten instances of once spectacular, hypervisible violence while others, like the disproportionate effects of climate change on islands, are slow-moving catastrophes. Through these connections, Svich suggests that the 2010 spill is not an isolated instance of spectacular violence but rather part of a pattern of exploitative slow violence. The play's production history further highlights the breadth of the spill: Svich, in collaboration with NoPassport Theatre Alliance & Press and Waterkeeper Alliance, created a free reading series, so that anyone could stage readings of the play in April and May of 2012. Throughout the US and several other countries—such as Brazil, Germany, South Africa, Australia, Canada, England, and Scotland—50 readings were staged at universities, theaters, and even homes.[15] The transnationality of the reading series speaks to the magnitude of the disaster and its resonance beyond US borders. Utilizing the temporary hypervisibility of the spill, Svich seeks to draw attention to the ongoing, invisible slow violence of environmental injustice both through her reading series and within the play itself. Firmly rooting the play in the local environment of Plaquemines Parish, Svich extends outward to expose the pervasive, irresolute slow violence of petrocapitalism.

The play is set several months after the 2010 spill and follows four characters still suffering its effects. Plaquemines Parish fishermen Jimmy and Yuki spend most of their time on their fishing boat dreaming of the next big catch or the next big meal, neither of which ever arrives. They know that they cannot survive as fishermen anymore, because the water is still contaminated, fish are scarce, and no one is buying what they occasionally do catch. However, the two men cannot give up their livelihood, so they sit in their boat and wait for their fishing lines to tug. Meanwhile, their spouses—Rosalie, married to Jimmy, and Neva, married to Yuki—alternate their time between thinking of creative ways to make money and falling into despair. Rosalie and Jimmy are already behind on their mortgage when the latter's health, deteriorating ever since the spill, puts him in the hospital. Without any health insurance, the couple goes further into debt, and their house falls into foreclosure. Meanwhile, Neva and Yuki also continue to struggle, their fear for the health of Neva's developing fetus largely unspoken but palatable. Protests against BP take place offstage and all of the characters except Jimmy, who doubts the protests' ability to effect change, consider participating in them. By the end of the play, Rosalie and Jimmy have crammed their car with as many meager belongings as they can manage and are about to leave for Waxahachie, Texas, where Jimmy's cousin, badly burned by a chemical fire at his plant, has said they can stay. On their way out of town, the couple decides to stop by the protest for the first time, marking a small but significant change in Jimmy's perspective. On the one hand, the play's ending may be said to provide a resolution of sorts: Jimmy finally begins to protest the injustice of the spill rather than resign himself to it. On the other hand, though, this small act of resistance indicates a deliberate irresolution, a refusal, several months after the spill, to pretend that an ecological or economic reparation has or can be reached. By ending *The Way of Water* with characters who demand justice for their ongoing health and economic woes, Svich contests the news media's drive toward resolution and suggests that the play's ending is only a continuation for impoverished Gulf residents whose futures remain precarious.

Not only does Svich create irresolution by ending with an act of rebellion, but she also does so by exposing the multifarious environmental injustices that preceded the spill and are exacerbated by it. For example, even before the characters are exposed to oil and Corexit, they are exposed to food injustices, particularly a lack of access to fresh produce and a lack of nutritional education. When Jimmy and Yuki are on the water and hungry, they fantasize about going to McDonald's; when Rosalie and Neva are thirsty, they reach for a soda. Trying to save money wherever she can, Rosalie buys the generic brand of cola, but, as a result, finds that she and Neva have to drink twice as many sodas to get the same effect. In one scene in particular, the two women discuss the lack of fresh produce available at their local corner store, which sells outdated, processed food. Since Rosalie and Jimmy only own one car, the former must bicycle to the grocery store when her husband takes the car to work; thus, the corner store is her only nearby option. Even were the characters to have access to better food, they could not afford it, as is made painfully obvious when Jimmy invites Yuki and Neva to dinner without telling Rosalie first, and all the couple has left in the kitchen is one Hot Pocket and popcorn.

The characters' plight reflects the actual reality for many in Plaquemines County, where more than 27% of the population has low access to a supermarket[16] and the poverty rate is 32.8% (Food Access Research Atlas 2019), as well as the reality in Louisiana as a whole which, as of 2020, was the second poorest state in the US ("Percent of Total Population in Poverty" 2020). Meanwhile, Louisiana is home to "Cancer Alley," an 85 mile-stretch of over 150 petrochemical plants between Baton Rouge and New Orleans (Castellón 2021, 15). The play's focus on preexisting social and environmental injustices in addition to the effects of the oil spill demonstrates how injustice tends to be compounded, "infused into the multi-scalar geographies in which we live" (Soja 2010, 20). Poverty-stricken people like the play's characters are doubly affected by the spill; already vulnerable because of their lack of fresh food, health insurance, and financial security, they are devastated by the toll the spill takes on their health and economic income. By highlighting the irony of a state rich in natural resources being unable to provide for its own residents, Svich reveals the ways in which poor people and the environment are mutually exploited.

Svich's inclusion of the slow violence that precedes the spill stands in stark contrast to typical disaster narratives, which often begin with an event that inter-rupts the status quo, bringing spectacular violence to what was otherwise an everyday, sleepy, or perhaps thriving town. By establishing the ordinary ubiquity of a setting, be it actual or fictional, disaster narratives serve to highlight the cata-clysmic effects of the "unanticipated" event. While such a technique may be dra-matically compelling, it nonetheless implies that the setting had no real problems prior to the disaster and, thus, the disaster could not have been avoided. *The Way of Water*, however, not only begins well after the perceived disaster—the gushing oil—is resolved, but also interweaves the characters' pre-spill injustices with their post-spill injustices. In her synopsis, Svich writes that the play is about the spill and "poverty in America" (2013, 18). In linking the two, she stresses the ways in which environmental disaster is connected to and anticipated by preexisting slow vio-lence—food injustice, low wages, healthcare inaccessibility, environmental exploi-tation, and drilling shortcuts. By showing how the spill greatly exacerbated existing injustices, rather than suggesting that it caused all of them, Svich exposes "lasting structures of unevenly distributed advantage and disadvantage" (Soja 2010, 20). Or, in other words, *The Way of Water* reveals the many ways in which the poor get poorer. Already infected by toxins in their highly processed food, the characters become doubly infected following the spill: it destroys their livelihood, further limits their ability to buy food, and exposes them to oil and highly toxic Corexit.

Embodying Transcorporeal Toxicity

In exposing the multiple forms of toxicity at play in Plaquemines Parish, *The Way of Water* tracks preexisting socio-environmental injustices and shows how the spill exacerbated them. Ecocritic Stacy Alaimo's term "trans-corporeality" is useful here in demonstrating the ways "in which the human is always intermeshed with the more-than-human world" (2010, 2). Traveling toxicities that mutually affect humans and nonhuman nature reveal the permeability and fragility of both. As Alaimo writes, "Tracing a toxic substance from production to consumption often reveals global networks of social injustice, lax regulations, and environmental degradation" (2010, 15). Svich traces the oil and the Corexit outward to other disasters and inward, materializing the ways in which the spill's toxins spread throughout the characters' bodies. For instance, while Jimmy, who often succumbs to hacking and shaking fits, is most visibly affected by the crude oil and Corexit, the other characters are clearly infected as well. Neva suffers from rashes, which likely affect her growing fetus; Yuki suffers from nausea; and Rosalie is mysteriously unable to conceive. Even as the characters succumb to the spill's side effects, there is a sense that the true extent of their infection remains unknown but ominous: Jimmy may die and Neva may miscarry. This speaks to the lack of transparency surrounding the toxicity of the combined effects of the crude oil and the dispersant agents. When BP first began treating the spill with dispersants made by Nalco Holding Company, the public—including unmasked clean-up workers—had no idea what chemicals were being used or what their effects might be (Schor 2010). One of ingredients in Corexit 9527 is 2-butoxyethanol which, by Nalco Holding Company's own admission, can be damaging to the kidneys, the liver, and red blood cells (Nalco 2012).

Nixon suggests that because chemical violence is "driven inward," it often goes unnoticed and untreated, especially within bodies of the poor (2011, 6). Thus, Svich performs vital work in giving transcorporeal form to these toxicities through her characters, revealing the ways in which the oil and Corexit not only spilled into the ocean but seeped into the surrounding land, air, and organisms. By materializing the multiple toxic threats her characters face, Svich makes visible embodied slow violence and what eco-theater scholar Theresa J. May calls the "shared vulnerability" of people and place (2017, 1). Jimmy, in particular, becomes increasingly aware that his poisoned state is shared by everything around him. For example, in a moment of magical realism, he vomits fish, but the other characters only see him heave up blood and bile. Poisoned by polycyclic aromatic hydrocarbons (PAHs) present in oil and Corexit, Jimmy, the ocean, and the marine life are similarly affected. As Jimmy's condition continues to deteriorate, his trembling fits and dizziness intensify. What begins as a subtle tremor rapidly turns into an uncontrollable shake, and, the more disorientated Jimmy becomes, the more he understands his interdependence with the ocean:

I see it. I fuckin' see…
A dream of water
Hot
Burnin'
Lettin' itself through me

> Floatin'
> Through the sludge of sticky crude on cane
> Down, down the way of no life
>
> *(Svich 2013, 69).*

Jimmy's vision speaks to the spill's remains, the oil and dispersant still left behind after skimming, burning, and evaporating techniques were employed.[17] As his toxicity level increases, the fisherman begins to see what none of the other characters do: embodied, mutual human, animal, and environmental deterioration. Identifying with the Gulf, now "the sludge of sticky crude on cane," Jimmy burns up much like the spilled oil. As toxins spread throughout his body, he senses them simultaneously spreading throughout everything around him, including the "bodies of dead baby dolphins" whose "skin becomes our own" (Svich 2013, 18). The imagery of spewing intact fish and taking on another animal's dead skin speaks to a porosity and interchangeability heightened by toxic exposure.

In the play's final scene, Jimmy witnesses an acid rainfall, while Rosalie, standing right next to him, sees nothing. The fisherman's infection gradually makes him aware of how the same infection runs through the Gulf, marine animals, and the atmosphere. Through his vulnerable state, Jimmy realizes, as Haraway suggests, that "to be one is always to *become with* many" (2007, 4, emphasis in original). While the other characters worry that Jimmy's visions mean that his health is worsening, his contamination lowers his constructed boundaries between himself and his environment, invoking a clarity that allows him to see his becoming with the dolphins, fish, and water. His hold on "reality" may be slipping, but, since his—and most people's—constructed reality is one in which humans are separate from and above the rest of their ecosystem, Jimmy may actually be seeing reality clearly for the first time. When he vomits whole fish, he is not only discharging the contents of his stomach but also the misconception that human and nonhuman toxicity are separate concerns. Becoming the skin of a dolphin and spewing forth fish from the ocean, Jimmy imagines an embodied exchange wrought by a mutual susceptibility to poison but maintained by a shared, mutant state of becoming other. In contrast, then, to a grand performance of spill resolution, where the numbered crisis seemed to be fixed once the well was sealed, Svich materializes unresolved slow violence in the largely invisible toxicity now embedded in the Gulf.

Translocal and Transnational Tentacularity

In addition to exposing the irresolution surrounding the effects of oil and Corexit on the Gulf and the multilayered environmental injustices exacerbated by the spill, Svich makes connections across past and future disasters. For example, one of the play's most prominent comparisons is between the 2010 BP spill and the 2011 Magnablend Chemical Plant explosion in Waxahachie, Texas. Long before Rosalie and Jimmy decide to relocate to Waxahachie, they are linked to the city. As Jimmy tells Yuki in the first scene, his cousin Ray was recently burnt in the explosion, for which he received "hush peanuts" (Svich 2013, 24). Tellingly, Yuki does not know where Waxahachie is and has heard nothing of the fire in the news; thus, Svich uses Yuki's unawareness of the event to show how even seemingly spectacular instances of violence can remain invisible, especially when there are no fatalities, as was the case with the Magnablend explosion. By putting the Magnablend explosion in conversation with the BP oil spill, Svich exposes the lax policies and underlying environmental indifference that link the two events. The fact that the Magnablend explosion occurred so soon after the BP disaster reveals how little changed in the US, despite the short-term hypervisibility of the spill. Although the incidents vary in their environmental magnitude, both were caused by deregulation. In the case of the oil spill, the fact that BP was able to drill what was, at the time, the deepest oil well in history only 41 miles offshore, even though its oil spill treatment plan was from the 1970s,[18] reveals a disregard for socio-environmental safety. Similarly, in the case of the plant explosion, Magnablend's freedom to mix large quantities of harsh, industrial chemicals—some of which are used in oil fields—and its lack of safety precautions led to the October 2011 explosion.

While the play's setting never shifts to Texas, Jimmy's and Rosalie's continual mention of Waxahachie as the site of another disaster and, eventually, as the only place to which they can relocate, establishes the city as a secondary setting. By relating the large-scale explosion in offshore Louisiana to the comparatively small-scale explosion in Waxahachie, Svich suggests that, regardless the magnitude, both are caused by environmental exploitation, a slow violence that underlies every instance of spectacular violence. Utilizing the short-term hypervisibility of the 2010 spill to draw attention to less publicized crises, Svich exposes the ongoing slow violence that precedes and follows each visible disaster. She also draws on the spill to make connections to previous disasters, once deemed catastrophic, too, before quickly being forgotten. For example, Jimmy says, "First in Valdez way back when...My daddy said, 'This time for sure somebody's gonna take them to task'... Big news for a while, then it faded away; like everythin' else.[...] Memories like sieves in this country" (Svich 2013, 21–2). Just as LLLR incorporates the 2005 Texas City oil refinery explosion to expose an ongoing pattern of violence, Svich relates the most recent numbered crisis to what was previously the largest spill in the US, the 1989 *Exxon Valdez* spill. In doing so, she urges us not to treat environmental disasters as glitches that can be resolved through short-term, technological fixes but as explosive instances of the deeply entrenched slow violence of environmental extractivism.

Extending farther outward, Svich alludes to the collective vulnerability of endangered islands. For instance, in one scene, Jimmy and Yuki, waiting for fish that will never come, pass the time by discussing the latter's Japanese heritage and the snow in Iceland. In another scene, they discuss "Aussie style" steak and eggs and the country's "red desert" (Svich 2013, 40). Subtly but significantly, Svich suggests that the toxins in the Gulf can spread to far-reaching waters and, more assuredly, that the oil spill is not an isolated or insulated incident. Islands like Japan, Australia, and Iceland are disproportionately threatened by climate change, because of rising sea levels from melting ice caps. Jimmy and Yuki, however, fail to recognize the connection between their parish and the islands they imagine. To the characters, the islands they casually discuss are remote, formed more fully in their imaginations than anywhere else; Japan is simply the land of *manga*, "Aussie" is merely the way Jimmy likes his steak, and Iceland is only snow. To Svich, though, the islands are deeply connected to Louisiana and one, if not all, of them could be the site of the next environmental disaster, as indeed Japan was in 2011.[19] Just as the spill's slow violence spreads inward, infecting humans and their environment with chemical toxins, it also spreads outward, to past and future catastrophes, all caused by a complete disregard for the shared, transcorporeal vulnerability of humans and nonhuman nature.

This Is Not a Conclusion

In the current political and environmental climate, reading the news each day is a struggle, let alone following a story with no end in sight. It is understandable that, when the gushing oil leak was plugged on day 87 of the spill, the US public and media alike were relieved to move on to the next disaster, to treat the sealed oil well like a sealed story—capped, cemented, resolved. In doing so, though, what is missed are the underlying patterns of relational slow violence that connect environmental "disasters" to one another. Although the *Deepwater Horizon* oil spill was a highly visible, and thus highly publicized, disaster, the slow violence of its long-term causes and effects is far more insidious, not least of all because it largely occurs out of sight. As oil rigs continue to proliferate in formerly inaccessible, earthly depths and distances and as the US continues to top the world in gas and oil production (Malm 2021, 7), creative détournements that disturb convenient economic narratives of disaster resolution become even more crucial. While it may not be entirely possible to think beyond the fossil economy (Szeman 2007, 806–7), a good first step is thinking beyond disaster narratives that characterize environmental catastrophes as unanticipated, isolated events narrated only in the present tense.

Both *NOLA* and *The Way of Water* do this by denying their audiences resolution, instead drawing their attention to less visible, tentacular aspects of slow violence, like environmental injustice, transcoroporeal toxicity, and climate change. Nixon argues for increased representation of "incremental and accretive" slow violence that does not erupt into "instant sensational visibility" (2011, 2). Such instant visibility can create tunnel vision, or a single-issue environmentalism that obscures less visible environmental crises. And, yet, the spectacular hypervisibility of disasters like the 2010 spill also creates a platform for artists to make connections to slower, more invisible forms of violence. The way of water is to move—to ebb and flow, to come in and out—and, as *NOLA* and *The Way of Water* suggest, even as oil spills spread their transcorporeal toxicity across several ecosystems, they also reveal a tentacular connectivity that extends across species and seas.

Notes

1 The well was sealed with a cap on day 87 of the spill, and this is when coverage of the spill began dwindling in the media. However, the well was not permanently sealed with cement until day 153.

2 As Anne McClintock argues, "In the year of media silence, from the fall of 2010 to the fall of 2011, voices from the Gulf kept crying out like Cassandras, trying to make themselves heard. The news remained dreadful, but no one outside the Gulf seemed to be listening" (2012).

3 Scientific studies of the spill suggest long-term effects on disaster responders' health (D'Andrea and Reddy 2018); on corals (Girard and Fisher 2018); on dolphins (Schwacke et al. 2021); and on fish (Ainsworth et al. 2018).

4 I am thankful to Elizabeth DeLoughrey for this suggestion.

5 A containment boom is a floating device temporarily placed in the ocean to keep oil from reaching the shore. However, waves and wind can easily cause oil to escape the boom.

6 New Orleans experienced a huge boom following a BP-sponsored ad campaign. Other areas, like Dauphin Island, Alabama, were much slower to recover (Jones 2011). By participating in BP-sponsored ads that insisted that tourism was better than ever, states undermined business owners' ongoing settlement claims (Robertson 2011).

7 Because @BPGlobalPR tweets were written by Josh Simpson and several unknown participants, I have cited the tweets by their Twitter handle.

8 The initial punitive damages figure was five billion, but Exxon Mobil repeatedly fought to have the number lowered, in the end to $287 million in actual damages and $507.5 million in punitive damages.

9 At the time of this writing, @BPGlobalPR's Twitter account was suspended.

10 Luke Broughton, Toby Manley, Nell Mooney, and Molly Taylor.

11 NOLA was researched and edited by LLLR's Artistic Director, Mimi Poskitt.

12 Take, for example, a 2004 spill not discovered in the Gulf of Mexico until 2019 (Mason, Taylor, and MacDonald 2019).

13 More than a decade after the spill, scientists are still discovering that the spill's effects are far more extensive than originally thought (Vaughn 2020).

14 I am thankful to artistic director Mimi Poskitt for sharing the production script with me.

15 I had the honor of directing a staged reading of The Way of Water at the University of California, Los Angeles, on May 29, 2012. It featured Adam Cropper, Kendal Evans, Linzi Juliano, Zeke Medina, and Medalion Rahimi.

16 Low access here is defined as being more than ten miles away from a large grocery store in a rural area.

17 Environmental policy specialist Jonathan L. Ramseur estimates that 22% of oil remains unaccounted for and is difficult to calculate (2010).

18 In The Rachel Maddow Show, episode "That Was Then, This Is Then," Maddow compares footage of the oil treatment of a spill in Alaska in 1979 with that of the 2010 spill. In both, the same treatment techniques are used: airplanes dropped hazardous chemicals on the oil that exacerbated the oil's toxicity.

19 The March 2011 Fukushima Daiichi nuclear disaster, the largest nuclear disaster since the 1986 Chernobyl disaster, was initiated by a tsunami and earthquake.

References

@BPGlobalPR. "One year ago, we thought that this terrible PR disaster would never go away. We were wrong. #StayStrongTEPCO." Twitter, April 20, 2010.

@BPGlobalPR. "Here's the thing: we made $45 million A DAY in profits in 2009. This really isn't a big deal." Twitter, May 10, 2010.

@BPGlobalPR. "We regretfully admit that something has happened off of the Gulf Coast. More to come." *Twitter*, May 10, 2010.

@BPGlobalPR. "We feel terrible about spilling oil in American waters, we'll make sure the next spill happens where the terrorists live. #bpcares." *Twitter*, May 25, 2010.

@BPGlobalPR. "Feeling down? Why not take a long drive and blow off some steam? #bpcares." *Twitter*, May 29, 2010.

@BPGlobalPR. "SPOILER ALERT: The leak stops eventually, everyone forgets about it and we all buy another vacation home. #cantwait." *Twitter*, June 4, 2010.

@BPGlobalPR. "We've modestly made modest changes to this modest gulf. This modest incident will blow over and you'll forget how modest we were. #MODEST." *Twitter*, June 4, 2010.

@BPGlobalPR. "DO NOT ask your reps to support Clean Energy. Buying their votes back will take a lot of money away from the cleanup effort. #bpcares." *Twitter*, June 10, 2010.

@BPGlobalPR. "We respect your outrage, we just don't believe it's sustainable. #exxon-valdez #bpcares." *Twitter*, June 13, 2010.

@BPGlobalPR. "If you want to help clean up, drive your cars fast and often. Let's melt those glaciers and dilute this mess! #bpcares." *Twitter*, June 14, 2010.

@BPGlobalPR. "We honestly didn't think this was going to be a huge deal. No one cares when this happens in Nigeria. http://ow.ly/1YuwZ." *Twitter*, June 14, 2010.

@BPGlobalPR. "We'd like to be remembered as the company that saved the Gulf. What we saved it from is not important. # bpcares." *Twitter*, July 23, 2010.

@BPGlobalPR. "Reports of 79% of the oil remaining in the Gulf are false according to the pie chart we made ourselves. http://ow.ly/2s889." *Twitter*, August 19, 2010.

"100 Days of Gushing Oil—Media Analysis and Quiz." 2010. *Pew Research Journalism Project*. August 25. https://tinyurl.com/2p8pxt6n.

Ainsworth, Cameron H., et al. 2018. "Impacts of the Deepwater Horizon Spill Evaluated Using an End-to-End Ecosystem Model." *PLOS One* 13 (1): e0190840.

Alaimo, Stacy. 2010. *Bodily Natures: Science, Environment, and the Material Self*. Bloomington: Indiana University Press.

Alaimo, Stacy. 2012. "Sustainable This, Sustainable That: New Materialisms, Posthumanism, and Unknown Futures." *PMLA* 127 (3): 558–564.

Bell, Andrew 2012. "NOLA (Look Left Look Right/Escalator East to Edinburgh)." *Three-WeeksEdinburgh.com*, August 14. https://tinyurl.com/2p86cuat.

Bellingrath Gardens and Home. 2012. "Come Back to the Gulf Coast." *YouTube*, March 15. https://tinyurl.com/mu4tmtve.

Castellón, Idna G. 2021. "Cancer Alley and the Fight Against Environmental Racism." *Villanova Environmental Law Journal* 32 (1): 15–43.

Chaudhuri, Una and Shonni Enelow. 2014. *Research Theatre, Climate Change, and the Ecocide Project: A Casebook*. New York: Palgrave Macmillan.

climatebrad. 2010. "BP Oil Disaster Ad Thanks Government for 'Strong Support.'" *You-Tube*, June 3. https://tinyurl.com/4nef8jd6.

"Crude Awakening." 2014. *VICE*. HBO. New York. May 16. Television.

D'Andrea, Mark A. and G. Kesava Reddy. 2018. "The Development of Long-Term Adverse Health Effects in Oil Spill Cleanup Workers of the Deepwater Horizon Offshore Drilling Rig Disaster." *Frontiers Public Health* 6 (117).

Debord, Guy. [1956] 2006. "A User's Guide to Détournement." In *Situationist International Anthology*. Trans. Ken Knabb. https://tinyurl.com/478ye3ez.

Debord, Guy. [1967] 2014. The Society of the Spectacle. Trans. Ken Knabb. *Bureau of Public Secrets*. https://tinyurl.com/y7tvzzyd.

Deepwater Horizon. 2016. Dir. Peter Berg. Perf. Mark Wahlberg and Kurt Russell. Lionsgate.

Durando, Jessica. 2013. "BP Spent $93 Million on Advertising After Gulf Oil Spill." *USA Today*, September 1. https://tinyurl.com/3pckj9t7.

Farber, Daniel. 2012. "The BP Blowout and the Social and Environmental Erosion of the Louisiana Coast." *Minnesota Journal of Law, Science, & Technology* 13 (1): 37–44.

Fondakowski, Leigh, in collaboration with Reeva Wortel. 2014. *Spill*. Swine Palace, Reilly Theatre. Baton Rouge, Louisiana, March 28.

Food Access Research Atlas. 2019. *Economic Research Services (ERS)*. *U.S. Department of Agriculture (USDA)*. Last modified April 27, 2021. https://tinyurl.com/2c8kfd6t.

Garrard, Greg. 2004. *Ecocriticism*. New York: Routledge.

Girard, Fanny and Charles R. Fisher. 2018. "Long-Term Impact of the Deepwater Horizon Oil Spill on Deep-Sea Corals Detected After Seven Years of Monitoring." *Biological Conservation* 225: 117–127.

Haraway, Donna. 2007. *When Species Meet*. Minneapolis: University of Minnesota Press.

Haraway, Donna. 2016. *Staying with the Trouble: Making Kin in the Chthulucene*. Durham: Duke University Press.

Hitchcock, Peter. 2012. "Everything's Gone Green: The Environment of BP's Narrative." *Imaginations: Journal of Cross-Cultural Image Studies* 3 (2): np.

Jardin, Xeni. 2010. "More Oil Spilled in Nigeria 'Every Year than Has Been Spilled in the Gulf of Mexico.'" *Boing Boing*, June 14. https://tinyurl.com/4ffcyvp7.

Jenkins, Henry, Sam Ford, and Joshua Green. 2013. *Spreadable Media: Creating Value and Meaning in a Networked Culture*. New York: New York University Press.

Jones, Charisse. 2011. "Tourism Returns a Year After the Gulf Spill." *USA Today*, April 22. https://tinyurl.com/5n79mxm7.

Kershaw, Baz. 2007. *Theatre Ecology: Environments and Performance Events*. Cambridge: Cambridge University Press.

LeMenager, Stephanie. 2011. "Petro-Melancholia: The BP Blowout and the Arts of Grief." *Qui Parle* 19 (2): 25–56.

Liebes, Tamar. 1998. "Television's Disaster Marathons: A Danger for Democratic Processes?" In *Media, Ritual, and Identity*, edited by Tamar Liebes and James Curran, 71–86. New York: Routledge.

"List of Oil Spills." 2022. *Wikipedia: The Free Encyclopedia*. Last modified July 1, 2022. https://tinyurl.com/y2vsravk.

Malewitz, Jim, Mark Collette, and Lisa Olsen. 2015. "Anatomy of Disaster: Studies pinpointed what went wrong in Texas City, but unsafe conditions persist." *The Texas Tribune*, March 22. https://tinyurl.com/4b5wcucv.

Malm, Andreas. 2016. *Fossil Capital: The Rise of Steam Power and the Roots of Global Warming*. Kindle ed. London: Verso.

Malm, Andreas. 2021. *How to Blow Up a Pipeline*. London: Verso.

Mascarenhas, Alan. 2010. "BP's Global PR vs. BPGlobalPR." *Newsweek*, June 3. https://tinyurl.com/5dt4a8w9.

Mason, A.L., J.C. Taylor, and I.R. MacDonald. 2019. *An Integrated Assessment of Oil and Gas Release into the Marine Environment at the Former Taylor Energy MC20 Site*. Silver Spring, MD: NOAA Technical Memorandum.

May, Theresa J. 2017. "Tú eres mi otro yo—Staying with the Trouble: Ecodramaturgy & the AnthropoScene," *The Journal of American Drama and Theatre* 29 (2): 1–18.

McClintock, Anne. 2012. "Slow Violence and the BP Oil Crisis in the Gulf of Mexico: Militarizing Environmental Catastrophe." *E-misférica* 9: 1–2.

Montagna, Paul A., et al. 2013. "Deep-Sea Benthic Footprint of the Deepwater Horizon Blowout." *PLOS One* 8 (8).

NALCO. 2012. "Safety Data Sheet." https://tinyurl.com/yc6pkkfw.

Nixon, Rob. 2011. *Slow Violence and the Environmentalism of the Poor*. Cambridge, MA: Harvard University Press.

NOLA: A Documentary Play about the BP Oil Spill. 2012. Look Left Look Right. Researched and edited by Mimi Poskitt. *Edinburgh Fringe Festival*, August 2–26.

"Percent of Total Population in Poverty." 2020. *Economic Research Service (ERS)*. *U.S. Department of Agriculture*. Last updated June 3, 2022. https://tinyurl.com/4b2hcfae.

Raley, Rita. 2009. *Tactical Media*. Minneapolis: University of Minnesota Press.

Ramseur, Jonathan L. 2010. *Deepwater Horizon Oil Spill: The Fate of the Oil*. Congressional Research Service Report for Congress. December 16.

Rico-Martínez, Roberto, Terry W. Snell, and Tonya L. Shearer. 2013. "Synergistic Toxicity of Macondo Crude Oil and Dispersant Corexit 9500A to the Brachionus plicatilis Species Complex (Rotifera)". *Environmental Pollution* 173: 5–10.

Robertson, Campbell. 2011. "No Vacancies, but Some Reservations." *New York Times*, July 15. https://tinyurl.com/6zswvupc.

Schor, Elana. 2010. "Ingredients of Controversial Dispersants Used on Gulf Spill Are Secrets No More." *New York Times*, June 9. https://tinyurl.com/2838d7n5.

Schwacke, Lori H., et al. 2021. "Modeling Population Effects of the *Deepwater Horizon* Oil Spill on a Long-Lived Species." *Conservation Biology* 36 (4).

Soja, Edward W. 2010. *Seeking Spatial Justice*. Minneapolis: University of Minnesota Press.

Strachan, Graeme. n.d. "NOLA." *British Theatre Guide*. https://tinyurl.com/y9jypeue.

Svich, Caridad. 2013. *The Way of Water*. NoPassport Press & Welsh Fargo Stage Company Edition.

Szeman, Imre. 2007. "System Failure: Oil, Futurity, and the Anticipation of Disaster." *South Atlantic Quarterly* 106 (4): 805–823.

Vaughan, Adam. 2020. "Deepwater horizon spill may have been a third bigger than estimated." *New Scientist*, February 12. https://tinyurl.com/54enyf7y.

Webb, Tim. 2010. "BP Boss Admits Job on the Line over Gulf Oil Spill." *The Guardian*, May 13. https://tinyurl.com/yc7czypz.

INDEX